C PROGRAMMING LANGUAGE

LANGUAGE

An Applied Perspective

LAWRENCE H. MILLER

University of Southern California,
Information Sciences Institute

ALEXANDER E. QUILICI

University of California,
Los Angeles

JOHN WILEY & SONS

New York • Chichester • Brisbane • Toronto • Singapore

To Our Families

Publisher: Stephen Kippur
Editor: Therese A. Zak
Managing Editor: Andrew B. Hoffer
Editing, Design & Production: G&H SOHO, Ltd.

Library of Congress Cataloging-in-Publication Data

Miller, Lawrence H.
    C programming language.

    1. C (Computer program language) I. Quilici,
Alexander E. II. Title.
QA76.73.C15M55 1986   005.13'3   85-17848
ISBN 0-471-82560-3

Preface

C is like a Porsche: powerful, efficient, compact. Programming in C, like driving a Porsche, can be interesting, exciting, and fun—once you have mastered the language and can use its capabilities to the fullest. In this book, we try to provide enough information to make programming with C as enjoyable for you as it is for us. Not only do we introduce each of C's features and describe the common ways they are put together, but we teach how to *use* the language, showing how to write readable, modifiable, efficient, and portable programs. While discussing the various language features we present the shortcuts, idioms, and stylistic problems the reader is likely to encounter in existing code. Our treatment of the language is thorough and includes complete coverage of the standard libraries and the preprocessor.

We do not assume any prior experience with C. However, we do assume some practice with a high-level programming language, or at least some knowledge of how variables, statements, and procedures work. As we go along, we note the similarities with and differences from other languages such as Pascal, FORTRAN, and BASIC. When our programs are drawn from topics that the reader may not be familiar with, we take care to explain not only the programs but the ideas and algorithms behind them as well. There are many illustrations to provide needed pictorial descriptions of pointers, data structures, and the behavior of algorithms.

EXAMPLES AND CASE STUDIES

Since the only way to learn how to write good C programs is to study well-written ones, we have included many examples and case studies.

Our examples not only illustrate language features but also reinforce general principles of good programming style. For instance, many of the functions written in our early examples are used to build more interesting programs later, illustrating modularity and the reusability of code—concepts central to C's philosophy. Our case studies consolidate and reinforce earlier material and illustrate real-world applications. Within all our programs, we avoid sacrificing clarity for conciseness.

The programs and functions used as examples and case studies are diverse and include:

- Interactive and display-oriented programs: an indexed data base and a histogram producer.

- Implementations of common sorting and searching algorithms: insertion sort, sequential search, and binary search.

- Our versions of useful tools for copying files, stripping duplicate lines, counting words, and line numbering.

- Implementations of standard libraries: the string library and the character-testing functions.

- Additional functions that we have found to be useful: an alternative to the standard library's input handling and a package that implements sets.

ORGANIZATION

Chapter 1 is a tutorial introduction to the language. Through a series of example programs, each adding several new language constructs, we present C's basic data types and control structures and introduce functions and parameter passing.

With this tutorial out of the way, we delve into the details of C's data types and control structures. Chapter 2 describes C's basic data types, emphasizing the differences in their ranges on different machines. This chapter introduces the character data type and presents character-at-a-time I/O. Chapter 3 presents C's rich set of operators, concentrating on the differences between C and other high-level languages. We give special attention to assignment, prefix, postfix, and bitwise operators, as well as automatic type conversions and casting. Chapter 4 discusses arrays, strings, and pointers, emphasizing the relationships between them. The standard string library functions are introduced and used in writing a tool that detects duplicate input lines. Chapter 5 examines C's statements, illustrating each with an example showing its most appropriate uses and concluding with a histogram program that ties together the concepts covered so far.

We then examine features of C that support the writing of larger programs. Chapter 6 discusses functions, examining the way they can communicate with each other through parameter passing and return values. In addition, the closely related topics of recursion and pointers to functions are described and illustrated with binary search and the nucleus of a function plotter. Chapter 7 discusses program structure, introducing storage classes, header files, separate compilation, and methods of implementing abstract data types. These concepts are illustrated with several useful modules including an alternative to the standard I/O library's input handling and an implementation of sets. Chapter 8 describes the preprocessor, showing its use in making programs easier to read and debug, as well as more efficient.

Next, we examine more complex user-defined data structures. Chapter 9 returns to arrays, concentrating on multidimensional and ragged arrays and the efficient use of pointers to access them. We also introduce dynamic storage allocation and use it in a program to sort strings. The chapter ends with a closer examination of C's declarations, explaining their often confusing syntax. Chapters 10 and 11 introduce structures and unions, illustrating their use in defining static data structures such as tables, and in constructing dynamic data structures such as linked lists. Chapter 11 ends with a program requiring dynamic data structures: a C program cross-referencer.

We conclude by discussing the writing of real-world programs. Chapter 12 focuses on the relationship between C programs and the outside world, describing command line arguments and files and providing complete coverage of the standard I/O library. The ideas of the chapter are brought together in the implementation of an indexed data base for names, addresses, and phone numbers. Chapter 13 provides techniques for writing more portable and efficient programs. The appendixes summarize library functions and describe the binary, octal, and hexadecimal base systems.

Acknowledgments

We are grateful to several insightful individuals who have had a significant influence on our views about programming and teaching. Dennis Ritchie's clear thinking has given us C and, as a result, has made program development a pleasant experience. Niklaus Wirth and Brian Kernighan, through their classic books, have shown us the power of structured programming and the intelligent development and use of tools. Lastly, Ken Thompson and Dennis Ritchie created UNIX, providing us with a comfortable environment for programming and for writing.

Special thanks go to our friends and colleagues for improving this book. In particular, David Smallberg has provided many perceptive comments and criticisms and in countless late night discussions has directed us to elegant solutions to our problems. Jeff Rothenberg at the Rand Corporation, Eric Anderson at the USC Information Sciences Institute, Arthur Goldberg at UCLA Extension, and Karen Dorato and David G. Kay at UCLA have been using drafts of the manuscript and have contributed helpful suggestions. David G. Kay's enthusiasm for teaching and writing is contagious, and his inspiration is noticeable throughout this book. Claire McKean and Robin Larsen did a wonderful job of copy-editing our manuscript. Marcy Swenson and Richard Wolpert aided us in putting together the appendixes. We would also like to thank our students at UCLA, especially Tai Lue and Bruce McCorkendale, and at other places we have taught, for their patience with our earlier drafts and for pointing out mistakes and painfully unclear explanations. We are particularly grateful for the generous use of resources at the UCLA computer science department, and at USC's Information Sciences Institute. Danny Cohen at ISI must be noted for his enthusiastic encouragement of this project.

Finally, we cannot imagine how we could have completed this book without the encouragement and support we received from Rita Grant-Miller and Colette Zee. And, as always, we are in debt to Colonel Vigorish for providing us with financial aid, and to Dr. Ruth Westheimer for making our evenings more exciting.

Contents

C H A P T E R 1

INTRODUCING
C PROGRAMMING

We begin with a tutorial introduction to C. Through a series of example programs, each using several new language constructs, we introduce many of C's fundamental data types, operators, and control structures. We also show how to use predefined library functions to perform formatted input and output, and introduce user-defined functions—the basic building blocks of sizeable C programs. As we do so, we examine the process of actually compiling, loading, and executing C programs. The chapter concludes by putting these pieces together in the implementation of a program that sorts its input using a technique known as *insertion sort*.

A FIRST C PROGRAM

Believing in the idea that we learn by seeing and doing, we start by examining a C program. The program in Figure 1.1 prints the interest accumulated in a bank account over a period of 10 years, with an initial deposit of $1000, assuming an interest rate of 10 percent.

When we compile and run this program, we produce the output shown in Figure 1.2. The program first writes a header giving the current year and the interest rate, and then prints the total amount of money in the account at the end of each year in the period. To do our calculations, we used a simple interest rate compounding formula:

Amount at end of year = *amount at start of year* × *interest rate* + *amount at start of year*

1

```
/*
 * Generate a table showing interest accumulation.
 */
#define PRINCIPAL     1000.00            /* start with $1000 */
#define IRATE         0.10               /* interest rate of 10% */
#define PERIOD        10                 /* over 10-year period */

main()
{
  int     year;                          /* year of period */
  float   sum;                           /* total amount */

  sum = PRINCIPAL;
  year = 0;
  printf("Year\tTotal at %5.2f%%\n\n", IRATE * 100.0);
  while (year <= PERIOD)
  {
    printf("%d\t$ %7.2f\n", year, sum);
    sum = sum * IRATE + sum;
    year = year + 1;
  }
}
```

FIGURE 1.1. A program that calculates interest.

ANALYSIS OF INTEREST PROGRAM

The first piece of the program, beginning with /* and ending with */, is a brief comment block describing the program. Anything between a /* and a */ is taken as a comment and ignored by the compiler. In general, comments can appear anywhere blank spaces can occur—at the end of a line, at the beginning, or even in the middle—as long as they do not appear in the middle of a keyword or identifier.

The next three lines begin with #define, C's mechanism for defining constants. The way C handles #defines is interesting and important; they are interpreted by a *preprocessor*. Each time a #define is seen by the preprocessor, the value associated with the name is remembered. Then, whenever the name occurs in the program, it is replaced with its corresponding value. After the preprocessor has finished its replacements, the program is passed to the compiler. The compiler never sees the names in the #define statements.

#define is so useful and its syntax (that is, the way the statement is constructed) is so simple that we will use it in virtually every program we write. In fact, #define is more powerful than we have indicated here; it is a general mechanism that allows the preprocessor to replace the given string of characters with another string. For now, we will use it to define constant values. In this simple form, its use requires the keyword **#define** to begin in column one, followed by the name we are defining, followed by its value:

    #define   *NAME*   *value*

We use italics (*NAME, value*) to indicate symbols that are generic; the programmer provides the name and its value.

    In Figure 1.1 we have used **#define** for the values that are constants for the program: the initial principal amount **PRINCIPAL**, the interest rate **IRATE**, and the number of years over which we wish to calculate the accumulating value, **PERIOD**. The preprocessor replaces each use of **PRINCIPAL** in the program with its defined value (1000.00) and performs a similar action for the other two defined constants. We have used all uppercase names for constants to make it easier to spot them when we read the program. The **#defines** can occur anywhere in a program but are usually placed at the beginning. Chapter 8 describes the preprocessor in detail.

The Main Program

The lines after the **#defines** define a function named **main**. Program execution begins with a call to **main**, so every program must have a function with this name. The parentheses that follow **main** indicate that it is a function that takes no parameters. Chapter 12 shows that **main** can indeed take parameters and shows how they are defined and used.

    Every program must have exactly one **main** function, but unlike many other programming languages it does not matter where it is defined. Other functions can appear before or after it. Our program consists of

```
Year    Total at 10.00%

0       $ 1000.00
1       $ 1100.00
2       $ 1210.00
3       $ 1331.00
4       $ 1464.10
5       $ 1610.51
6       $ 1771.56
7       $ 1948.72
8       $ 2143.59
9       $ 2357.95
10      $ 2593.74
```

FIGURE 1.2. Output generated when running the interest rate accumulator.

just the one function, main, which, in turn, consists of data declarations and statements. We group the declarations and statements that belong together under main using the statement grouping symbols { and }.

Data Definitions

In C, the types of all variables must be declared before they are used. Variable declarations appear at the beginning of a function. In Figure 1.1, the declarations

```
int        year;
float      sum;
```

tell the compiler that year is an int (an abbreviation for the word *integer*) and sum is a float (a *floating point* or *real* number). These declarations are required because the amount of storage actually used by a variable depends on its type and because accuracy and the range of values differ between types. Explicit variable declarations also make our programs more readable.

There are two basic numerical representation forms: integer and real (or floating point). Among these, there are also multiple forms. For integers, they are short, int, and long; for reals, they are float and double. Integer forms are used when exact "whole" numbers are needed, since their representation is exact within the range of integers that a given word size can represent. They are also used when speed of arithmetic operations is important, since most operations are faster with integers. Different sizes are provided for storage efficiency and for program portability, a topic we discuss in considerable depth in Chapter 13.

Reals are numbers with a decimal point. Their accuracy depends on the machine's representation. Typically, a float represents about 7 significant digits, with exponents generally ranging from about −38 to +38. The doubles allocate more storage for the real, and this storage is usually given to the fractional part of the number. Thus, doubles usually represent about 14 significant digits. There are both automatic and explicit ways to convert from one form to another.

In Chapter 2 we will consider built-in data types in more detail, pointing out that the range of values of a particular type can vary from machine to machine. The basic integer representation varies from 16 to 32 bits. With one bit required for the sign, the range of an int using a 16-bit representation is from $-32,768$ to $+32,767$ (that is, -2^{15} to $+2^{15} - 1$). On a 32-bit machine, however, ints range from $-2,148,483,648$ to $+2,148,483,647$ (that is, from -2^{31} to $+2^{31} - 1$). Care must be taken to select an appropriate data type if a program written on one computer is to run on another.

In addition to int and float, C provides character and pointer (address) data types, allows arrays and structures of any data type, and allows us to devise new data types from the standard types, topics we will examine in later chapters.

Executable Statements

The statements that are executed when a function is called follow any variable declarations. The first statements in main in Figure 1.1 are

```
sum = PRINCIPAL;
year = 0;
```

These are assignment statements and work in the conventional way. The first assigns the value defined for the constant PRINCIPAL (1000.00) to the variable sum; the second sets the variable year to 0.

printf

The next statement is an output statement that writes the header line.

```
printf ("Year\tTotal at %5.2f%%\n\n", IRATE * 100.0);
```

printf is a predefined function for performing formatted output. *Predefined* means that it is a function that has already been written and compiled for you, and is linked together with your program after it compiles. In C, all input and output is performed by library functions. Together, these functions comprise the standard I/O library.

Formatted output means that printf takes a formatting control string and a list of values to be printed according to the formatting control. In general, anything in the format specification (between the quotation marks) is printed as is. However, instructions for formatting numerical and string output are indicated using the % formatting codes: %d is used to print a decimal integer, and %f is used to print a floating point value. If no size is given, enough space is used to print the entire value. In the interest program, we have specified a format of %5.2f for the interest rate, which tells the compiler that we want floating point output, with five places in all and two places to the right of the decimal point. Leaving off the initial 5 would cause the field to be just wide enough to print the value. In our example, the value of the expression IRATE * 100.0 is calculated and printed according to our formatting specification. Since we also want to print a percent sign in the heading, we use two percent signs (%%) to indicate that a single percent is to be printed. Appendix 6 contains detailed descriptions of the various formatting instructions.

Perhaps you have noticed the obscure \n at the end of the formatting string. Characters with backslashes are special nonprinting characters. \n is used to indicate that a newline is wanted. Without this, output continues on the same line as the previous output. There are many nonprinting characters in any machine's character set, and the backslash quoting method is used to indicate a desired function. For example, \t indicates the tab character. We will see other special characters in Chapter 2.

For each value to be printed, there must be a corresponding formatting instruction. We see this in the second `printf` statement

```
printf("%d\t$ %7.2f\n", year, sum);
```

where we print the values of year and sum. First, year is printed using the %d specification, followed by a tab character (the \t code). Then, after a dollar sign and a blank are written, sum is printed using the %7.2f format. Finally, a newline is written (via the \n code).

`printf` is powerful and easy to use. However, in certain cases there are more efficient ways to produce output. We present these methods in Chapter 12, along with other functions in the standard I/O library.

The while Loop

Most of the work of the program is accomplished in a while loop:

```
while (year <= PERIOD)
{
  printf("%d\t$ %7.2f\n", year, sum);
  sum = sum * IRATE + sum;
  year = year + 1;
}
```

while is a mechanism for repeating a statement or a group of statements. The syntax of a while loop is

```
while (expression)
  statement
following-statement
```

The expression in parentheses is evaluated; if the condition is true, *statement* is executed. The process repeats until the condition is false, when we skip to *following-statement*.

In this case, whenever year is less than or equal to PERIOD, we want to execute the three statements

```
printf ("%d\t$ %7.2f\n", year, sum);
sum = sum * IRATE + sum;
year = year + 1;
```

We do this by grouping the statements together using the statement grouping indicator { to start the group and } to end it. The first statement in the group does the printing; the second updates sum, and the last updates year. We exit the loop when year is greater than PERIOD.

C has the usual arithmetic operators (+ , − , *, /), along with several others, which we will examine in Chapter 3. The operators * and / have higher precedence than + and − , but as with most other programming languages, we can change the order of evaluation by using parentheses.

Before we leave our first program, there are two additional points we should make. The first is that every line does not terminate with a semicolon. Although each statement is followed by a semicolon, statement groups, function definitions, and #defines are not. The other point is that C is free format. We have used one particular indentation style, but you are free to use others—just be careful to format your programs consistently. For those who need help with program layout, many C environments include program formatters that can be used to reformat programs that were indented in an unreadable way. On UNIX, these include *cb* (standing for "C Beautifier") and *indent*.

COMPILING AND RUNNING A PROGRAM

Creating a program typically requires the use of several facilities, such as text editors, compilers, file system utilities, and others. Figure 1.3 diagrams the typical program-building, compiling, and running cycle, showing the use of some of these tools.

The program is first created with an *interactive text editor*. Then the source file is compiled using the C *compiler*. Before compiling, the program is automatically run through a *preprocessor* that expands the #defines and replaces their names with their values throughout the program. The preprocessor also does preliminary *syntax* checking.

At this point, the expanded version of the program is passed to the compiler proper. If there are no errors in the compilation of the program, an intermediate form of the program, known as an *object module*, is

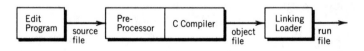

FIGURE 1.3. Typical process of building, compiling, and running a C program.

produced. An object module or object file contains the compiled code, but this code may contain references to functions that the code did not define, called *externals* (such as `printf` in Figure 1.1).

Now the *linking loader* must reconcile any externals. It does this by looking in a standard location that contains a library of precompiled standard functions. The compiled definition of the `printf` function is found in this library and is linked together with the object module by the linking loader (usually invoked automatically by the C compiler) to produce a runnable program. The runnable program is the sole output of this pipeline.

Many of these steps can be modified by the use of flags to the compiler. You should read your compiler documentation to discover the details of your own system.

PROGRAMMING PRACTICE

1-1. Compile and run the interest rate program (Figure 1.1) on your own computer.

1-2. Remove a terminating semicolon or needed parenthesis from one of the statements in the interest rate program (Figure 1.1) and then try to compile it. How helpful are the compiler's error messages? You will probably discover that the error messages from your C compiler are not very helpful. Start keeping a list of messages and their true meaning.

1-3. Experiment with different values for the constants `PRINCIPAL`, `IRATE`, and `PERIOD`.

EXTENDING THE SAMPLE PROGRAM—
INPUT AND ADDITIONAL CONTROL STRUCTURES

We would like to have a more flexible interest accumulation program. Rather than hard-wiring the initial amount of money (`PRINCIPAL`), the interest rate (`IRATE`), and the number of years (`PERIOD`), we request these values from an interactive user and read them as input. To do this, we use another function from the standard I/O library, `scanf`, the input analog of `printf`. As with `printf`, `scanf`'s arguments are a formatting control string, enclosed in quotation marks, and a list of variables. The control string uses conventions similar to those of `printf`: `%d` indicates a decimal integer, %f a floating point, and so on. Unlike printf, however, scanf does not recognize the special formatting descriptions that start with \ such as \n. In fact, when searching for a value, scanf ignores line boundaries and simply looks for the next appropriate character.

Importantly, scanf indicates whether the input has been completed successfully and whether the end of the input file has been reached. scanf does this because it is a function that returns a value—the number of values correctly read from the input, or the special value EOF (a predefined constant), meaning that the end of the input file has been reached. Since scanf returns the number of values correctly read, we can compare this value with the expected number, to determine if an error has occurred. An error may occur, for example, when we are reading an integer value and an alphabetic character is entered.

When we read a value into a variable, scanf does not use the *name* of the variable, but rather its *address*. Fortunately, there is a simple operator for indicating a variable's address. If we have declared year to be an int and we wish to read a value for year, we use scanf as follows:

```
scanf("%d", &year);
```

The symbol & before the variable name year is an operator that returns the variable's address. If you forget the address operator &, unexpected results will occur. We will see why when we consider how parameters to functions work in Chapter 6.

With this preliminary review out of the way, we can extend the interest accumulator to allow input from the user. This time, we ask the user to enter the interest rate, principal, and period. We then read these values using scanf. Since we are reading three values, we expect scanf to return a value of three. If scanf returns something other than three, either there has been an error in the input or we have reached the end of the input file. In either case, we print a simple message and terminate the program. This version is shown in Figure 1.4.

When we run the new version of the program, we produce output similar to that from before, shown in Figure 1.5. What the user types is shown in italics.

ANALYSIS OF THE INTERACTIVE INTEREST PROGRAM

Since the values used in the program are now variables, we no longer use the #defines for IRATE, PRINCIPAL, and PERIOD. Instead, we make them variables by declaring their types along with the program's other variables:

```
int    period,        /* length of period */
       year;          /* year of period */
float  irate,         /* interest rate */
       sum;           /* total amount */
```

```
/*
 * Generates a table showing interest accumulation.  Allows the
 * user to input the interest rate, principal and period.
 */
main()
{
  int    period,                          /* year of period */
         year;                            /* length of period */
  float  irate,                           /* interest rate */
         sum;                             /* total amount */

  printf("Enter interest rate, principal and period: ");
  if (scanf("%f %f %d", &irate, &sum, &period) == 3)
  {
    printf("Year\tTotal at %.2f%%\n\n", irate * 100.0);
    year = 0;
    while (year <= period)
    {
      printf("%5d\t$ %10.2f\n", year, sum);
      sum = sum + sum * irate;
      year = year + 1;
    }
  }
  else
    printf("Error in input.  No table printed.\n");
}
```

FIGURE 1.4. Second implementation of the interest rate accumulator. Here the information is input from the user.

```
Enter interest rate, principal and period: .10    10000    10
Year    Total at 10.00%

   0  $  10000.00
   1  $  11000.00
   2  $  12100.00
   3  $  13310.00
   4  $  14641.00
   5  $  16105.10
   6  $  17715.61
   7  $  19487.17
   8  $  21435.89
   9  $  23579.47
  10  $  25937.42
```

FIGURE 1.5. Output from the second implementation of the interest rate accumulator.

We have declared `period` and `year` to be `int`s and `irate` and `sum` to be `floats`.

The first executable statement in the program is a `printf`, asking the user to enter values of the interest rate, the principal, and the period. Since we want to write the prompt and leave the cursor on the same line, the format string of the `printf` does not contain the newline character `\n`.

```
printf("Enter interest rate, principal and period:  ");
```

Input into the variables `irate`, `sum`, and `period` is accomplished using `scanf`. To see if the input was read correctly, we test `scanf`'s return value with an `if` statement:

```
if (scanf("%f %f %d", &irate, &sum, &period) == 3)
{
  printf("Year\tTotal at %.2f%%\n\n", irate * 100.0);
  year = 0;
  while (year <= period)
  {
    printf("%5d\t$ %10.2f\n", year, sum);
    sum = sum + sum * irate;
    year = year + 1;
  }
}
else
  printf("Error in input.  No table printed.\n");
```

The `if` statement has a simple form:

```
if (expression)
    statement1
else
    statement2
```

First, the expression in parentheses is evaluated (the parentheses are required). If the condition is true, *statement1* is executed; if it is false, *statement2* is executed. Notice that there is no keyword `then` before *statement1*. The `else` *statement2* is optional. As with the `while` statement, braces can be used around a group of statements whenever we show a single statement.

In Figure 1.4 we want to read values for the three variables `irate`, `sum`, and `period`, so we expect `scanf` to return three. We test the value of `scanf` using the test-for-equality operator, the double equal sign (`==`). In addition to testing for equality, we can test for inequality (`!=`), less than (`<`), greater than (`>`), less than or equal (`<=`), and greater than or equal (`>=`).

Putting all this together, if `scanf` in Figure 1.4 returns three, we execute the group of statements that follows it, writing the heading and computing the balances for the various years—the body of our earlier interest rate program. If `scanf` does not return three, we have an input error, and we execute the else part of the if statement, printing an appropriate error message.

The relational operators (tests for equality, inequality, and the others) are conventional in their use, except that they return an integer value: *true* is represented by one, *false* by zero. Consequently, C is more general than other programming languages in its use of tests within a while or if statement. Any arithmetic expression may be used, not just one of the relational tests. If the expression is zero, it is interpreted as false; if it is nonzero (positive or negative) it is interpreted as true.

An Aside on scanf

scanf is a useful function, but there are several limitations that may preclude its use in production programs. Unfortunately, because of the way scanf is written, there is no easy way to scan over illegal input; it remains on the illegal character, returning the same error indication over and over. In addition, because scanf can read an arbitrary number of values with differing types, the underlying implementation is extremely large and cumbersome. In subsequent chapters, we examine low-level input in detail and develop solutions to these problems, writing our own special-purpose versions of scanf. The methods needed are brief and surprisingly simple, and they can reduce the size of the compiled code by one-third or more, and the running times of programs by equally large amounts.

PROGRAMMING PRACTICE

1-4. The input-directed interest accumulator (Figure 1.4) did not do any range or error checking on the values entered by the user. Add a constant MAXPERIOD and check (with an appropriate if statement) that the number of years entered is less than or equal to MAXPERIOD. Similarly, add a check to see that the principal amount entered is greater than 0.0. If either of these bounds is violated, print an appropriate error message and terminate the program.

ARRAYS

C supports arrays of the predefined data types and constructed types (we will consider constructed types in later chapters). An array is a collection of values, all of which are of the same underlying type, such as int or float. We will illustrate the use of arrays by writing a program that reads integers and prints them in reverse order. One use for this program, shown in Figure 1.6, is to take the values from a sorting program that sorts in ascending order only and to print them sorted in descending order.

ANALYSIS OF REVERSE

The program in Figure 1.6 reverses its input by reading the input values into an array and then printing the array in reverse order. We declare an array by giving the type of its elements, its name, and the number of elements. The declaration

```
int     table[MAXVALS]
```

declares table to be an array, consisting of MAXVALS ints (1000 here).

We access an array element by specifying its index. The index within the square brackets can be any expression that can be interpreted as an integer. In C, arrays are indexed from 0, so in this example we access table from table[0] to table[999]. There is no run-time array bounds checking, unlike languages such as Pascal, where an illegal array access causes the program to terminate. In C, if you attempt to access a location such as table[−10], neither the compiler nor the run-time environment

```
/*
 * Read values and print out in reverse order.
 */
#define MAXVALS          1000            /* max values in array "table" */

main()
{
  int table[MAXVALS],           /* input array */
      i,                        /* index used in writing values */
      n;                        /* number of values in "table" */

  n = 0;
  while (n < MAXVALS && scanf ("%d", &table[n]) == 1)     /* read values */
    n = n + 1;
  printf("Values in reverse order:\n\n");
  for (i = n - 1; i >= 0; i = i - 1)                      /* write values */
    printf ("%d\n", table[i]);
}
```

FIGURE 1.6. Print the input in reverse order.

will complain. You are responsible for doing your own bounds checks during the running of your program.

The `while` Loop

We control reading of *reverse*'s input values with a `while` loop. There are two conditions that must be true for the loop body to be executed: n must be less than `MAXVALS` (so that we do not insert past the upper array bounds), and `scanf` must return one (so that we know we successfully read another value).

```
n = 0;
while (n < MAXVALS && scanf("%d", &table[n]) == 1)
  n = n + 1;
```

The double ampersands (`&&`) represent the logical AND operator. Logical OR is also available and is indicated by double vertical bars (`||`). When we are testing more than one conditional combined with logical AND, the leftmost one is tested first. Only if this one is true (nonzero) is the next conditional tested. A similar situation holds for logical OR: only if the first conditional is false (zero) is the second tested. As a result, in the `while` loop we first test n `< MAXVALS`. If this is false, we do not perform the second test, and `scanf` is not called. Only when the first test is true is `scanf` called and compared with one. The result is that we read a value only if there is room to store it in the array.

Notice again that `scanf` takes a formatting string, followed by a list of variable addresses. In this case, we want to read a single decimal integer, which is indicated by `"%d"`. We want to read this value into `table[n]`, so we pass `scanf` its address, indicated by `&table[n]`.

The for Loop

Once we have read the values into the array, we want to go through the array backwards, printing each value it contains. We capture this notion of statement repetition with a `for` loop. Most other programming languages have a similar construct, which contains the idea of a loop index that is initialized to some starting value and is incremented or decremented each time through the loop. The loop terminates when a stopping condition is met. The C `for` loop contains these ideas but is really much more general. Its basic form is:

```
for (Start ; Test ; Action)
  statement
```

Start, *Test*, and *Action* can be any C expressions. As with the `while` and `if` statements, braces are used if there are multiple statements within the loop body.

When a <u>for</u> is executed, *Start* is evaluated first (usually a loop initialization, such as i = 0). *Test* is evaluated next (usually the loop index bounds test, such as i <= n). If *Test* evaluates to true (or any nonzero value), the statements in the loop body are executed; if it evaluates to false (or zero), the <u>for</u> loop exits. If the loop does not exit (that is, if *Test* is nonzero), after the loop body is executed, *Action* is evaluated and the cycle is repeated. Usually *Action* increments the loop counter.

In Figure 1.6, we initialize i to the index of the last element (the number of elements in the array, n, minus one), and then compare to see whether it is greater than or equal to zero (the index of the first array element). If it is, we enter the body of the loop; if not, we exit the loop. After the loop body has been executed (in this case, when an element has been printed), we subtract one from i, evaluate the test condition again, and repeat the process:

```
for (i = n - 1; i >= 0; i = i - 1)
  printf("%d\n", table[i]);
```

FUNCTIONS

Our programs so far have consisted of only the single function **main**. When we write larger programs, however, it becomes necessary to break them up into smaller, more efficient, more manageable pieces. Functions provide a way of packaging code and giving the package a name that can be referred to by other functions and the main program. A program in C is actually a collection of one or more functions, including **main** (which must be present in each program). Functions are used because they allow common, single purpose routines to be neatly packaged and their capabilities made available to the main program, without the main program having to know how their task is accomplished internally. In fact, we have already used functions that were prewritten and compiled for us, such as **printf** and **scanf**, without knowing how they perform their jobs.

We illustrate the creation and use of user-defined functions by rewriting our input reversal program to use two new functions—one reads data into an array, counting the number of elements read, the other prints an array in reverse order. Although simple, these functions demonstrate the different aspects of function use and will prove instructive as a guide for writing your own functions. The entire program, showing where the functions are defined and how they are called, is shown in Figure 1.7.

```
/*
 * Read values and print in reverse order.
 */
#define MAXVALS        1000            /* max values in array "a" */

main()
{
  int table[MAXVALS],                  /* input array */
      n;                               /* number of values in "table" */

  n = get_data(table, MAXVALS);        /* read values */
  printf ("Values in reverse order:\n\n");
  print_reverse(table, n);             /* print values */
}

int get_data(a, max)                   /* read up to "max" values into "a" */
int a[], max;
{
  int count;

  count = 0;
  while (count < max && scanf("%d", &a[count]) == 1)
    count = count + 1;
  return count;
}

print_reverse(a, num)                  /* print "a" in reverse order */
int a[], num;
{
  int i;

  for (i = num - 1; i >= 0; i = i - 1)
    printf ("%d\n", a[i]);
}
```

FIGURE 1.7. Program that reads values and prints them in reverse order.

ANALYSIS OF THE NEW VERSION OF REVERSE

The task of the main program in this version of *reverse* is the same as that of the previous version: read values into an array and print them in reverse order. However, it accomplishes this task by calling two functions, get_data and print_reverse. The underscore (_) is part of the function name; it is a legal character and can occur anywhere in a name. We use the underscore to make the function name more readable. An alternative is to use uppercase and lowercase, such as GetData.

Unlike scanf and printf, get_data and print_reverse are not defined in a library, so we must define them ourselves. The syntax of a function definition is quite similar to the syntax of the `main` function that occurs in every program:

type-of-return-value   *function-name*(*parameter-1*, *parameter-2*, . . . , *parameter-n*)
  type parameter-1;
  type parameter-2;
        . . .
  type parameter-n;
{
  local declarations

  function body
}

All functions in C are assumed to return a value (type `int` unless we declare them to be otherwise). We can ignore the returned value, in which case a function behaves like a procedure in other languages (such as Pascal). *type-of-return-value* is the type of the value that the function returns. The function is assumed to return an `int` if no type is specified. If the function has parameters, they are indicated in the parameter list; if there are no parameters, the parentheses are still needed to indicate to the compiler that this is a function definition. The parameter list names the parameters but gives no type information; this is indicated in the next part of the function, where the type of each parameter is declared.

Any variables that are local to the function (such as loop counters and array indexes) are declared in the *local declarations*. A local variable's value can be accessed only within the function where it is declared. Finally, the body of the function is written. Notice the use of statement grouping brackets (`{` and `}`), which are required even if the function has no body.

The Function get_data

`get_data` is a function that takes two parameters: the array where the input values are to go and the maximum number of values to read, in this case the size of the array. In addition, the function returns `count`, the number of values in the array (the array `a` contains values at `a[0]` through `a[count-1]`). Notice that in Figure 1.7 the parameters to the functions are named in the function header, which is followed with the declarations of the function's parameters, `a` and `max`. `a` is an array of integers and `max` is an integer.

```
int get_data(a, max)
int a[], max;
```

To call a function, we specify its name and provide a list of values, the function's arguments. The arguments are copied and supplied as the value of the function's parameters. Therefore, any changes to the argument value apply only to the copy within the function, and the function *cannot* access the argument itself. This parameter-passing mechanism is known as *call by value* because the argument's *value* is copied to the function. In Figure 1.7, for example, max can be changed within get_data without affecting the argument MAXVALS passed to the function.

When an array is passed, however, only a pointer to its first element is passed and copied, not the entire array. This means that modifying an array element within the function changes the array that is passed to the function. If get_data is called with

```
get_data(table, MAXVALS)
```

an assignment within get_data, such as

```
a[0] = 10;
```

changes the value of table[0]. Because a pointer is passed instead of the array, it is not necessary to declare the size of a one-dimensional array parameter. Within the function, the compiler need only allocate the amount necessary to hold a single address, and sufficient storage to hold the entire array is allocated in the main program.

Parameters are one form of communication between functions, return values are another. To return a value from a function, we use the return statement. When we call get_data we are interested in the number of values read, which get_data returns as its value.

```
return count;
```

The expression following return is evaluated and its value returned to get_data's caller. In Figure 1.7, we call get_data and assign its value to a variable n in main with

```
n = get_data(table, MAXVALS);
```

When get_data exits, n is set to the number of values read into a; that is, the elements a[0] through a[n-1] contain valid data. If no values have been entered, n will be zero.

The Function print_reverse

print_reverse takes two arguments, the array to be printed and the number of values in the array. The array is printed in reverse order using i as an index. Since i is declared within print_reverse's body, it is local to print_reverse.

Since the size of an array parameter is not specified in the declaration, any size array (of the specified type) can be passed. This makes `print_reverse` fairly general; it can be used to print any size array of integers in reverse order.

PROGRAMMING PRACTICE

1-5. Write a function, **search**, that finds the location of a value in an array. The function should take three parameters: the value to be found, the array to be searched, and the size of the array. The function should return an **int**, the index where the value is found. If the value is not in the array, the function should return minus one.

1-6. Write a function, **sum**, that computes and returns the sum of the first n elements in an array of **int**s.

CASE STUDY—INSERTION SORT

We tie together the ideas we have presented in this chapter by writing a program that reads integers and keeps them sorted in an array. We use a sorting technique known as *insertion sort*; it is easy to understand and to program, and usually works with little debugging effort. Its drawback is that it is not the fastest sorting routine; the computing time increases as the *square* of the number of values to be sorted. Double the number of values and the computing time goes up by a factor of four, triple the number and the computing time goes up by a factor of nine. However, insertion sort is suitable when the number of values to sort is fewer than about 50 to 100.

Insertion sort works by assuming that the array is already sorted and then trying to find the appropriate place to insert a new value. We compare the new value with the last, "largest" element in the array. If the value is less than the largest one, we shift it over one place and compare it with the next value. When the new number is finally larger than some value in the array, we have found the appropriate place to insert it. If the new value is smaller than every value in the array, it will go into the first position. Therefore, the entire operation can be characterized as "compare, shift; compare, shift . . ." until we find the appropriate place. The technique is diagrammed in Figure 1.8. Insertion sort is an enjoyable algorithm to implement because it is so natural. If you give someone one suit of a deck of cards and ask that the cards be sorted, the person will usually do something resembling insertion sort—compare the next card

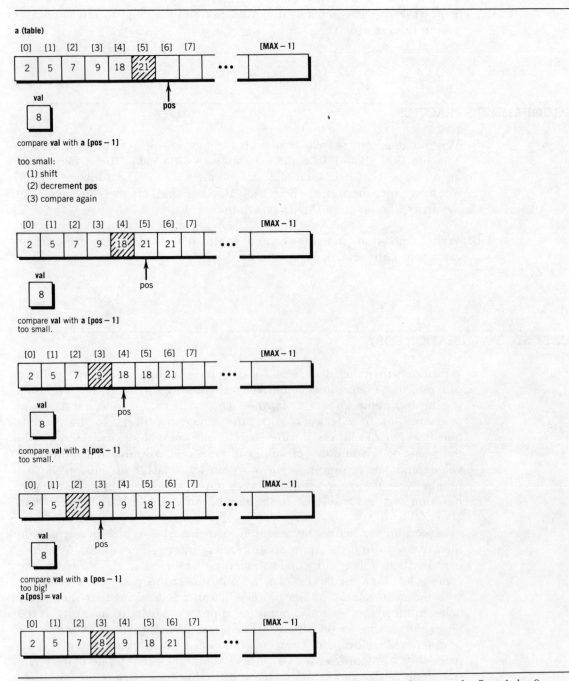

FIGURE 1.8. Stages in insertion sort. The new value is eventually put between the 7 and the 9.

with each in turn, until the right place is found and then move everything over to make room for the new card.

Figure 1.9 is the program used to accomplish insertion sort. In Figure 1.10 we show a sample collection of input values and the output generated by the program. As long as we have more numbers to read, we will continue reading them and inserting into the array. Of course, we may eventually run out of room, since we only preallocate MAX array elements, so we include an additional check during input to be certain that we read only MAX numbers (MAX is a program constant and is set to 100 via a #define statement). When we exceed MAX numbers or reach the end of the input file, we print the array elements in order.

```
/*
 * Read a table of values and sort them using "insertion sort."
 */
#include <stdio.h>
#define  MAX        100               /* maximum number of values to sort */

main()
{
  int num,                            /* number of values currently in table */
      res,                            /* value returned by scanf */
      table[MAX],                     /* table of values */
      next;                           /* current value */

  for (num = 0; num < MAX && (res = scanf("%d", &next)) == 1; num = num + 1)
    insert(table, next, num);
  if (res != EOF && num < MAX)        /* check for errors in input reading */
    printf("Error while reading input.\n");
  print_table(table, num);
}

/*
 * Place value in correct place in array.
 */
insert(a, val, n)
int a[], val, n;
{
  int pos;

  for (pos = n; pos > 0 && val < a[pos - 1]; pos = pos - 1)
    a[pos] = a[pos - 1];
  a[pos] = val;
}
```

(continued)

```
/*
 * Print array in sorted order.
 */
print_table(a, n)
int a[], n;
{
  int i;

  for (i = 0; i < n; i = i + 1)
    printf("%d\n", a[i]);
}
```

FIGURE 1.9. Insertion sort program—builds an array of integers in sorted order.

ANALYSIS OF INSERTION SORT

Insertion sort's main program is simple, consisting of a loop that reads a value in with scanf and then inserts it into the correct place in the array with the function insert. When all values have been read, we use another function, print_table, to print the values in the array.

As we pointed out earlier, when the end of the input is reached, scanf returns a special value, EOF. EOF is defined in a file named *stdio.h* (usually as minus one, but this is system dependent). To use this definition, we need to introduce a new statement:

```
#include <stdio.h>
```

#include is another preprocessor directive, which causes the preprocessor to *include* or process a file as if it were part of the source file. In this case, the file named *stdio.h* is included in the program. *stdio.h* is a system-supplied *header* file (thus the suffix name *.h*) that contains many of the def-

15	−45
97	9
−45	15
123	18
18	21
9	97
21	123

(a) Sample input data   *(b) Output from the insertion sort program*

FIGURE 1.10. Sample input and output produced by the insertion sort program, Figure 1.9.

initions used by the library functions for low-level input and output processing (thus the prefix *stdio*, which stands for standard input/output). The exact location of this file is system dependent, but the angle brackets surrounding its name instruct the preprocessor to look in various standard locations where header files are likely to be found.

In previous programs, if scanf did not read the number of values we expected it to, we assumed we had reached the end of the file successfully. However, it is possible that an illegal input value was entered, and we would like our program to give some indication if an error occurred. We do so by recording scanf's return value and, if it fails to equal one, we can compare it against EOF to determine whether an error occurred or we reached the end of the file successfully.

```
for (num = 0; num < MAX && (res=scanf("%d", &next)) == 1; num = num + 1)
  insert(table, next, num);
if (res != EOF && num < MAX)      /* check for errors in input reading */
  printf("Error while reading input.\n");
```

This works because assignment (=) is an operator; it performs an assignment and returns the value assigned. In this case, scanf is used to read a value and its return value is assigned to res. After the assignment, the value of res is compared with 1 to determine if the loop should exit. If res is 1, the loop body is entered and we insert the value into the table.

The Function insert

To insert a value in the array, we want to compare it with each entry in the array, starting with the largest, or last, entry and shifting values one place whenever val is smaller than the entry we are comparing. Eventually, val will be greater than or equal to an entry in the array, or we will have reached the beginning of a. In that case, we insert val into the newly created hole. We do this with a for loop, whose entire body consists of a single statement:

```
    for (pos = n; pos > 0 && val < a[pos - 1]; pos = pos - 1)
      a[pos] = a[pos - 1];
```

A great deal is taking place within this for loop; we suggest that you try working through it by hand to see its effect.

The Function print_table

print_table is similar to print_reverse; the only difference is in the order the table is printed. Notice that like print_reverse, print_table is passed the number of elements in the array it is printing, so it works for any size array.

PROGRAMMING PRACTICE

1-7. Add additional code to the insertion sort program, Figure 1.9, that counts the number of elements moved. After printing the entire sorted array, print out this count of the number of element movements. For a random set of n input values, this number should be approximately $n(n + 1)/2$. Compare your result with this expected result.

1-8. Rewrite the insertion sort program so that it sorts the values from high to low. There are two ways to do this, so try to implement both methods.

1-9. Write an insertion sort program that first finds the appropriate place to insert the new value, and then shifts everything after it one place before inserting the value.

1-10. How can we use *call by value* to make our insertion sort more compact? (*Hint*: Because parameters are copied, we can use the parameter as a local variable, so we can often easily avoid having additional index variables.)

C H A P T E R   2

BASIC DATA TYPES

There are three built-in data types in C, with several variations: integers, reals, and characters. The differences in the numerical types (integers versus reals) result from different storage representations and different machine instructions for handling them. Each numerical type comes in different sizes, allowing you to select the number of bits (or range of values) that is appropriate for your needs. In Chapter 1 we introduced the basic data types `int` and `float`. In this chapter we discuss these data types and their variations in more detail, introduce a new data type `char`, and examine C's automatic conversions between the various types. We also illustrate character-at-a-time input and output, and conclude the chapter by using it to build an alternative to `scanf` for reading numeric input.

INTEGERS

Integers, as we saw in Chapter 1, are whole numbers with a range of values supported by a particular machine. Generally, integers occupy one word of storage, but since the word size of machines varies over a wide range (typically 16, 32, or 36 bits), we are not certain how big an integer can be. To provide some control and to save storage space when values are in a more restricted range, C has three classes of integer storage: `short`, `int`, and `long`, in both signed and unsigned forms. Usually a `short` is 16 bits, an `int` is 32 bits, and a `long` is also 32 bits, but this depends on the machine your program runs on. Thus, a `short` can be used to save space when you can guarantee that a value will always be in a small

TABLE 2.1. Integer representation on typical computers.

Data Type	Number of Bits			
	DEC PDP-11	DEC VAX	IBM-PC	Apple Macintosh
short	16	16	16	16
int	16	32	16	16
long	32	32	32	32

range, and a long can be used to store larger values. Table 2.1 lists the sizes of shorts, ints, and longs on typical machines.

Integers can be either signed or unsigned. Signed integers use one bit for the sign of the number. A signed int (or just int, the default) uses one bit for the sign and 15 bits for the magnitude of the number on 16-bit machines or 31 bits for the magnitude on 32-bit machines. On a 16-bit machine, an int can store a value in the range from $-32,768$ to $+32,767$ (that is, -2^{15} to $+2^{15} - 1$).

Unsigned integers use all the bits for the magnitude and are always nonnegative. On a 16-bit machine all 16 bits are used, so any value in the range from 0 to 65,535 (0 to $2^{16} - 1$) can be represented. Unsigned types are used to increase the range of representable values when it is known that a variable will always be nonnegative, as, for example, in a loop counter. We declare unsigned integers with unsigned int, unsigned short, or unsigned long. Most compilers allow the type of integer to default to int, so a variable declared as unsigned is assumed to be an unsigned int. Unsigned integer arithmetic is described in Chapter 3.

Integer constants are expressed as a string of digits, with a leading minus sign indicating a negative number. If the number is too large for an int, it is automatically stored as a long. You can force a number to be a long by placing the letter 'l' or 'L' after it. For example, 32767L is a long constant. There is no such thing as a short or unsigned constant; C will automatically make it an int.

In addition to decimal (base 10) numbers, integers can be specified in either octal (base 8) or hexadecimal (base 16). A leading zero indicates an octal number; a number prefixed by '0x' or '0X' indicates a hexadecimal (hex for short). Regardless of how a value is indicated, however, it is stored in its binary equivalent. For example, the decimal value 63, the octal 077, or the hex 0x3f are all stored as 0...0111111. The octal and hexadecimal number systems are described in Appendix 1.

The data types short, int, and long are called *integral* types. They can be read or printed using scanf and printf using the %d formatting string. Normally, integers are printed in decimal (base 10) format, even if they have been defined as octal or hex values. To read or print an integral value in octal with scanf or printf, use %o; to read or print in hex, use %x. Unsigned integers are printed using the %u format specifier. Reading or printing a long requires the modifier l (%ld for a long decimal, %lo for a long octal, %lx for a long hex value, and %lu for a long unsigned value).

```
main ()
{
  int          a, b, c, d;
  short        s, t, u;
  long         l, m, n;
  unsigned int ui, uj, uk;

  a = 17;      b = -197;
  c = 0xa7c;   d = 01777;
  printf("a: %d\tb: %d\tc: %d\td: %d\n", a, b, c, d);

  s = 32;      t = -32767;   u = -1;
  printf("s: %d\tt: %d\tu: %d\n", s, t, u);

  m = -455;    l = -15L        /* redundant "L" */
  n = 156765341;               /* too big for 16-bit int */
  printf("l: %ld\tm: %ld\tn: %ld\n", l, m, n);

  ui = 157;  uj = 0xff;
  uk = -15;                    /* careful - machine dependent */

  printf("ui: %u\tuj: %u\tuk: %u\n", ui, uj, uk);
  printf("uj (octal): %o\tuj (hex): %x\n", uj, uj);
}
```

(a) Sample declarations and `printf` *formats*

```
a: 17     b: -197   c: 2684    d: 1023
s: 32     t: -32767 u: -1
l: 15     m: -455   n: 156765341
ui: 157   uj: 255   uk: 4294967281 ✓
uj (octal): 377     uj (hex): ff
```

(b) Output when run on a 32-bit machine

FIGURE 2.1. Sample declarations and assignments using shorts, ints, and longs.

Similarly, reading a short requires the modifier <u>h</u> (%hd, %ho, %hx, and so on), but printing a short does not.

Figure 2.1a shows typical declarations and assignments of these data types, along with `printf` statements for printing some of the values. Figure 2.1b shows the output of the program in Figure 2.1a.

PROGRAMMING PRACTICE

2-1. Write a program to determine the largest and smallest values for an int, short, and long on your computer. Modify the program to work for unsigned values.

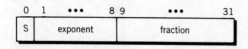

FIGURE 2.2. A typical floating point representation. Bit 0 is the sign of the fraction; bits 1-8 are the exponent (excess 128); bits 9-31 are the fraction.

2-2. Write a program that reads a value using `scanf` and prints it in base 10, hex, and octal.

REALS

Reals, or floating point numbers, are stored in 32 bits (on all 16-bit and 32-bit machines), with a machine dependent number of bits for the fraction and for the exponent. A typical representation uses 24 bits, including the sign, for the fraction and 8 bits for the exponent, as in Figure 2.2.

Real numbers are normally written with a decimal point, such as 13.45 or −211.0, but they may also be written in "e" notation, giving both a fraction and an exponent to base 10, as shown in Figure 2.3. "e" notation is similar to scientific notation with the letter "e" replacing the times sign and the base.

Reals are defined using the `float` declaration and have about seven significant digits. When greater significance is needed, a `double` can be used. `doubles` use 64 bits per value, with additional bits going to the fraction. Typical representations for `doubles` give 14 significant digits.

`floats` and `doubles` are specified in floating point notation, and are read with `scanf` using the `%f` formatting string for `floats` and `%lf` for `doubles`. Both types can be printed with `printf` using the `%f` formatting string. If the "e" notation is desired (1.3e5 instead of 130000), use `%e`. The default number of digits printed using these formats is compiler

Floating Pt.	Scientific Notation	"e" notation
12.45	1.245×10^1	1.245e1
−211.0	-2.110×10^2	−2.110e2
0.0056	5.600×10^{-3}	5.600e−3
−0.000123	-1.230×10^{-4}	−1.230e−4

FIGURE 2.3. Examples of floating point notation and equivalent scientific and "e" notation.

```
main()
{
  float    f = 0.1245e2,
           g = -0.123e-3,
           h = 0.00013;

  double   d = 2.0,
           e = -371.2164982e17;

  printf("f: %f g: %f h: %f\n", f,g,h);    /* print f, g, h as floats */
  printf("d: %f e: %f\n", d,e);            /* print d, e as floats */
  printf("d: %e e: %e\n", d,e);            /* print d, e using "e" notation */
}
```

(a) Examples of declarations and use of floats *and* doubles

```
f: 12.450000 g: -0.000123 h: 0.000130
d: 2.000000 e: -37121649820000000000.000000
d: 2.000000e+00 e: -3.712165e+19
```

(b) Output from the program in part (a), run on a 32-bit machine

FIGURE 2.4. (*a*) Examples of declarations and use of floats and doubles. (*b*) Output from the program in part (*a*), run on a 32-bit machine.

dependent. The examples in Figure 2.4*a* and *b* were run on a DEC VAX, a 32-bit machine. Try them on your own machine to see what the defaults are.

CHARACTERS

C allows us to manipulate characters as well as numbers. We usually think of characters as letters of the alphabet, but they encompass more than that. In fact, a character value can be any member of a machine's character set. The available characters and their internal representations depend on the machine on which the program runs. The most common character sets are ASCII (American Standard Code for Information Interchange) and EBCDIC (Extended Binary Coded Decimal Interchange Code). ASCII is the character set used on most personal, micro, and minicomputers, as well as several large mainframes, while EBCDIC is used on large IBM mainframes. ASCII characters are seven bits but are usually put into an eight-bit byte, while EBCDIC is an eight-bit set. There are 128 ASCII and 256 EBCDIC characters. They are shown in Appendixes 2 and 3, respectively.

A character variable is declared using the type identifier `char`:

```
char c;
```

Single characters are indicated using single quotation marks. Here are examples of assignments to `c`:

```
c = 'A';             /* uppercase A */
c = 'a';             /* lowercase a */
c = '7';             /* the character code for the digit 7 */
c = '!';             /* character code for an exclamation point */
```

Since all compilers store a `char` in a representation corresponding to the local character set, these assignments are machine independent.

To write a character in its integer representation, write it as an integer. In ASCII, for example,

```
c = 'a';
printf("%d", c);
```

prints the number 97. To read or print a character as a *character*, use the `%c` format. The output of

```
c = 'a';
printf("%c", c);
```

is the single character **a**. Characters are usually stored in single bytes, the size that is appropriate for most machines.

Some character codes do not yield a printable character, and are represented using escape sequences. An escape sequence is a backslash (\) followed by a code letter for the particular function. Figure 2.5 shows the character escape codes.

The last code in Figure 2.5 (`'\xxx'`) is provided because we need a flexible mechanism to specify all the available characters, including nonprinting ones. Here `xxx` represents a (maximum) three-digit octal number. A leading zero is not needed because the value is always interpreted as octal, but it aids readability. A maximum of three digits is permitted; if the number of bits is greater than that needed for a single character (such as `'\0777'`), machine dependent results occur. Usually the rightmost bits are used, but caution must be exercised.

In ASCII, the code to ring the terminal bell on most terminals is a *control-g*, or seven. Therefore, we can define this as a constant `BELL` and use `printf` to ring someone's bell:

```
#define  BELL     '\007'               /* ASCII bell code */
    ...
    printf("Wake up! %c", BELL);        /* ring terminal bell */
```

`'\0'`	null character
`'\b'`	backspace
`'\f'`	form feed (top of next page)
`'\n'`	newline
`'\r'`	carriage return
`'\t'`	tab
`'\v'`	vertical tab
`'\''`	single quotation mark
`'\"'`	double quotation mark
`'\\'`	backslash
`'\xxx'`	octal value

FIGURE 2.5. Character codes using the backslash quoting mechanism.

Figure 2.6 is a program that prints all the characters in a machine's character set (assuming a maximum of 128 characters), showing the decimal, octal, and character values. Caution is needed in running this program, though, because some of the nonprinting characters do strange things to a terminal (such as erase the screen) or to a printer (such as eject the paper to the top of the next page). For this reason, we have chosen the inelegant method of placing each character on a separate line.

CHARACTERS VERSUS INTEGERS

Characters seem strange, because they are machine dependent and because there does not appear to be a strong distinction between them

```
/*
 *      Print character set in decimal, octal, and character form.
 */
#define  MAXCHAR        128     /* change to 256 for EBCDIC machines */

main()
{
  char c;

  for (c = 0; c < MAXCHAR; c = c + 1)
    printf("%4d\t%4o\t%c\n", c, c, c);
}
```

FIGURE 2.6. Program that prints the local character set.

and integers. In the previous program, for example, we incremented a character variable and printed it as both an integer and a character. Characters give us the first hint that C is not a strongly typed language, since we can often use characters and integers interchangeably. Unlike more strongly typed languages, C allows us to do arithmetic on characters and treat integers as if they were characters.

In a strongly typed language such as Pascal, built-in functions are needed to convert between characters and integers, and it is an error to try to convert an integer to a character if the integer is outside the local character set. In C, however, no explicit conversion from one to the other is needed. If c is a char and n is an int, the assignment

```
n = c;        /* assign char to int */
```

causes n to be an integer with the value of the local set's code for c. In ASCII, if c is 'a', this assigns 97 to n. Similarly, the assignment

```
c = n;        /* assign int to char */
```

causes the rightmost bits (depending on the character set and the machine) of c to be the same as the rightmost bits of n.

A char can be safely converted to an int on any machine and will give the integer character code equivalent of the character. The reverse conversion, from int to char, is also safe, as long as the int is a valid integer representation for a character. If, for example, the int is larger than any legal character's integer representation, the conversion is machine dependent and should be avoided when portability of code is desired.

Because of these automatic conversions, we can use int variables to store characters. In Figure 2.6, for example, c could have been declared as an int with no change in the program's behavior. This means that char variables are less useful than one might think, and are ordinarily used only with arrays of characters, a topic discussed in Chapter 4.

PROGRAMMING PRACTICE

2-3. Write a program that reads a char and prints its integer equivalent in the local character set.

2-4. Write a program that reads an integer and prints the corresponding character. Be sure to do appropriate error/range checking.

CHARACTER INPUT AND OUTPUT

Just as there are prewritten routines for formatted input and output of numerical and string data, there are predefined functions for character input and output. The two character-equivalent functions of scanf and printf are getchar and putchar, respectively.

getchar takes no arguments and returns as its value a single character—the next character in the input stream. Like scanf, getchar will return the special value EOF if the end-of-file character is entered. getchar is guaranteed to return a value that is the integer representation of the character in the local character set, or the special value EOF. As we saw earlier, EOF is usually minus one, a value that does not represent a character.

Similarly, putchar takes an integer that represents a legal character, and writes it as a character to the standard output. If the number does not represent a legal character, anomalous results will occur. Usually the least significant bits (equivalent to the local character representation) are examined, but the results vary from machine to machine. It is the programmer's responsibility to provide a value that represents a legitimate character. putchar does not return a value and should not fail (although it can fail if the character is being written to a file). Handling input and output failures is discussed in detail in Chapter 12.

As a result of the need for an "extended" character set (that is, one that includes all of the machine's characters, plus EOF), we usually deal with variables declared as ints when reading character data. We can see this in Figure 2.7, a program that echoes its input to its output, one character at a time. Such a program is useful if we have the ability to direct the standard input or standard output to different files, since it can then

```
/*
 * Copy the input to the output.
 */
#include <stdio.h>

main()
{
  int c;                  /* next character */

  while ((c = getchar()) != EOF)
    putchar(c);
}
```

FIGURE 2.7. A program that copies its input to its output.

be used to copy one file to another. (For example, the UNIX file-copying program *cp* functions almost in this way, except that it includes additional code to handle named files or directories on the command line.) This program is interesting because many programs that transform their input are straightforward extensions to it.

The program itself simply reads characters using getchar and writes them with putchar until getchar returns EOF. We have included *stdio.h* because getchar and putchar, as well as EOF, are defined there. Because of the need for the extended character set, the variable c, which holds the character being read or written, is declared as an int. Note that reading the character and assigning it to c occur within the loop's test, taking advantage of C's assignment operator's ability to return the value that it has assigned.

Try compiling and running the program in Figure 2.7 to see how it works on your system. Some operating systems buffer the characters from the terminal until carriage return is typed. In that case, after typing a complete line plus carriage return, the entire line will be echoed (Figure 2.8*a*). If your operating system does not buffer lines, each character will be repeated as it is typed (Figure 2.8*b*).

A PROGRAM TO LINE NUMBER ITS INPUT

To further illustrate character handling, as well as the now familiar printf, we will write a small program (Figure 2.9) that prints each line in

---

```
Now is the time                    NNooww  iiss  tthhee  ttiimmee
Now is the time
for all good men                   ffoorr  aallll  ggoooood  mmeenn
for all good men
to come to the aid                 ttoo  ccoommee  ttoo  tthhee  aaiidd
to come to the aid
of their party.                    ooff  tthheeiirr  ppaarrttyy..
of their party.
```

(a) Output from the copy program   *(b) Output from the copy program*
in line buffered mode   *when lines are not buffered*

FIGURE 2.8. (*a*) Output from Figure 2.7 when input is being line buffered. (*b*) Output when lines are not buffered.

```
/*
 * Copy the input to the output, giving each line a number.
 */
#include <stdio.h>

main()
{
  int c,                              /* next character */
      lastch,                         /* previous character */
      lineno;                         /* lines printed so far */

  lastch = '\n';
  lineno = 0;
  while ((c = getchar()) != EOF)
  {
    if (lastch == '\n')
    {                                 /* hit end of line */
      lineno = lineno + 1;
      printf("%6d ", lineno);
    }
    putchar(c);
    lastch = c;
  }
}
```

FIGURE 2.9. Program that copies its input to its output, placing a line number at the start of each line.

the input with a line number. Like Figure 2.7, this program will read one character at a time until the end of the file, and write the character to the standard output. We will also remember the previous character typed. When a character is ready to be printed, if its previous character was a carriage return (\n), we will know that we are at the start of a new line and print the line number. Notice that this is just an extension of the function provided in Figure 2.7, the program that copied its input to its output.

Figure 2.10 shows the result of running the line-numbering program on itself. Line numbering is a useful capability and is surprisingly simple to accomplish. However, it makes sense only if the operating system buffers its input lines and if we have the ability to redirect the standard input and output. In UNIX or PC-DOS, for example, if we have compiled the program into a file named *number*, we can create a line-numbered version of *infile*, called *outfile*, by entering *number < infile > outfile*.

```
 1 /*
 2  * Copy the input to the output, giving each line a number.
 3  */
 4 #include <stdio.h>
 5
 6 main()
 7 {
 8   int c,                            /* next character */
 9       lastch,                       /* previous character */
10       lineno;                       /* lines printed so far */
11
12   lastch = '\n';
13   lineno = 0;
14   while ((c = getchar()) != EOF)
15   {
16     if (lastch == '\n')
17     {                               /* hit end of line */
18       lineno = lineno + 1;
19       printf("%6d ", lineno);
20     }
21     putchar(c);
22     lastch = c;
23   }
```

FIGURE 2.10. Output with line numbers added by the program.

PROGRAMMING PRACTICE

 2-5. Notice that blank lines are numbered in Figure 2.10. Rewrite the line-numbering program (Figure 2.9) so that blank lines are counted but not numbered.

 2-6. Add page numbering to the line-numbering program (Figure 2.9). That is, place a line with ''PAGE *N*'' at the beginning of each page, with a blank line between the page-numbering line and the next line of output. Assume that a page has a maximum of 66 lines (use a constant PGLINE).

IDENTIFIERS AND NAMING CONVENTIONS

Declarations have two parts: a name and a type. We have examined the different types; we now examine the rules for constructing names.

Variable and function names are known as *identifiers*. Not every com-

TABLE 2.2. C reserved words.

auto	break	case	char	continue
default	do	double	else	enum
extern	float	for	goto	if
int	long	register	return	short
sizeof	static	struct	switch	typedef
union	unsigned	void	while	

bination of characters is a legal identifier, however. Identifiers are composed of any sequence of lowercase and uppercase letters, digits, and underscore (_) characters, with the restriction that the first character must not be a digit. Case is significant in identifiers: count refers to a different identifier than Count. Some operating systems use identifiers that start with an underscore. To prevent conflicting use of names, our identifiers should begin with a letter.

To provide access to certain system functions, some compilers allow the dollar sign ($) to appear in identifiers. This feature is not portable, however, and may cause conflicts with the use of names already defined at the systems level.

Certain identifiers are reserved as keywords and cannot be used as normal identifiers; these reserved identifiers are listed in Table 2.2. Other identifiers may be reserved by a particular compiler; among the more common ones are asm, entry, and fortran.

The maximum number of characters in an identifier is not restricted by the language, although most compilers place a limit on the number of significant characters. In the original definition of C, only the first eight characters were significant, implying that var_name1 and var_name2 referred to the same identifier. In most modern C compilers, the first 31 characters are significant, although to be portable to all current compilers, it may be necessary to restrict names to six, seven, or eight characters. This topic is covered in Chapter 13.

CASE STUDY—CONVERTING CHARACTERS INTO NUMBERS

We have been using scanf to read input, but as we have pointed out, scanf is useful only when the input has no errors in it. In Chapter 7, we will implement an alternative to scanf that allows us to skip over bad data. Now, however, we will write a small program, shown in Figure 2.11, that copies its input to its output, filtering out any inappropriate characters appearing in its input, and writing the total of its input values.

```
/*
 *    Convert characters representing digits to a long integer.
 */
#include <stdio.h>

main()
{
  long total, sum;                          /* running total, sum of digits */
  int  c, sign;                             /* next character, sign of number */

  c = ' ';
  total = 0;
  while (c != EOF)
  {
    while (c == ' ' || c == '\t' || c == '\n')
      c = getchar();                        /* scan over "white space" */
    sign = c;
    if (c == '+' || c == '-')
      c = getchar();                        /* skip over the '+' or '-' */
    if (c >= '0' && c <= '9')
    {
      sum = 0;
      while (c >= '0' && c <= '9')          /* accumulate sum */
      {
        sum = 10 * sum + (c - '0');
        c = getchar();
      }
      if (sign == '-')                      /* is it neg? */
        sum = -sum;
      printf("%ld\n", sum);                 /* the value */
      total = total + sum;
    }
    else
      if (c != EOF)
        c = getchar();
  }
  printf ("Total %ld\n", total);
}
```

FIGURE 2.11. A program that converts character input into a long integer, then uses the value to keep a running total.

To do so, we read the input one character at a time. Groups of characters representing a single number are converted to an integer, which is then added to a running total. Since numbers can be separated by *white space* (spaces, tabs, and carriage returns), the program begins by skipping over white-space characters until a non-white-space character is read. If the character is a **+** or a **-**, a flag is set and the remaining characters are assumed to be digits.

Once we have the first digit in a number, we use a **while** loop to convert the sequence of characters, reading and converting one character at a time, and adding its value to a sum representing the value of the sequence. The loop stops when a nondigit is read. If the next character (c) is a digit (that is, a character greater than or equal to '0' and less than or equal to '9'), we add it to the sum representing the number. We do this by taking the current value of the sum and multiplying it by 10, and then adding the digit that the new character represents.

```
sum = 10 * sum + (c - '0');
```

Note that to perform the conversion, we do not really need to know the machine representation of the character. We can convert a digit character to an integer by subtracting the character '0' from it. (This assumes that all digits are represented by contiguous codes, which is the case with both ASCII and EBCDIC.) For example, in ASCII, the code for '7' is 55 and the code for '0' is 48; the subtraction yields the integer value 7. Trace out the conversion of a number such as 812 by hand to see the operation of the program clearly.

The idea of reading numerical data one character at a time and doing our own conversions may seem extreme when we already have **scanf**. However, **scanf** has several problems: it compiles into a large amount of runnable code, and it is slower than using our own conversions. More importantly, **scanf** makes it difficult for the programmer to handle errors because it tells us only how many values were correctly converted, giving us no information as to why any failure might have occurred. If a failure occurs (the number is less than expected), we still have to deal with the input one character at a time in order to provide suitable error messages or error recovery.

PROGRAMMING PRACTICE

2-7. The character-to-integer program (Figure 2.11) implements part of what scanf does—it reads values from the input stream. **printf** performs the opposite function; it converts numbers to character strings and writes them. Write a program that converts an integer (perhaps defined by **#define**) to characters and writes them to the output, without using **printf**.

2-8. Modify the function **get_data** from Chapter 1 so that it does its own character scanning and conversion to longs (as in Figure 2.11), eliminating scanf from the program. Compare the size and speed of the compiled code in both versions.

2-9. Modify the program in Figure 2.11 so that it reads and converts real numbers (that is, numbers containing a decimal point) as well as integers. Extend the program so that it reads and converts numbers in scientific notation as well.

CHAPTER 3

OPERATORS

C provides an especially rich set of operators. We have already introduced several of them, such as the arithmetic and logical operators. In this chapter, we go over these operators in more detail, noting any unusual behavior or restrictions on their use, and discuss those operators we have ignored up to this point. We pay special attention to C's shorthand and bit manipulation operators, which are not found in most other programming languages. The chapter concludes with a case study implementing several important functions that use these operators.

OPERATORS, OPERANDS, AND PRECEDENCE

Table 3.1 summarizes the C operators, the types of operands expected, and their relative precedence. Parentheses can be used to override the default precedence, although the compiler is allowed to arbitrarily rearrange expressions involving only commutative operators (+, *, &, |, and ^), for which temporary variables must be used to force the desired order of evaluation. The rest of this chapter elaborates on the table.

Many operators require operands to be of a certain type. If an operand of an incorrect type is given, the operation may still be performed but the results may be different from those expected. It is *your* responsibility to guarantee that operands are the correct type, in range, and that the result has not produced overflow or underflow. The alternative is for the compiler or run-time environment to capture incorrect operand types, as with languages such as Pascal. When this is done at compile time, we can change the incorrect operation and recompile. When it occurs at run

TABLE 3.1. C operators summarized in order of decreasing precedence.

Operator	Description
x[i]	Array subscripting.
f(x)	Function call.
.	Structure field selection.
->	Indirect structure field selection.
++, --	Postfix/prefix increment/decrement. If both occur in the same expression, postfix has higher precedence.
sizeof	Size of a variable or type (in bytes).
(type)	Cast to type.
~	Bitwise negation.
!	Logical NOT.
-	Unary minus.
&	Address of.
*	Indirection (dereferencing).
*, /, %	Multiply, divide, modulus. All are equal in precedence.
+, -	Addition, subtraction. Equal in precedence.
<<, >>	Left, right shift. Equal in precedence.
<, >, <=, >=	Test for inequality. Equal in precedence.
==, !=	Test for equality, inequality. Equal in precedence.
&	Bitwise AND.
^	Bitwise exclusive OR.
|	Bitwise OR.
&&	Logical AND.
||	Logical OR.
? :	Conditional operator.
=, +=, -=, *=, /=, %=, <<=, >>=, &=, ^=, |=	Assignment operators. All are equal in precedence.
,	The comma operator—sequential evaluation of expressions.

time, many languages do not provide tools for capturing errors and attempting to correct them. When using C, we must know our own code and monitor the operations ourselves. The benefit is that the need for run-time type checking is eliminated; if our programs run, they will run more efficiently.

ARITHMETIC OPERATORS

The arithmetic operators are addition (+), subtraction (-), multiplication (*), division (/), remaindering (%), and unary minus (-). As expected, all except % operate on integer, character, and floating point operands.

TABLE 3.2. Precedence of C arithmetic operators.

high	unary −, ++ −−
	∗, /, %
	+, −
low	= (assignment)

The arithmetic operators associate (are evaluated) left to right and follow the usual precedence rules. Table 3.2 shows the precedence, from high to low, of the arithmetic operators, including assignment (which is also an operator). In this table, operations of equal precedence are applied left to right.

Operands should agree in type. If they do not, automatic conversions occur; these are natural and are discussed later in the chapter. After the expression on the right side of the assignment is evaluated, it is converted to the type of the left (known as *assignment compatibility*) whenever possible.

INTEGER ARITHMETIC

Integer arithmetic is always exact within the limits of the number of values that can be represented in the data type. Integer addition (and subtraction) is carried out without regard to overflow. On most machines, adding one to the largest positive number yields the largest negative value. For unsigned integers, one added to the largest value yields zero.

With multiplication, division, and remaindering (the *multiplicative operators*), problems can occur if the result of integer operations is assigned to a variable of a shorter type. Given the assignments

```
long    i, j;
short   answer;

i = 10000;   j = 10000;
answer = i * j;
```

the calculation of **answer** will correctly evaluate to 100,000,000. However, the assignment of the **long** result to a **short** produces machine-dependent results. Generally, the least significant bits are assigned. In the following illustration of the assignment

```
short s
    . . .
s = -1691154500L;
```

notice that the **long** is a negative number (the sign bit is 1): -1,691,154,500; the truncated **short** (assuming that conversion from **long** to short uses the least significant bits) is a positive number: 1980. Conversion from a longer type to a shorter type leads to loss of significance, or worse, meaningless results.

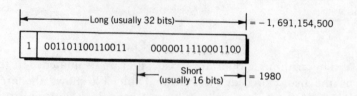

Integer division (both operands are integers) produces a *truncated* result. If both operands are integers with the same sign, the result is truncated toward zero. If only one of the operands is negative, the direction of truncation is implementation dependent. Since integer division truncates toward zero, "fractional" division of integers always returns zero. Whether a and b are ints or floats,

```
a = 1/3;
b = 6/7;
```

assigns zero to both a and b.

The remaindering operator % takes two integer operands and returns the remainder when the first is divided by the second. If both are positive, this is the familiar modulus operation. The sign of the result is always the sign of the dividend (the first operand, or the one "upstairs"). Here are some examples:

```
 10 %   5 =  0
 10 %   7 =  3
  5 %  12 =  5
-20 %  12 = -8
-20 % -12 = -8        ← WATCH OUT—machine dependent
```

Regardless of the sign of a and b, (a / b)*b + a % b will always equal a.

FLOATING POINT ARITHMETIC

Floating point arithmetic is an approximation of the correct result, since floating point values are rounded to the number of significant digits allowable in the representation. Typically, this is 7 digits for floats and 14 digits for doubles. Adding to the largest possible float will produce overflow, and the results are machine dependent. The hardware of most machines traps floating point overflow, causing a run-time error and termination of the program.

All floating point arithmetic is carried out with double precision operands. This means that floats are always "widened" to doubles before the arithmetic occurs (at the expense of machine efficiency). After the expression is completely evaluated, the result is converted to the type of the left hand side of the assignment. This may involve loss of precision when converting back to a float, or overflow when converting to an int. Overflow and underflow can occur with real arithmetic; the action taken is machine dependent.

Floating point division differs from integer division. If either operand of the division is a float, both operands are converted to double (for the purpose of the arithmetic), and the division is carried out in double precision with no truncation of the result. If x and y are floats,

```
x = 1.0/3.0;
y = 6.0/7.0;

w = 1.0/3;
z = 6/7.0;
```

assigns 0.333333 to both x and w and 0.857143 to both y and z.

UNSIGNED ARITHMETIC

Unsigned arithmetic is similar to integer arithmetic, except that there are no negative results and no overflow. Instead, all unsigned arithmetic takes place modulo 2^n, where n is the number of bits in the unsigned operands. This means that adding one to the largest unsigned value gives zero, and conversely, subtracting one from zero gives the largest unsigned value. We illustrate unsigned arithmetic with the program in Figure 3.1a. Figure 3.1b shows the program's output, assuming the program is run on

---

```
main()
{
  unsigned int i;

  i = 4294967295;    /* (2^32)-1, the largest unsigned int */
  printf("i: %u, i + 1: %u, i + 2: %u\n", i, i + 1, i + 2);
}
```

(a) A program to illustrate unsigned arithmetic

```
i: 4294967295, i + 1: 0, i + 2: 1
```

(b) The program's output assuming 32-bit ints

FIGURE 3.1. A small program that illustrates unsigned arithmetic.

a machine with 32-bit ints. We have hard-coded the largest unsigned integer in our program; later in the chapter we will see how to determine its value automatically.

UNARY MINUS

The minus sign in front of an expression is an operator. Since all constants are positive in C, the unary minus is equivalent to multiplying by −1, which is straightforward with ints and floats. With unsigned data, however, we must carefully consider the effect of multiplying by −1. Consider the following small program that assigns negative values to an unsigned variable.

```
main()
{
  unsigned int a = -1;

  printf ("unsigned a: %u\n", a);
  printf ("signed a: %d\n", a);
}
```

The program was run on a 32-bit machine, and produced this output:

```
unsigned a: 4294967295
signed a: -1
```

To understand why this output occurs, recall that unsigned values are considered to be positive (or zero). Because −1 is represented as a word of all ones (at least on two's complement machines) and because −1 is interpreted as a signed integer (using the %d formatting in the second printf), we printed −1. However, a word of all ones is the largest positive value when interpreted as an unsigned int. So, as in this example. using 32 bits for an int, 4,294,967,295 is printed.

RELATIONAL OPERATORS

The relational operators compare values for equality (==), inequality (!=), greater than (>), less than (<), greater than or equal (>=), and less than or equal (<=). The result of a relational operator is an int, one (true) if the specified relation between the operands holds and zero (false) if not.

The inequality operators (>, >=, <, <=) all have the same precedence, which is higher than the precedence of == and !=. All of these operators have precedence higher than assignment, however, so it is often necessary to use parentheses in order to be certain that comparisons and assignments are made in the correct order, as in

```
while ((c = getchar()) != EOF)
    putchar(c);
```

In general, it is a good idea to parenthesize relational operators, since they are in the middle of the precedence hierarchy.

LOGICAL OPERATORS

Logical operators perform the logical AND (**&&**), logical OR (**||**), or logical negation (**!**) of their operands. The logical operators take any numerical argument and return <u>true</u> or <u>false</u> (represented by one for true, zero for false) according to the truth table in Table 3.3. Nonzero values are interpreted as true and zero as false. Negation returns one if its operand is zero, and zero otherwise.

The logical operators associate left to right, and their precedence is low, so we rarely need to parenthesize (AND has higher precedence than OR). Figure 3.2 shows how expressions using **&&** and **||** are evaluated.

EVALUATION ORDER

The operands of logical operations can be any expression and may have side effects that change the values of their parameters. To use logical operators correctly, we must understand the order of evaluation and the resulting possibility that a clause might not be evaluated at all.

Without parentheses, logical operations are performed left to right, and evaluation stops as soon as the <u>result</u> can be determined. For logical AND, such as in the statement

```
while (i < MAX && scanf("%d", &value) != EOF)
    ...
```

the clause i < MAX is evaluated first. If it is false, the value of the entire

TABLE 3.3. Truth table showing results of logical AND and logical OR.

Operands		Result	
Op1	Op2	&&	||
Nonzero	Nonzero	1	1
Nonzero	Zero	0	1
Zero	Nonzero	0	1
Zero	Zero	0	0

Declarations and Initial Values:

```
int     a = 1, b = 2, n = 1, m = 2;
char    c = 'm';
```

Expression	Equivalent Expression	Value
a && b && n	(a && b) && n	1
a || b || n	(a || b) || n	1
c >= 'a' && c <= 'z'	(c >= 'a') && (c <= 'z')	1
c >= 'A' && c <= 'Z'	(c >= 'A') && (c <= 'Z')	0

FIGURE 3.2. Examples of evaluation of logical operators.

logical expression is false, regardless of how the second clause would evaluate, and therefore the second clause is *not* evaluated. More to the point, the call to scanf does not occur; no reading or assignment to value occurs. If there are multiple clauses connected by logical AND, the first false one terminates the evaluation. In this example, only when i < MAX evaluates to true is the second clause,

```
scanf("%d", &value) != EOF
```

evaluated.

In logical OR, the first true clause terminates evaluation of all succeeding clauses. In the following statement, the function scanf is not called if x is greater than zero.

```
while (x > 0 || scanf("%d", &x) == 1)
    ...
```

BITWISE OPERATORS

While the operators we have seen so far are common to most higher-level programming languages, C also provides less common bit manipulation operators for shifting bits left or right; for bitwise AND, OR, and exclusive OR of two operands; and for the bitwise inversion of a single operand. These operations are provided to allow us to deal with the details of the machine. They can be used when the hardware requires individual bits within a machine word to be set or read and can also provide faster versions of some numerical operations. All these operators require their operands to be an integral type, although some compilers forbid their use on longs.

BIT SHIFTS

The left and right bit shift operators shift an operand left or right by a specified number of bits. The form of the operator is

left shift: *right shift:*
op << n   op >> n

As an example,

```
a = val << 1;
```

assigns val, shifted one bit to the left, to a, multiplying val by two. Similarly,

```
a = val >> 1;
```

shifts val one bit to the right, assigning the result to a, dividing val by two. If val is originally 6, which in binary is 0..00110, here is what val looks like, shifted left by one bit and shifted right by one bit:

```
val << 1          val >> 1
0..01100          0..00011
```

The number of bits to shift must be positive and be an int expression or an expression convertible to an int. Bit shift operations are not defined for negative shifts. The number of bits to shift should also be less than or equal to the number of bits in an integer. The result of a large shift is machine dependent.

On *left* shifts, zeros are always shifted into the vacated bits on the right. On *right* shifts, the bit shifted in depends on the variable's type. If the variable is unsigned, zeros are shifted in; if the variable is signed, *usually* the sign bit is extended, but this operation is machine dependent. It is possible that on some machines zeros are shifted in for signed values, which would have the (most likely undesired) effect of changing the sign of the value. Caution is the general rule when using right shifts on signed values.

BITWISE LOGICAL OPERATORS

There are three bitwise logical operators: bitwise AND (&), bitwise OR (|), and bitwise exclusive OR (^). These operators work on their operands bit by bit, setting each bit in the result, as shown in Table 3.4. The bitwise AND is one only when both bits are one; otherwise it is zero. The bitwise OR is one if either operand is one. The exclusive OR is one if exactly one of the bits is one.

TABLE 3.4. Result of bitwise AND, OR, and exclusive OR.

Operands		Result		
Op1	Op2	&	|	^
1	1	1	1	0
1	0	0	1	1
0	1	0	1	1
0	0	0	0	0

As an example of the results of these bitwise operations, Figure 3.3 shows the result of AND, OR, and exclusive OR on two ints, assuming 16-bit integers. OR is sometimes called the "either" or "any" function, AND the "both" or "all" function, and exclusive OR the "odd" or "only one" function.

Bit operations are useful because they allow the selection of individual bits or groups of bits in a word. They are needed when special devices use individual bits as flags or controlling signals. We can use combinations of logical AND, logical OR, and bitwise negation to create a *mask* that allows selected bit fields to be manipulated. The following program fragment sets a particular bit (the second bit from the right) in a variable flag; the last piece tests whether the particular bit has been set. Parentheses are needed because the precedence of the test-for-inequality operator (!=) is higher than that of bitwise AND (&).

```
#define   FLAGBIT1      01            /* equiv to 00..0001 */
#define   FLAGBIT2      02            /* equiv to 00..0010 */
          ...
    int    flag;
          ...

    flag = flag | FLAGBIT2;            /* turn on appropriate flag */
          ...
    if ((flag & FLAGBIT2) != 0)        /* test if flag is set */
          ...
```

```
A:     1 0 0 1 0 1 1 0   1 1 1 0 0 0 0 1
B:     0 0 0 1 1 0 1 0   1 1 0 1 1 0 0 1


A | B:  1 0 0 1 1 1 1 0   1 1 1 1 1 0 0 1
A & B:  0 0 0 1 0 0 1 0   1 1 0 0 0 0 0 1
A ^ B:  1 0 0 0 1 1 0 0   0 0 1 1 1 0 0 0
```

FIGURE 3.3. AND, OR, and exclusive OR on two 16-bit integers.

Notice that the meaning and use of the bitwise operators **&** and **|** are much different than those of the logical operators **&&** and **||**.

There is one final bitwise operator, negation (̃), which inverts each bit in its operand; that is, each one bit becomes zero, each zero becomes one. The operand must be an integral type. If x is represented as eight bits, here is ˜x:

```
x:    10011001
˜x:    01100110
```

ASSIGNMENT OPERATORS

Assignment operators are used to assign the result of an expression to a variable. The type of the right-hand side of the assignment should match the type of the left. If it does not, the type of the right is converted to that of the left before the assignment is made (although no change is made in any variables on the right).

As we have seen, assignment is an operator that returns a value—the value assigned. Thus, assignment operators may be used more than once in a single statement. To initialize more than one variable to INITVAL, use

```
a = b = c = INITVAL;
```

The assignment operator is evaluated right to left, so this multiple assignment is equivalent to

```
a = (b = (c = INITVAL));
```

In addition to the usual assignment, =, there are shorthand assignment operators of the form

lhs op = rhs

where *lhs* is the left-hand side of the assignment, *rhs* is an expression, and *op* is a C binary operator. The shorthand form is equivalent to

lhs = lhs op (rhs)

with *lhs* evaluated once. *op* can be any of the arithmetic or bit-shift operators (but not **&&** or **||**), so the shorthand assignment operators are **+=**, **-=**, ***=**, **/=**, **%=**, **<<=**, **>>=**, **&=**, **|=**, and **^=**. Like =, the shorthand assignment operators return the value assigned and can be used in other expressions.

Using the shorthand operators, we can easily divide val by two with

```
val /= 2;
```

which is equivalent to

```
val = val / 2;
```

Another way to accomplish this division (if val is nonnegative) is

```
val >>= 1;
```

the shorthand for

```
val = val >> 1;
```

which is a right shift of one bit.

These assignment operators are convenient and lead to more concise, more efficient, and perhaps surprisingly, more readable code. For example, consider the assignment

```
table[2 * i * j] = table[2 * i * j] + newval;
```

Using the assignment operator +=, this assignment can be written more concisely as

```
table[2 * i * j] += newval;
```

The latter is more efficient because the expression 2 * i * j is evaluated only once. It is more readable because it makes it clear that only one array element is involved in the computation. And it is less likely to be in error because we have to enter the subscripting expression only once.

POSTFIX AND PREFIX ASSIGNMENT OPERATORS

Two special sets of shorthand operators are provided for the common operations of incrementing and decrementing by one. ++ adds one to its operand; -- subtracts one from its operand. For example, a++ and ++a are equivalent to a += 1. Similarly, a-- and --a are equivalent to a -= 1.

There are two forms of these operators, *prefix* (preceding its operand) and *postfix* (following its operand). As either a prefix or a postfix operator, ++ adds one to its operand. However, when used as a postfix operator, ++ first evaluates the operand, providing its value to the rest of the statement or expression and then adds one to it. When it is used as a prefix operator, the addition occurs first and then the new value of the variable is used in the expression. Prefix and postfix -- behave similarly to ++, except that they decrement their variable by one.

As an example, if n is five, then the postfix assignment a = n++ assigns five to a and then increments n. After the assignment, a is five and n is six. The corresponding prefix assignment, a = ++n, first increments n and then makes the assignment. After the assignment, both a and n are six.

We will often use one form or the other when going through an array. Because an assignment using the ++ or -- operator causes two assignments to occur, we can often save an instruction and produce more efficient code. The assignment

```
max = a[i++];
```

assigns the current a[i] to max and then increments i, equivalent to the two statements

```
max = a[i];
i++;
```

Similarly, max = a[++i] first increments i, then makes the assignment, and is equivalent to the two statements

```
i++;
max = a[i];
```

Notice that as a statement not involving other side effects,

```
i++;
```

is the same as

```
++i;
```

We can use either form to make our for and while loops more compact, as we have done in the following loops that print the first n values in an array vals:

```
i = 0;
while (i < n)
  printf("%d\n", vals[i++]);
```

OR

```
for (i = 0; i < n; ++i)
  printf("%d\n", vals[i]);
```

OTHER OPERATORS

There are two other operators of interest, the comma operator and the sizeof operator. The *comma operator* is used to link related expressions together as a single expression, making programs more compact. A comma-separated list of expressions is treated as a single expression and evaluated left to right, with the value of the rightmost expression returned as the expression's value. A program fragment to exchange the values of two variables x and y

```
temp = x;                        /* swap the values of "x" and "y" */
x = y;
y = temp;
```

can be written more compactly using the comma operator as

```
temp = x, x = y, y = temp;     /* swap the values of "x" and "y" */
```

We can also use the comma operator to eliminate embedded assignments from tests. For example,

```
while ((c=getchar()) == EOF)
```

can be rewritten as

```
while (c = getchar(), c == EOF)
```

separating reading the character from testing for end of file. Because the comma operator evaluates left to right, the rightmost expression's value (here, the test for end of file) controls the while's execution. Either method is acceptable; use the one that is easier for you to read.

The comma operator has the lowest precedence of any of C's operators, so it can safely be used to turn any list of expressions into a single statement. However, the comma used to separate the parameters in function calls is not a comma operator and does not guarantee left to right evaluation.

The sizeof operator returns the number of bytes in its operand, which may be a constant, a variable, or a data type. A byte is somewhat loosely defined as the size of a character, which is eight bits on most but not all machines. If the variable is an array or another constructed type (structure, union, or enumeration type; see Chapter 10), the value returned is the total number of bytes needed. For arrays, sizeof returns the size of the base type (whether it is a built-in or a constructed type) times the declared size of the array. If a is an array of 100 ints, sizeof(a) is 400, assuming 4-byte (32-bit) ints, and 200, assuming 2-byte (16-bit) ints.

```
main()
{
    int a[100];

    printf ("Size of array a:\t %d \n", sizeof (a));
    printf ("Size of short: \t %d \n", sizeof (short));
    printf ("Size of int:   \t %d \n", sizeof (int));
    printf ("Size of long:  \t %d \n", sizeof (long));
    printf ("Size of float: \t %d \n", sizeof (float));
    printf ("Size of double: \t %d \n", sizeof (double));
}
```

(a) Program that prints the size of various data types

```
Size of array a:     400
Size of short:         2
Size of int:           4
Size of long:          4
Size of float:         4
Size of double:        8
```

(b) Output from part (a)

FIGURE 3.4. (*a*) Program that prints the size of various data types. (*b*) Output from part (*a*).

The syntax of `sizeof` requires parentheses around a type, but they are optional around a variable.

`sizeof(`*type*`)`

`sizeof` *variable*   *OR*   `sizeof(`*variable*`)`

If a variable x is of some type T, `sizeof(T)` returns the same as `sizeof x`. The `sizeof` operator is unique because it is evaluated at compile time, not when the program is running. The compiler replaces the call with a constant.

The program in Figure 3.4*a* prints the size of several different data types, including the standard types `short`, `int`, `long`, and so on. (We did not print the size of a `char` since by definition that is one byte.) The output is shown in Figure 3.4*b*.

AUTOMATIC TYPE CONVERSION

We have seen how C automatically converts between characters and integers when we assign one to the other. Whenever there is an assignment

1. If both operands are the same type, no conversions are performed.
2. If one operand is a double, the other is converted to a double.
3. If one operand is an unsigned long, the other is converted to an unsigned long. (Note: This means that signed values are converted to unsigned values.)
4. If one operand is a (signed) long int and the other is an unsigned int, then *both* are converted to unsigned long. (Note: This means that signed values are converted to unsigned values.)
5. If one operand is an unsigned int, the other is converted to an unsigned int. (Note: Again, this means that signed values are converted to unsigned values.)
6. Otherwise, both operands are of type int: no additional conversion takes place.

FIGURE 3.5. Automatic conversions between data types.

operation, C converts the type of the value of the expression on the right-hand side to the type on the left. This may involve truncation or internal representation changes, such as when we convert a real to an integer. C also performs conversions whenever it does arithmetic; Figure 3.5 gives the rules. The rules are intuitive, except when dealing with conversions involving chars and unsigned ints. Further discussion of automatic conversions is covered in Chapter 6.

CONVERSIONS AND CASTS

As we have just seen, C performs some type conversions automatically. However, there are times when we want to force a type conversion in a way that is different from the automatic conversion. We call such a process *casting* a value. A cast is specified by giving the cast-type in parentheses followed by the expression to be cast:

(*cast-type*) *expression*

As an example, to force the floating point number 17.7 to be treated as an int, we use a cast:

```
a = (int) 17.7 * 2;
```

This casts 17.7 (and only 17.7, not the entire expression) to an int by truncation. The result of this assignment is that a receives the value 34. Here 17.7 is cast to an int, 17, rather than the entire product, since the precedence of the cast operator is higher than that of most other operators.

We normally cast a variable to ensure that the arithmetic is carried out with the type of the left-hand side. We can round (rather than truncate) a variable to an integer by adding 0.5 to it and then casting to an int, as we do here by again assigning to the variable a:

```
a = (int) (val + 0.5);
```

If val is 37.8, adding 0.5 to it yields 38.3; casting this to an int truncates the result to 38, the value that is then assigned to a. Of course, the _variable_ or _expression_ being cast is not changed; a cast simply returns a value of the cast type. Because of the high precedence of the cast operator, the expression to be cast must be parenthesized, as we did above. Contrast this to the effect of writing

```
a = (int) val + 0.5;
```

A typical use of a cast is in forcing division to return a real number when both operands are ints. For example, a program to average a series of integers might accumulate a total in an integer variable sum, and a count of the number of values read in the integer n. To compute the average, we divide:

```
ave = (double) sum / n;
```

Casting sum to a double causes the division to be carried out as floating point division. Without the cast, truncated integer division is performed, since both sum and n are ints. Here are some other examples of casts and their results. Many of these are machine dependent and may seem unintuitive; they should therefore be used with caution.

(unsigned short)	−1	=	65535
(short)	65000	=	−536
(char)	65000	=	'h'
(double)	5	=	5.00
(unsigned long)	−1	=	4294967295

CASE STUDY—BIT MANIPULATION FUNCTIONS

Routines that need to manipulate individual bits or strings of bits within a word can often be written in a portable way by appropriately combining C's shift, negation, ANDing, and ORing operators. We will examine short functions to determine the number of bits in various data types on a particular machine, to extract a given bit from a word, and to turn on or off (that is, to set to ones or zeros) a specified string of bits in a word.

```
/*
 *  Returns the number of bits in a word.
 */
int wordlength()
{
  unsigned int    word;                 /* used to find word length */
  int             bits = 0;             /* bits in the word */

  for (word = ~0; word != 0; word <<= 1)
    bits++;

  return bits;
}
```

FIGURE 3.6. A function to determine the number of bits in an int.

Figure 3.6 contains the function wordlength, which returns the number of bits in an int. The function initializes word to all ones (by setting it to ~0) and then shifts left one bit at a time, until word is zero. A counter is kept of the number of shifts, and this is returned as the number of bits in the word.

Figure 3.7 contains the function getbit, which gets the value of the nth bit in word (a zero or one), assuming that the *rightmost* bit in the word is bit number zero. Thus, the call getbit(word, 2), where word looks like

```
bit:       3 2 1 0
 0  ...  0 1 0 1
```

will return one. The function works by shifting word *right* n places, and then ANDing the entire word with a mask consisting of all zeros, except for the rightmost bit (01).

Lastly we review a method used to turn on a bit string in a single word. Specifically, we want to set n bits in a word to ones, starting with a position i from the right (again, the rightmost bit is zero). We can do so with the expression

```
word = word | ~ (~0 << n) << i;
```

For example, if we have a word that looks like

```
bit:           7 6 5 4 3 2 1 0
 0  0  ...  1 0 1 0 1 1 0 1
```

```
/*
 * Gets the value of bit "n" in "word". Assumes that the rightmost
 * bit of the word is bit zero, and that "n" will be between zero and the
 * word length of the machine, minus one.
 */
int getbit(word, n)
unsigned int word;
int         n;
{
  return (word >> n) & 01;
}
```

FIGURE 3.7. A function to determine the nth bit in a word.

and we would like bits seven, six, and five to be ones (the rest unchanged), so that the word then looks like

we use an n of three and an i of five. Tracing the result of this expression by hand will help you see how it works.

PROGRAMMING PRACTICE

3-1. Write a program that determines the number of bits in an int, short, and char on your machine, using the function wordlength of Figure 3.6 as a model.

3-2. Write an expression that takes a word, a location, and the number of bits, and sets the bits to zero, starting at the location from the right of the word (counting the rightmost bit as bit zero). All other bits remain the same.

3-3. Write an expression that takes a word, a location, and the number of bits, and inverts the bits, starting at the location from the right of the word (counting the rightmost bit as bit zero). All other bits remain the same.

3-4. Write a function that takes a word (assumed to be an unsigned int) and prints its binary representation. Use the function getbit in Figure 3.7 to get the individual bits in the word.

```
0 1 0 1 0 0 0 0    DATA    (ASCII 'P')
0 0 0 1 0 0 1 0    KEY
```
```
0 1 0 0 0 0 1 0    DATA exclusive OR KEY = encrypted data
```
```
0 0 0 1 0 0 1 0    KEY
```
```
0 1 0 1 0 0 0 0    encrypted data exclusive OR KEY = DATA
```

FIGURE 3.8. Data encryption and decryption using the exclusive OR function.

CASE STUDY—A SIMPLE ENCRYPTION PROGRAM

Exclusive OR is an operator that is useful in data encryption. Encrypting data in such a way that it takes a substantial amount of time (many weeks) to decipher a file without knowing the encryption key, is obviously an important property of any secure encryption scheme. But there are

```
/*
 *    Encrypt the standard input using a built-in encryption key.
 *    The encryption key is "The encryption key."
 */
#include <stdio.h>
#define MAXKEY   19

main ()
{
  char    key[MAXKEY];
  int     c, j = 0;

  key[0]  = 'T';     key[1] = 'h';    key[2] = 'e';    key[3] = ' ';
  key[4]  = 'e';     key[5] = 'n';    key[6] = 'c';    key[7] = 'r';
  key[8]  = 'y';     key[9] = 'p';    key[10] = 't';   key[11] = 'i';
  key[12] = 'o';     key[13] = 'n';   key[14] = ' ';   key[15] = 'k';
  key[16] = 'e';     key[17] = 'y';   key[18] = '.';

  while ((c = getchar ()) != EOF)
  {
    putchar (c ^ key[j % MAXKEY]);
    j++;
  }
}
```

FIGURE 3.9. Program to encrypt a file, using exclusive OR with a key. In this version the key is built into the program, but this would not be done in a "secure" encryption scheme.

some surprisingly simple methods that produce good results as long as the encrypting key is long enough.

Perhaps the simplest method is to take the exclusive OR of the text to be encrypted with the encryption key. If the text is larger than the key (which is usually the case), just cycle through the key repeatedly until the entire file has been encrypted. The nice aspect of this scheme is that the encrypted version of the file can be decrypted with the same key using the same method: take the exclusive OR with the key.

As an example, Figure 3.8 shows an eight-bit piece of data to be encrypted and an eight-bit key. Taking the exclusive OR with the key produces the encrypted data. Taking the exclusive OR with the key again produces the original data.

A program used to encrypt or decrypt a file is shown in Figure 3.9; it is virtually identical to the character-copying program from Chapter 2. Instead of copying each character directly to the output (via putchar), we take the exclusive OR of the current character with the next character of the key. To simplify the structure of the program, we build the key into the program. In a truly secure encryption program, the key would be provided independently by the user of the program. Notice the use of the remaindering operator % for cycling through the elements in the key.

CHAPTER 4

POINTERS, ARRAYS, AND STRINGS

In this chapter we introduce a new data type, *pointer*; discuss the special relationship between pointers and arrays; and examine a special kind of array, *strings*. In doing so, we examine two important uses of pointers: accessing specific memory locations, and traversing arrays efficiently. We also discuss the differences between arrays and strings, and present the standard library functions for manipulating strings. We conclude with a program that eliminates duplicate lines from its input, building a useful new program from small, existing functions.

POINTERS

Pointers are a basic data type in C, and we cannot hope to use the complete capabilities of the language unless we are thoroughly familiar with them. Pointers are needed to take full advantage of parameter passing with functions; they are used in dynamic memory allocation for a wide range of data structures and algorithms; they are intimately related to arrays; and their use often results in more compact, faster code compared to alternative methods.

A pointer is a value that indicates where another value is stored. These storage locations represent the address of a variable in memory. If a variable val is defined as an int, the compiler allocates an appropriate amount of storage at the time this definition occurs. For example, the compiler might allocate memory location 10000 for val. After the assignment

```
val = -15;
```

memory location 10000 will contain the integer value -15.

The address of val, indicated as &val, is 10000. We can print addresses (as well as the contents of addresses) with printf. To print the address of val, we use

```
printf("Address of val: %d\n", &val);
```

On some machines, addresses are long integers and the %ld form is necessary. Of course, we can be more portable and use a cast:

```
printf("Address of val: %ld\n", (long) &val);
```

The address-of operator (&) returns the location where its operand is stored. The operand must be a variable, but not an array or function name.

A variable can be declared as an address (or pointer) type. That is, it can contain the address (and thus a pointer to) another value. A pointer variable must have a type, just like an ordinary variable. Pointers are usually thought of as pointing only to an int, a float, a char, and so on. In addition, because the storage requirements for all pointer types need not be the same, we must be certain that a pointer variable of one type is not used to contain the address of a variable of another type.

We declare a variable as a pointer to a given type with

```
type    *name;
```

This declares name as a pointer to *type*. The following declares iptr as a "pointer to int," fptr as a "pointer to float," cptr as a "pointer to char," and dptr as a "pointer to double."

```
int       *iptr;          /* iptr is "pointer to int" */
float     *fptr;          /* fptr is "pointer to float" */
char      *cptr;          /* cptr is "pointer to char" */
double    *dptr;          /* dptr is "pointer to double" */
```

Each of these declarations allocates space for the named pointer variable, but *not* for what it points to. Once a pointer variable has been declared, it must still be made to point to something. This can be done with an assignment such as

```
iptr = &val;
```

which causes `iptr` to point to `val`. That is, `iptr` now contains the address 10000, the location of `val`. Before a pointer is given an address, it should not be used, since pointer variables are not automatically initialized and therefore contain garbage values.

With this declaration of `iptr`, Figure 4.1 traces an assignment to `val` (the same `val` declared earlier) by assigning through `iptr`. Accessing the underlying storage location (in this case `val`, or 10000) through a pointer variable is called "dereferencing." Dereferencing uses the indirection operator `*`, which returns the value pointed to by the pointer variable operand. The assignment

```
val = *iptr;
```

assigns to `val` whatever `iptr` points to, 10 in the case of Figure 4.1. Similarly, the assignment

```
*iptr = val;
```

assigns the current value of `val` to whatever `iptr` points to. In fact, a dereferenced pointer can be used in any context in which the underlying type can occur. The assignment

```
val = *iptr + 10;
```

adds 10 to whatever `iptr` points to and assigns the result to `val`. Again, `iptr` is of type "pointer to `int`," and we can and should think of `*iptr` as if it were a single variable of type `int`. Therefore, this assignment is interpreted to mean that `val` is assigned some `int` value plus 10.

We can initialize or assign a constant value to a pointer, although we would probably not want to. Since a pointer must be the correct type, it is necessary to cast the constant to a pointer. The assignment

```
iptr = (int *) 100000;
```

although legal, is obviously machine dependent and likely to lead to memory violations. It is only when we must address specific memory locations, such as for device drivers, that such constructs are suitable. Even though in most systems pointers are integers (that is, they use the same amount of storage as an `int`), we should still cast the address to the type "pointer to `int`" or `(int *)` if `iptr` is a pointer to an `int`; a direct address assignment to a `float` pointer should be cast to `(float *)`, and so on.

```
fptr = (float *) 200000;
```

These assignments and casts are used when we need to examine a specific memory location or assign it a value. Rather than code these

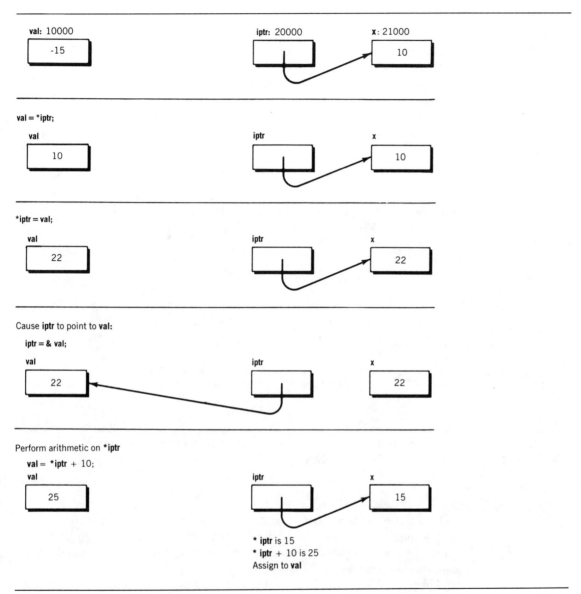

FIGURE 4.1. Examples of referencing val through iptr.

instructions inline, we use functions. Two useful routines are called peek, to print the value in a location, and poke, to put a value into a location. These routines, shown in Figure 4.2, are machine dependent, and they must be given addresses that are reasonable, or the run-time system will cause a memory exception error and terminate the program.

```
/*
 * Examine the contents of a specific memory location "where" containing an int.
 * Assume addresses are longs.
 */
peek(where)
long  where;
{
  printf("%d\n", * (int *) where);
}
```

(a) Function to print the contents of a specific memory location

```
/*
 * Put a specific int "val" into memory location "where".
 * Assume addresses are longs.
 */
poke(val, where)
int   val;
long  where;
{
  * (int *) where = val;
}
```

(b) Function to place a value into a specific memory location

```
peek(100000L);          /* Print the value in address 100000 */
poke(-32, 100000L);     /* Place -32 in that address */
```

(c) Example calls to peek and poke

FIGURE 4.2. (*a*) Function peek to print the contents of a specific memory location. (*b*) Function poke that assigns a value to a specific location. (*c*) Examples of the use of these functions.

It is permissible to assign one pointer to another, and it is also possible (although there can be difficulties on some machines) to assign a pointer of one type to that of another, using appropriate casts. We will examine such operations in later chapters.

There is a special pointer, NULL, that points to nowhere. More specifically, NULL is a guaranteed illegal address (the constant zero, which C guarantees to convert to the NULL pointer) that can be used for any pointer type. The constant NULL is defined in the include file *stdio. h*, so any program that uses the NULL pointer should have the preprocessor directive

```
#include <stdio.h>
```

As an alternative, the program can use zero in place of NULL, or can add the statement

```
#define NULL 0
```

We will see several uses of the null pointer later in the book.

ARRAYS AND THEIR RELATIONSHIP TO POINTERS

In Chapter 1 we saw that we declare an array by giving its underlying type (or "base type"), name, and size.

type   name[*size*]**;**

The size of an array tells the compiler how much storage to allocate for it. The actual amount of storage allocated depends on the base type; the amount of storage is at least *size* times the amount required for a single variable of *type*. *type* can be any type (except **void**, discussed in Chapter 6); *size* must be an integral expression, known at compile time.

We also saw that all arrays are indexed beginning at zero. That is, if we declare **a** to be an array of 100 **int**s by:

```
int   a[100];
```

the compiler allocates 100 storage locations, each holding an **int**, and we can (legally) access elements of **a** by giving an index in the range of 0 to 99, done by specifying the index of the element in brackets. A common mistake is to assume that array subscripting begins at one, and thus to attempt to access **a[100]**. Accessing out-of-bounds elements is not required to be caught by the compiler and may not even cause a run-time error.

What we did not see was that when we declare an array, the array name is defined as a constant pointer to the first (zeroth) element of the array. In the above declaration, not only is space for 100 integers allocated, but **a** is defined as the address of the zeroth element (equivalent to **&a[0]**). In Figure 4.3, **a** is the constant 1000, the location where **a[0]** is stored. Since **a** is a constant address, the assignment

```
int    a[100];
int    *iptr;

iptr = a;
```

is well defined and is shown in Figure 4.3. This assignment is equivalent to

```
iptr = &a[0];
```

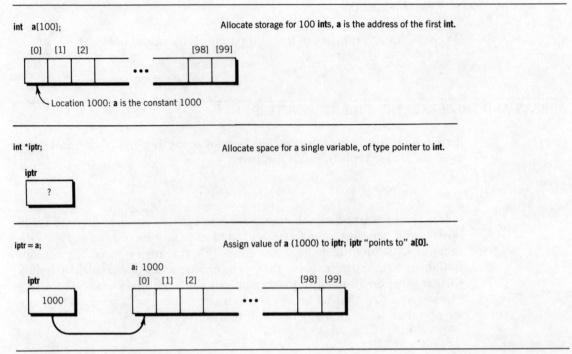

FIGURE 4.3. Trace of array allocation and pointer assignments.

Either assignment could be used to set `iptr` to point to `a`'s first element (`a[0]`).

Instead of using array indexing, we can use pointers to access array elements. This is because pointer arithmetic (that is, adding integers to or subtracting integers from a pointer) is always done in units of the pointer's underlying base type. To illustrate, suppose we declare an integer pointer `iptr` and make it point to `a`'s first element (`a[0]`) as before. Then `iptr + 1` is the address of the second element (`a[1]`), `iptr + 2` is the address of the third element (`a[2]`), and in general, `iptr + i` is the address of element `a[i]`. More specifically, given `iptr` declared as a pointer to `a[0]`, we can assign the value 10 to `a[3]` either by array indexing or by pointer dereferencing. Since `iptr` has been assigned `a`'s address

        a[3] = 10;

is equivalent to

        *(iptr + 3) = 10;

In our programs we can use any of the forms:

        iptr[3]   *or*   *(iptr + 3)   *or*   a[3]   *or*   *(a + 3)

In fact, the compiler translates all array subscripting into pointer dereferences:

```
a[i]   becomes  *(a + i)
```

In the pointer dereference, `*(a + i)`, the addition `a + i` is carried out in `sizeof(int)` increments. Selecting the ith element involves calculating the address of the element, given the base address (the location of `a[0]`). For example, to access `a[2]`, C computes

```
a[2]    →  address of a[0] + 2 × sizeof(int)
        →  a + 2 × sizeof (int)
        →  1000 + 2 × 4 = 1008
```

This calculation is based on the assumption that **a** is stored beginning at memory location 1000, with an integer size of 4 bytes.

Because incrementing a pointer causes it to point to the next array element, we can traverse an array using a pointer. The following loop prints the first n values in an array of `int`s, one per line, using the usual array accessing and pointer accessing methods.

Array Accessing	*Pointer Accessing*

```
                            int  *iptr = a;
    ...                         ...
i = 0;
while (n-- > 0)             while (n-- > 0)
{                          {
  printf("%d\n", a[i]);        printf("%d\n",*iptr)
  i++;                         iptr++;
}                          }
```

To increment `iptr` along **a**, we need only to add one to `iptr` each time we go through the loop. The pointer accessing method is often faster because, at the hardware instruction level, the pointer dereferencing and incrementing is done with a single machine instruction, avoiding the additional calculations needed in array subscript accesses.

Since pointer arithmetic is performed in units of the base type, we can use this method to traverse any kind of array. If another array **d** is declared as an array of **doubles**,

```
double  d[MAX];
```

then indexing through **d** involves arithmetic in units of eight (bytes). An assignment such as

```
d[i] = 2.0e3;
```

is always converted to

```
*(d + i) = 2.0e3;
```

and if d[0] is stored at location 2000 (equivalently, &d[0] is 2000, or equivalently, d is the constant value 2000), the assignment is made into location 2000 + 8i. As with a earlier, we can print an element of d directly using d[i] or indirectly using a pointer. If we want dptr to be a pointer to a double (that is, to point to an element of array d), we can declare and use it as in the following piece of code, which prints the first *n* elements of d:

```
double    *dptr = d;
      . . .
while (n-- > 0)
{
  printf("%f\n", *dptr);
  dptr++;
}
```

C allows us to add integers to or subtract integers from pointers, as well as to subtract one pointer from another, yielding the number of elements between them (but only if they point to the same array). However, other arithmetic is not allowed (specifically, no multiplying or dividing pointers and no arithmetic involving reals).

The restrictions on pointer arithmetic are occasionally irritating, such as when we need to find the middle element in a subarray, bounded below by an index L and above by an index H. With array indexing, the middle element can be found at location (H + L) / 2. However, if lp is a pointer to a[L] and hp is a pointer to a[H], we cannot find the middle element at (ip + lp) / 2, since pointer *addition* is illegal. However, pointer *subtraction* is legal and well defined, so we use an equivalent method, lp + (hp - lp) / 2. Although this looks like pointer addition, it is not. The difference between two pointers is an integer, and the division by two returns an integer. Adding an integer to a pointer is allowed. In summary, to obtain the value of an array's middle element, the following are equivalent:

```
int   value = a[(H - L) / 2];
```

is equivalent to

```
int   value;
int   *lp, *hp;
    . . .
lp = &a[L];   hp = &a[H];
    . . .
value = *(lp + (hp - lp) / 2);
```

ARRAY ADDRESS COMPARISONS USING POINTERS

In addition to participating in the arithmetic operations we have described previously, pointers can be compared for equality (==), inequality (!=), less than, less than or equal, greater than, or greater than or equal (<, <=, >, >=). Table 4.1 summarizes the valid comparisons and operations on pointers. These comparisons are portable only if the pointers access the same array.

We illustrate the comparison operators by using them in two simple tasks—printing the elements in an array and printing them in reverse order (*traversing* an array). Because accessing arrays using pointers is often faster than accessing directly through indexes, we should be familiar with the use and restrictions of pointers for this purpose.

If **a** is an array of **MAX** ints, it is straightforward to print **a**'s elements using a pointer. We declare **iptr** to point to **a[0]** and then use a **for** loop, stopping when **iptr** points to the last element, **a[MAX - 1]**.

```
int    a[MAX];
int    *iptr;
    . . .
for (iptr = a; iptr <= &a[MAX - 1]; iptr++)
  printf ("%d\n", *iptr);
    . . .
```

TABLE 4.1. Pointer operations and their meanings.

Pointer Operator	Operation	Return
p1 == p2	Test for equality	One if the two pointers point to the same location; zero if they do not.
p1 != p2	Test for inequality	Zero if the two pointers point to the same location; one if they do not.
p1 < p2, <=	Test for less than, less than or equal	One if p1 points to an array element with a lower (less than or equal) index; zero otherwise.
p1 > p2, >=	Test for greater than, greater than or equal	One if p1 points to an array element with a higher (greater than or equal) index; zero otherwise.
p1–p2	Pointer subtraction	If p1 and p2 point to the same array, it returns the number of elements between them (if p2 points to a higher indexed element, it returns the negative of the number of elements between them).

We can print the array in reverse order by making appropriate changes in the for loop:

```
int    a[MAX];
int    *iptr;
    . . .
for (iptr = &a[MAX - 1]; iptr >= a; iptr--)
  printf ("%d\n", *iptr);
    . . .
```

Notice that in these examples we do not test a counter to determine when the array has been traversed; instead, we compare the indexing pointer with the address of the array's first (or last) element.

We can write the loop that prints the values even more concisely:

```
iptr = a;
while (iptr <= &a[MAX - 1])
  printf("%d\n", *iptr++);
```

Because of the precedence and evaluation order of * and ++, *iptr++ means "obtain the character that iptr points to (i.e., *iptr). After obtaining that character, increment the pointer (i.e., perform iptr++ in terms of pointer arithmetic)." The following diagram illustrates the accessing of the array indirectly through a pointer.

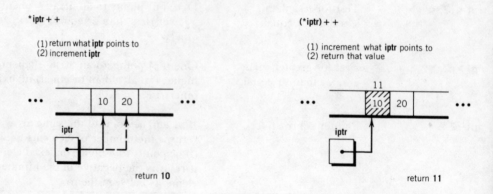

*iptr + +

(1) return what **iptr** points to
(2) increment **iptr**

return 10

(*iptr) + +

(1) increment what **iptr** points to
(2) return that value

return 11

PROGRAMMING PRACTICE

 Write a program that sums the elements in an array, using only pointers (no extra array indexing).

 Rewrite the reverse printing program from Chapter 1 (Figure 1.6), using pointers rather than array indexes.

PASSING ARRAYS AS PARAMETERS TO FUNCTIONS

We saw in Chapter 1 that when an array is passed as a parameter, the address of the array's first element is passed, not the entire array. That is, when we pass an array we are really only passing a pointer, and the following parameter declarations are equivalent:

```
int func(table)          int func(table)
int  table[];            int *table;
{                        {
    . . .                    . . .
}                        }
```

If `a` is an array, when we call `func(a)` the address of `a[0]` is copied and given to `f`. Because we are only passing a pointer, there is no need to indicate bounds on `table`.

Within the body of `f`, we can access `table` by using either the array (square bracket) form or the pointer form (using the dereferencing operator `*`). The following assignments are equivalent:

```
table[i] = 15;               *(table + i) = 15;
```

Pick your favorite, though it is customary to use the form corresponding to the way the object was defined—either a pointer or an array.

Since C's parameters are passed by value (copied), we can use the passed pointer to traverse the array, instead of declaring an additional local variable. We illustrate this in Figure 4.4a, a function `print_table` that prints the elements in an array. Figure 4.4b shows an example call that prints an array `table` containing **MAX** elements.

When `print_table` is called, `tab_ptr` is initialized with the address of the array's first element and then used to traverse the array, and incremented after each element is printed. `table` is a constant and is not affected by the call to `print_table`. As we do not explicitly declare an array parameter's size, any function passed an array should also be passed the number of elements in the array or should have some other

```
/*
 * Print table of "num" integers.
 */
print_table(tab_ptr, num)
int *tab_ptr, num;            /* pointer to first element, element count */
{
  while (num-- > 0)
    printf("%d\n", *tab_ptr++);
}
```

(a) Print an array's elements

```
{
  int table[MAX];
      . . .
  print_table(table, MAX);
}
```

(b) Example use of `print_table`

FIGURE 4.4. Printing an array's elements using the parameter to traverse the array.

way to determine how many elements to process. We cannot use `sizeof` in `print_table` because `sizeof(table)` returns the size of a pointer, not of the entire array, which is not necessarily known at compile time.

Because an array is passed as a pointer, we can pass the address of any array element, which effectively allows us to pass only part of an array. As an example, either

> `print_table(&table[i], k);`   *OR*   `print_table(table + i, k);`

prints k elements, starting with `table[i]`. In both cases, the address of `table[i]` is passed, and all elements of `table` are still accessible to `print_table` through appropriate negative or positive offsets of `tab_ptr`.

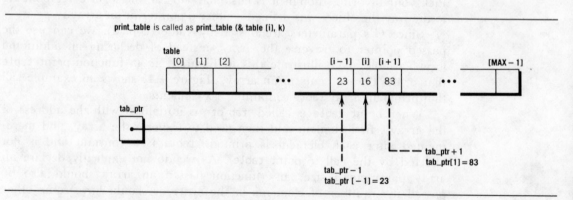

It is a common mistake to pass an array element, instead of its address, to a function expecting an array parameter. The call

```
print_table(table[i], k);    /* incorrect: pointer not passed! */
```

is a serious mistake, since print_table is expecting a pointer and is instead receiving an int. A function expecting an array *must* be passed an array name or an element's address.

PROGRAMMING PRACTICE

4-3. Write a function, insert, that takes a sorted array of longs and a long value and inserts the value in its correct place in the table. Write both pointer and array versions. Which is more efficient? Which is more compact?

CHARACTER ARRAYS—STRINGS

A string is an array of characters, terminated with an extra character, the null character, '\0'. Any group of characters defined between double quotation marks is a constant string; for example,

```
"By the light of the silvery moon."
```

To place a double quotation mark in a string, precede it with a backslash:

```
"Have you seen \"Gone with the wind\"?"
```

When the compiler sees a constant string, it terminates it with an additional null character, allocates space for it, and returns a pointer to its first character. Thus, we can have s contain a string by declaring it as a pointer and assigning the string to it.

```
char *s;
   . . .
s = "By the light of the silvery moon.";
```

s now points to a string containing 34 characters: the 33 between the double quotation marks, and the additional null character inserted by the compiler:

B	y		t	h		...		o	n	.	\0	

Even though the string is constant, the pointer to it is not. However, it is bad practice to change the assignment, such as

```
s = "I love rock and roll.";
```

since that leaves the space occupied by the old string dangling in memory.

When the compiler initializes a string constant, the trailing null (`'\0'`) is supplied automatically, but when we build strings ourselves, we have to supply it. The reason for the terminating null is that C has a library of useful string functions, which expect a string to be null terminated, including printing a string using the %s format for printf. We can always declare the elements in a string array in a similar way to other arrays—by specifying the individual elements. In this case, however, we must provide the trailing null ourselves.

```
char  error_msg[14];      OR   char *error_msg = "Illegal Value";
    . . .
error_msg[0]  = 'I';
error_msg[1]  = 'l';
error_msg[2]  = 'l';
    . . .
error_msg[11] = 'u';
error_msg[12] = 'e';
error_msg[13] = '\0';
```

Figure 4.5 is a short function that reads a string of characters (up to a maximum of max) into a string line. It then places a null at the end of the string. Since there must be room for the extra null character, we are careful to terminate reading when max − 1 characters have been read. The function returns the number of characters read, not counting the added null character, or it returns EOF on end of file.

This is a practical function that we will use again and again in various forms. We read characters, placing them into the array line. Since there are two stopping conditions (too many characters or end of line reached), we must continue reading characters, even though we do not save them, until the end-of-line character (`'\n'`) is entered. This guarantees that the next time the function is called, it will begin reading characters from the start of a new line, not from the last character before max characters on the previous line.

```
/*
 * Get a line, terminating on CR, or more than "max" chars entered.  DOES
 * NOT include the ending newline.  Returns EOF if end of file detected;
 * otherwise, the number of characters read (not counting trailing NULL).
 */
int  get_line(line, max)
char line[];
int  max;
{
  int    c, i;                      /* current char, count of chars */

 /* Read until max chars; ignore all chars after max until CR. */

    i = 0;
    while ((c = getchar ()) != '\n' && c != EOF)
            if (i < max - 1)
                line[i++] = c;
    line[i] = '\0';                 /* terminate with null */
    if (c == EOF)
      return EOF;
    else
      return i;
}
```

FIGURE 4.5. Function get_line gets a line and terminates with a null character.

PROGRAMMING PRACTICE

4-4. Write a pointer version of get_line (Figure 4.5). Is it more efficient than the array accessing version?

4-5. Write a function, stoi (for string to integer), that takes a null terminated string (array of char) and converts the characters to an integer. Use a method similar to that in Chapter 2.

4-6. Write a function, itos, that takes two parameters. The first is an integer, and the second is a character array. The function converts the integer into characters (null terminated) and places them into the array parameter. Assume that the array is large enough to hold the necessary characters.

STRING FUNCTIONS FROM THE STANDARD LIBRARY

C does not provide operators that work on strings directly. If we do not initialize a string, assigning one string to another requires the assignment to be done on a character-by-character basis. This seems a bit strange at first, because strings are just arrays of characters, and arrays are in fact pointers to the first location. Although it seems as if the following set of declarations and assignments should work, they do not.

```
char *s = "Hi Mom.  Hi Dad.";
char t[100];
    . . .
t = s;
```

The reason is that even though t is indeed a pointer to the first character location in the array, it is a *constant*. Its value (the address of t[0]) may not change. If we really want to copy the characters in s into t, we have to do so one at a time. Luckily, there is a built-in function called strcpy (for *string copy*) provided in the standard string library that does the string copying task for us. Other functions in this library compute a string's length, concatenate two strings, and compare two strings.

strcpy takes two arguments, both strings, and copies the second to the first. It assumes that the second string is null terminated and that the first string is large enough. To copy string s to string t, as we tried to do above, we use

```
strcpy(t, s);
```

Notice that the order of the parameters mimics that of the assignment t = s.

It is instructive to examine how a function such as strcpy is written. Figure 4.6 shows us one way; the actual code differs from one machine to another and a more compact example will be given at the end of the chapter. In addition, these versions are a slight simplification. Most versions of strcpy return a value, a pointer to the destination string. (The details

```
/*
 * Copy string "source" to string "dest".
 */
strcpy(dest, source)
char dest[], source[];
{
  int    i;

  for (i = 0; source[i] != '\0'; i++)
    dest[i] = source[i];
}
```

FIGURE 4.6. One version of strcpy from the standard library.

TABLE 4.2. String functions from the standard string library.

Name	Function
strcat(s1,s2)	Concatenates s2 to the end of s1.
strncat(s1,s2,n)	Concatenates at most *n* characters from s2 to the end of s1.
strcpy(s1,s2)	Copies s2 to s1.
strncpy(s1,s2,n)	Copies *n* characters from s2 to s1.
strcmp(s1,s2)	Compares s1 and s2; returns less than zero, zero, or greater than zero, depending on whether s1 is less than, equal to, or greater than s2 respectively.
strncmp(s1,s2,n)	Compares at most *n* characters; returns the same as strcmp.
strlen(s)	Returns the number of characters in s, *not* counting the trailing null.
index(s,c)	Returns a pointer to the first occurrence of c in s, or NULL. It is sometimes called strchr.
rindex(s,c)	Returns a pointer to the last occurrence of c in s, or NULL. It is sometimes called strrchr.

of the returned values of functions in the standard string library are shown in Appendix 5.) The advantage of having the string functions provided for us is not that they implement hard-to-code routines—strcpy is short and straightforward—but instead that they implement frequently used routines and therefore simplify our job of program construction.

The string-handling functions provided with most C compilers are shown in Table 4.2. To use the string library functions, include the file *strings.h* with:

```
#include <strings.h>
```

This is a header file that declares the types of the standard string functions. On some systems the file is named *string.h*; other systems do not have the header file available at all. If the file is not available, the types of the functions must be declared in programs where they are used.

One function that we will use in a case study at the end of the chapter is strcmp. This function takes two strings, s1 and s2, and returns a value that is less than zero if s1 is alphabetically less than s2, zero if they are equal, and greater than zero if s1 is alphabetically greater than s2. As with strcpy, the function is short and quite simple to write. But because it is used so often, we see the value of having it provided in a standard library.

Figure 4.7 shows strcmp. It works by walking through the two strings and comparing corresponding characters (s1[i] and s2[i]). If the characters are the same and are also null, we are at the end of the string. Since we know the strings are equal, we return zero. However, if at any point

```
/*
 * Compare two strings.  Returns: 0 if they are the same, negative value if s1 < s2,
 * or a positive value if s1 > s2.
 */
int  strcmp(s1, s2)
char s1[], s2[];                          /* strings to compare */
{
  int    i;

  for (i = 0; s1[i] == s2[i]; i++)        /* as long as the same */
    if (s1[i] == '\0')                    /* see if we hit the end of one */
      return 0;                           /*    and return equality */
  return s1[i] - s2[i];                   /* return difference between characters */
}
```

FIGURE 4.7. A version of strcmp from the standard string library.

in the comparison the characters differ, we know that one of the strings is alphabetically less than the other, and we return the difference between them.

```
        return s1[i] - s2[i];
```

This returns a negative value when s1[i] is alphabetically less than s2[i] and a positive value when it is greater.

ADDITIONAL STRING FUNCTIONS

The standard I/O library provides two functions, extensions to printf and scanf, that allow output to and input from a string. These functions are sprintf and sscanf, respectively. Each of these functions takes a string for input or output, a control string, and a list of variables.

```
        sprintf(string, format, var-list);
        sscanf(string, format, var-list);
```

As with scanf, sscanf returns the number of values correctly converted, or EOF on end of file.

We can use sscanf together with get_line to avoid some of the problems associated with illegal input using scanf. We can read an entire input line using get_line and then use sscanf to extract the values of the variables, as outlined in the following code fragment.

```
      . . .
while ((n = get_line(line, MAX)) != EOF)
   if ((inpres = sscanf(line, "%d %f %f", &hours, &rate, &overtime)) == 3)
      process_data(...);                /* process valid input */
   else
      printf("Bad line encountered\n");    /* report bad input data */
```

In this way, only those lines containing invalid or missing data items are ignored; we no longer have to quit the first time bad data is encountered.

Despite their usefulness, the string functions in the string and standard I/O libraries are not part of the language definition. These functions are now considered part of the entire environment, but are *not* guaranteed to be provided with every C compiler; some compilers provide only a few of these routines, and others provide them with slightly different names. If your compiler does not have them, they should be written and used whenever their capabilities are needed.

PROGRAMMING PRACTICE

4-7. Another useful string function from the standard library is the length function, strlen. Write a function strlen that takes a string terminated by a null ('\0') and returns the number of characters in the string, *not counting* the null. Assume s is null terminated and that the length of the empty string (a string consisting of just a null) is zero. Test your function on a program using strings of various lengths, including the empty string. Use get_line from Figure 4.5 to get a line of input from the terminal.

4-8. Modify the insertion sort program in Chapter 1 to read its input with get_line and sscanf.

4-9. Find the string-handling functions available on your system. Implement any useful missing ones.

USING POINTERS TO TRAVERSE STRINGS

Strings are arrays and therefore can be traversed using either pointers or traditional array indexing. Earlier, we wrote a version of strcpy, the string copying function (Figure 4.6), by accessing the arrays source and dest through an array index i. An alternative way to write the function is to treat source and dest as pointers (initialized to the first element of the respective arrays) rather than as arrays. When we do this, we access the elements indirectly through pointers rather than directly through array indexes. This version is shown in Figure 4.8.

```
/*
 * Copy "source" string into "dest".
 */
strcpy(dest,source)
char *dest, *source;
{
  while ((*dest = *source) != '\0')
    dest++, source++;                    /* incr ptrs */
}
```

FIGURE 4.8. Copying two strings using the passed pointers to traverse them.

dest and source are used to traverse the destination and source strings, respectively. During each pass through the loop, the character that source points to is assigned to the character that dest points to; the assigned character is compared against the null character to see if the end of the string has been reached, and if not, the two pointers are incremented. Notice that even though the parameters dest and source are modified as the copy is performed, the pointers passed to strcpy remain unchanged. However, the character string that dest points to is modified, becoming a copy of the character string pointed to by source.

What advantage do we gain by accessing storage through pointers rather than through array indexing? The answer, in most computers, is speed. We ran both the original array version and the pointer version of strcpy on a DEC VAX 11/750, copying a string of 15,000 characters. The array version (Figure 4.6) required about 0.32 seconds of CPU time. The pointer version (Figure 4.8) needed only 0.13 seconds, a saving of almost 60 percent!

PROGRAMMING PRACTICE

4-10. Using pointers and avoiding unnecessary local variables, write a function, rmchr, that takes a string and a character as arguments, removing all occurrences of the character from the string. rmchr should not leave holes in the string. What should rmchr return?

4-11. Write a function, rmstr, that takes two strings as arguments, removing all occurrences of any characters in the second string from the first string. Like rmchr, rmstr should not leave holes in the string. What should rmstr return?

4-12. Write compact pointer versions of the standard string library functions. Are these more efficient than straightforward array versions?

CASE STUDY—A PROGRAM TO ELIMINATE DUPLICATE LINES

To illustrate the use of arrays and string functions from the standard string library, we will write a program (called *Uniq*) that takes text as input and copies it to its output, minus any lines that are the same as the line they follow. For example, if the input consists of the lines

```
There was a young lady from Norway
There was a young lady from Norway
There was a young lady from Norway
who hung by her heels in the doorway
she said to her man,
she said to her man,
        . . .
```

We want the output to be

```
There was a young lady from Norway
who hung by her heels in the doorway
she said to her man,
        . . .
```

The program has a number of uses, and a variation suggested in the programming practice has been used to help remove duplicated words in large text files created with a text editor. The sentence *"I told him not to go and and he went anyway,"* contains two "and"s. We can eliminate one of them by running two programs over the text: first, a program that breaks the input into individual words, one per line, and second, a program that only prints the first line of any set of duplicated lines.

Importantly, this program illustrates how a useful function can be created from small, already existing pieces. The program uses get_line, strcmp, and strcpy, each of which we have already written or is provided for us as a library function.

The program processes its input a line at a time, storing both the current and previous lines (using get_line, Figure 4.5, and not repeated here). The current and previous lines are compared using the library function strcmp (see Figure 4.7), and if they are not the same, the current line is printed; if they are the same, the program continues. For this program, we are interested in whether the previous and current lines are equal: we test strcmp for a nonzero return.

```
/*
 *  Uniq - A program to strip duplicate lines.
 */
#include <stdio.h>
#include <strings.h>                        /* declares types of strcpy, etc */

#define MAXLINE     256                     /* longest line program can handle */
#define FALSE         0
#define TRUE          1

main()
{
  char    curr_line[MAXLINE + 1],           /* current line */
          prev_line[MAXLINE + 1];           /* previous line */
  int     first;                            /* first time through? */

  first = TRUE;
  while (get_line (curr_line, MAXLINE) != EOF)
  {
    if (first || strcmp(prev_line, curr_line) != 0)
    {
      printf ("%s\n", curr_line);
      first = FALSE;
    }
    strcpy (prev_line, curr_line);          /* copy curr_line to prev_line */
  }
}
```

"get__line" goes here

FIGURE 4.9. *Uniq*—a program to remove duplicate lines from its input.

The current line is then copied to the previous one using strcpy, and the loop continues. We terminate when get_line returns EOF. The main program is shown in Figure 4.9. Note the use of the two include files: *stdio.h*, which defines EOF, and *strings.h*, which declares the types of the string functions.

PROGRAMMING PRACTICE

4-13. Write a variation of *Uniq* that prints only duplicated lines, and then only the first occurrence of each repetition.

4-14. Write a variation of *Uniq* that prints one instance of each line, preceded by a count of the number of times the line is repeated.

4-15. Write a program that reads the input and breaks it up into individual words, which are then printed one per line. Words are strings of alphabetic or numeric characters separated by non-alphanumerics.

4-16. Write a function, `put_line`, that takes a string and writes it and a trailing newline. Use `putchar` in a loop, rather than `printf`, to do this. The standard I/O library defines a function, `puts`, that does just this. Compare the size and running time of a test program that uses your own `put_line` rather than `printf`.

4-17. Finish the "girl in the doorway" limerick on page 83. Be creative.

C H A P T E R 5

STATEMENTS

We have already introduced many of C's statements. However, our previous descriptions were brief, so we will now explain more fully the statements already used and give detailed descriptions of those we have ignored. In this chapter we begin combining language features to write larger programs, including a simple calculator and a palindrome checker. We conclude by tying everything together in a program that produces a histogram of its input values.

EXPRESSION STATEMENTS

C's simplest statement is the *expression statement*, an expression followed by a semicolon. An expression statement can be used anywhere the language syntax requires a statement, and is executed by evaluating *expression* and ignoring its result. Both function calls and assignment statements, such as

```
printf("sum is %d\n", sum);
sum += value;
```

are merely expression statements; they are not separate kinds of statements, as in FORTRAN or BASIC. Notice that the semicolon terminates statements instead of separating them, as in Pascal.

Any useful expression statement must have a side effect, such as invoking a function, incrementing or decrementing a variable, or assigning a value to a variable. Expression statements with no side effects accomplish nothing, and although syntactically legal, should be avoided. The legal but useless expression statement

```
sum / entries;
```

causes sum to be divided by entries, with the result ignored. Smarter compilers recognize useless expression statements and give a warning, or fail to generate code for them.

COMPOUND STATEMENTS

Any group of statements surrounded by braces is a *compound statement* or *block* and, like an expression statement, can be used wherever the language syntax requires a statement. Compound statements should not be followed by a semicolon.

A compound statement composed entirely of expression statements, such as a series of assignment statements, is often rewritten as a single more compact expression statement using the comma operator. For example, we can replace

```
{
  lineno = 0;
  pageno = 1;
  lastch = '\n';
}
```

with

```
lineno = 0, pageno = 1, lastch = '\n';
```

Changing a compound statement into a single expression statement can make the program more compact, although not necessarily more readable. Generally, compound statements should be left alone unless the expression statements contained in them are closely related or unless the lines saved make the function fit on a single page, aiding readability.

SIMPLE DECISION STATEMENTS—IF

We have already introduced the if statement.

```
if (expression)
    true-statement
else
    false-statement
```

It is executed by first evaluating *expression*; then, if it is not zero, *true-statement*; otherwise, *false-statement* is executed. The `else` and *false-statement* are optional.

One common combination of `if`s is the *nested if*, one `if` inside another, as shown in the following fragment that converts military time (`mhour`) to standard time (`stdhour`). Hours in military time range from 0 (midnight) to 23 (11 P.M.).

```
if (mhour <= 12)
  if (mhour == 0)
    stdhour = 12;              /* midnight */
  else
    stdhour = mhour;           /* morning */
else
  stdhour = mhour - 12;        /* afternoon */
```

Problems can arise when the inner `if` statement does not have an `else` clause. Consider an alternative to the previous `if`:

```
/* BUG: Does the wrong thing despite the misleading indentation. */

stdhour = mhour;               /* assume morning */
if (mhour <= 12)
  if (mhour == 0)
    stdhour = 12;              /* midnight */
else
  stdhour = mhour - 12;        /* afternoon */
```

There is an ambiguity over which `if` the `else` belongs to. The compiler resolves the ambiguity by arbitrarily assuming that any `else` is attached to the closest nonterminated `if`. Therefore, despite this program's indentation, the `else` is associated with the *inner* `if` and the program does not do the time conversion correctly. To avoid the association of an `else` with the closest `if`, that `if` must be placed in braces. The following produces the desired result:

```
stdhour = mhour;               /* assume morning */
if (mhour <= 12)
{
  if (mhour == 0)
    stdhour = 12;              /* midnight */
}
else
  stdhour = mhour - 12;        /* afternoon */
```

PROGRAMMING PRACTICE

5-1. Using nested `if`s, write a function `min3` that returns the smallest of the three `int` values passed to it as parameters. Use the function declaration

```
int min3(value1, value2, value3)
int value1, value2, value3;
```

Are there other reasonable ways to accomplish this?

ASSIGNMENT DECISIONS—THE CONDITIONAL OPERATOR

When an `if` decides which one of two values a particular variable should be assigned, the conditional operator `?:` is a convenient shorthand. For example, using the conditional operator, an `if` that assigns `min` the smaller value of `x` and `y`

```
if (x < y)
  min = x;
else
  min = y;
```

can be rewritten as

```
min = (x < y) ? x : y
```

The conditional operator is C's only ternary operator; all three of its operands are expressions:

expression **?** *true-expression* **:** *false-expression*

The conditional operator is evaluated by first evaluating *expression*. If the result is not zero, *true-expression* is evaluated and returned as the conditional expression's value. Otherwise, *false-expression* is evaluated and returned. It is a good idea to parenthesize *expression*; though usually not necessary, the parentheses help distinguish the test from the values returned.

More complex assignment decisions can also be rewritten using the conditional operator. Here is our conversion from military time to standard time rewritten using the conditional operator:

```
stdhour = (mhour != 0) ? ((mhour > 12) ? mhour - 12 : mhour) : 12
```

In addition to parenthesizing the expressions tested by the conditional operators, we parenthesized the nested conditional operator. Again, although not strictly necessary, this is a good habit to get into, since it protects against possible precedence problems.

When the conditional operator is used, the code will be more concise and possibly more efficient, but not as readable. Anything with more than a single nested conditional operator is better written using ifs.

PROGRAMMING PRACTICE

5-2. Using the conditional operator, write a function, max, that returns the larger of its two integer arguments.

5-3. Rewrite the function min3 (from Programming Practice 5-1) using the conditional operator instead of a nested if statement. Is this function as understandable as the version written using nested if statements?

MULTIWAY DECISIONS—ELSE-IF

There is one other common way to put ifs together, the *multiway decision*. A multiway decision is a chain of ifs in which the statement associated with each else happens to be an if:

```
if (first-expression)
    first-statement
else if (second-expression)
    second-statement
    ...
else if (final-expression)
    final-statement
else
    default-statement
```

The final else and its associated *default-statement* are optional.

When a multiway if is executed, each of the expressions is evaluated in turn until one of them evaluates to something other than zero. Then the statement associated with it is executed and the multiway if is exited. If all the expressions evaluate to zero and *default-statement* is present, it is executed.

Figure 5.1, a program to find the smallest and largest values in its input, contains two examples of the multiway if. The first multiway if, within the while, is executed once for each value read and updates the variables min and max. The first time through, max = min = value is exe-

```
/*
 *  Find maximum and minimum values in input.
 */
#include <stdio.h>

main()
{
  int inpres,              /* result of reading in input value */
      max, min,            /* maximum and minimum values so far */
      value,               /* next value in input */
      valuecnt = 0;        /* number of values so far */

  while (((inpres = scanf("%d", &value)) == 1)
    if (valuecnt++ == 0)   /* first value? */
      max = min = value;
    else if (value > max)  /* new maximum? */
      max = value;
    else if (value < min)  /* new minimum? */
      min = value;
  if (inpres != EOF)
    printf("Error after %d values\n", valuecnt);
  else if (valuecnt == 0)
    printf("No values read\n");
  else
    printf("Maximum: %d\nMinimum: %d\nValues: %d\n", max, min, valuecnt);
}
```

FIGURE 5.1. Finding the smallest and largest input values.

cuted. For subsequent values, the new value is compared with max; if it is larger, max is assigned value. Otherwise, the new value is compared with min; if it is smaller, min is set equal to value.

The second multiway if is used for error handling. When there are several error conditions to check, a multiway if is often convenient. The tests for the various errors come first, and the default statement (the final else) is executed when no errors are found.

PROGRAMMING PRACTICE

5-4. Write a program to read numeric scores and assign letter grades based on the traditional scale: 90-100 is an A, 80-89 is a B, 70-79 is a C, 60-69 is a D, and anything less is an F. Print an error message for any scores greater than 100 or less than 0. Be sure to test for improper input data by checking the return value of scanf or by using get_line and sscanf.

5-5. Write a program to find the two largest and the two smallest values in its input.

CONSTANT MULTIWAY DECISIONS—SWITCH

When each of the comparisons in a multiway `if` checks for different values of the same expression, we have a constant multiway decision. This occurs, for example, in programs that process single-letter commands; the user-entered command is compared with the program's legal commands to determine the appropriate action to be taken. The `switch` statement is often a more convenient, more efficient, and more readable way to make such decisions than a multiway `if`.

```
switch(expression)
{
  case first-constant-expression:
    statement-list
  case second-constant-expression:
    statement-list
    ...
  case final-constant-expression:
    statement-list
  default:
    statement-list
}
```

`switch` is similar to the `case` and computed `goto` statements found in other languages. A `switch` can contain zero or more cases appearing in any order with an optional `default` case. Each of the case labels must be an expression evaluable at compile time to an integral constant, and all case labels within a single `switch` must be unique. A *statement-list* can contain zero or more statements; there is no need to put braces around them.

When `switch` is executed, *expression* is evaluated and control passes to the case labeled with the expression's value. When the `case`'s statement list has been executed, control falls through to the next case label. Since this is almost always undesirable, a `break` statement is usually placed at the end of each `case`'s statement list; `break` causes the enclosing `switch` to exit, passing control to the statement following the `switch`.

We illustrate the use of `switch` with a simple calculator program shown in Figure 5.2. The calculator's input is a series of operator-operand pairs. Each pair contains a single character operator (such as +, -, *, or /) followed by a floating point operand. A running total is updated as each pair is processed, and the total is printed when the end of input is reached. Given the input

```
+ 3.1415926
  * 30.56  * 30.56
  / 2.0
```

the calculator's output is

1466.988027

We use scanf to read both the operator and the operand. Because scanf skips white space before character strings but not before single characters, the operator is read as a string instead of as a character. Allowing operators and operands to be surrounded by white space makes the calculator easier to use. Notice that when scanf is used to read a string, the string's name is passed and the & operator is not used.

```
/*
 * Simple calculator program.
 */
#include <stdio.h>

#define MAXLINE 256

main()
{
    int     inpres;            /* return value when reading in value */
    char    operator[2];       /* read in operator: op followed by null */
    double  operand,           /* read in operand */
            result;            /* result of computation */

    result = 0.0;
    while (inpres = scanf("%1s%lf", operator, &operand), inpres == 2)
        switch(operator[0])
        {
        case '+':  result += operand;
                   break;
        case '-':  result -= operand;
                   break;
        case '*':  result *= operand;
                   break;
        case '/':  if (operand != 0)
                       result /= operand;
                   else
                       printf("Division by zero, ignored.\n");
                   break;
        default:   printf("Unknown operator: %c\n", operator[0]);
                   break;
        }
    if (inpres == EOF)
        printf("%f\n", result);
    else
        printf("Error in input.\n");
}
```

FIGURE 5.2. A simple calculator program illustrating switch.

A `switch` uses the string's first character to select the appropriate operator-labeled case. The default case prints an error message and is executed whenever there is an invalid operator. We have ended the actions for each case with a `break` statement; without it, control would automatically pass to the following case. Although we do not need the `break` after the `default`, we have used it as a defensive measure, preventing an accidental fall-through if additional case labels are added.

Although falling through cases automatically can lead to serious problems when `break` is forgotten, it is useful when we want numerous cases to select the same action. The program fragment

```
case 'a':                         /* fall through */
case '+':   result += operand;
            break;
```

makes `a` an operator equivalent to `+`. Since there are no actions for its case and no `break`, when the operator is an `a` its operand is added to the running total.

Falling through should be used only when the same action occurs for many different constants, and should not be used to execute statements in one case followed by statements in another. Even though we could combine the actions of the calculator's addition and subtraction operators,

```
case '-':   operand = -operand;   /* here we fall through, */
case '+':   result += operand;    /* but this is GROSS! */
            break;
```

it is not good style, since the program becomes less readable and more difficult to modify. Falling through can occasionally simplify code, but these cases are rare, and should be well commented.

PROGRAMMING PRACTICE

5-6. Modify the calculator program to include various synonyms for the existing operators (such as d for /, m for *, s for -, and a for +) and the two additional operators, % (remainder) and ^ (exponentiation).

5-7. The calculator will print out incorrect results if any of the computations overflow. Modify the calculator to print an error message if overflow occurs.

5-8. Rewrite the calculator to use a multiway `if` instead of a `switch`.

5-9. Write a simple program to aid in balancing a checkbook. The input to the program should be a single-letter command followed by an amount. The legal commands are **d** (deposit), **c** (check), **s** (service charge), **w** (withdrawal), and **b** (set starting balance). After each command, the account's new balance should be printed. To aid robustness, use `get_line` and `sscanf`, both from Chapter 4.

SIMPLE LOOPS—WHILE AND DO-WHILE

The simplest looping mechanisms in C are the `while` and `do-while` statements. We have used `while` in many of our programs.

```
while (expression)
    statement
```

When `while` is executed, a cycle of evaluating *expression* and executing *statement* is entered. The cycle ends when *expression* evaluates to zero.

Unlike the `while`, which tests before its body is executed, the `do-while` tests afterward.

```
do
    statement
while (expression);
```

When a `do-while` is executed, a cycle of executing *statement* and evaluating *expression* is entered. As with the `while`, the cycle ends when *expression* evaluates to zero. But unlike the `while`, *statement* is always executed at least once.

Although `do-while` is used much less often than `while`, it can be convenient. Figure 5.3*a* uses it in the function `yesorno`, which encapsulates the common operation of asking a yes-or-no question, verifying the response, and returning it. An example use of `yesorno` is shown in Figure 5.3*b*. When `yesorno` is called, a `do-while` is entered after the question is asked. Within the loop, a prompt is written, the first character typed is taken as the answer, and the remainder of the current input line is discarded. The loop terminates when an appropriate character is entered. We are careful to test for end of file because on systems where a program's input can be redirected, this prevents an infinite loop if the end of file is hit before a correct response is entered. Our example use of `yesorno` simply treats **EOF** as a no. We use a `do-while` since at least one response will be entered, and we want to loop until we get a correct response.

When the body of a `do-while` consists of a single statement, it should be made into a compound statement by surrounding it with braces. The

```
/*
 * Write prompt, wait for 'y', 'n' or EOF as the user's answer
 * (include <stdio.h> before this function)
 */
int yesorno(question)
char question[];
{
  int answer,               /* user's response */
      junk;                 /* used to skip characters */

  printf("%s? ", question);
  do
  {
    printf(" (y for yes, n for no): ");
    junk = answer = getchar();   /* get user's answer */
    while (junk != EOF && junk != '\n')
      junk = getchar();          /* skip rest of line */
  } while (answer != 'y' && answer != 'n' && answer != EOF);
  return answer;
}
```

(a) *Get a yes or no answer from the user*

```
if (yesorno("Are you smart") == 'y')
  printf("Me too.\n");
else
  printf("Too bad.\n");
```

(b) *An example use of* yesorno

FIGURE 5.3. A function to get a yes or no answer from the user.

braces are not required by the language syntax, but their use clearly
shows that the do and the while are associated. For example,

```
do    /* Ignore the rest of the line */
{
  c = getchar();
} while (c != '\n' && c != EOF);
```

is preferred to the more compact but less readable

```
do    /* Ignore the rest of the line */
    c = getchar();
while (c != '\n' && c != EOF);
```

MORE GENERAL LOOPS—FOR

We have also used the **for** statement before.

>   **for** (*Start*; *Test*; *Action*)
>   *statement*

for is executed by evaluating *Start*, discarding the result, and entering a cycle of evaluating *Test*, executing *statement*, and evaluating *Action*. The cycle terminates when *Test* evaluates to zero.

Usually, *Start* and *Action* are assignments or function calls and *Test* is a relational test. These expressions are all arbitrary, however, and can be omitted. When *Start* is omitted, it is generally because any needed initializations have already been done. As an example, Figure 5.4 contains a function **print_tab**, which prints out a table of integers, given pointers to its first and last elements. **tab_ptr** is used to traverse the array, but is initialized when the function is called, rather than in the loop.

A missing *Test* is assumed to evaluate to nonzero; such a loop is infinite and will normally be exited by a **return** or other control-flow altering statement. For example,

```
for (;;)
    printf("Reflex test - hit the terminal interrupt key\n");
```

repeatedly writes the same message until the terminal interrupt key is pressed. Notice that the semicolons remain even when the expressions are left out.

Because the **for** is so general, we often write **for** loops with multiple index variables, as well as index variables that are pointers instead of integers. Figure 5.5 shows examples of both in a program (called *Pal*) that

```
/*
 * Print table given pointers to start and end of table.
 */
print_tab(tab_ptr, end_ptr)
int *tab_ptr, *end_ptr;                 /* the pointers */
{
    for (; tab_ptr <= end_ptr; tab_ptr++)
        printf("%d\n", *tab_ptr);
}
```

FIGURE 5.4. A function to print an array of integers.

```
/*
 *  Palindrome checker (assumes get_line from Chapter 4).
 */
#include <stdio.h>

#define MAXLINE 81                      /* longest input line + ending null */
#define TRUE    1                       /* the usual booleans */
#define FALSE   0

main()
{
  char line[MAXLINE],                   /* user input line */
       copy[MAXLINE];                   /* copy of user input line */

  while (printf("line? "), get_line(line, MAXLINE) != EOF)
  {
    strcpy(copy, line);                 /* make copy of user line */
    printf("%s: %spalindrome.\n", line, ispalin(copy) ? "" : "not ");
  }
}

/* Is a string a palindrome? */

int ispalin(test)
char *test;                             /* string to check for palindrome */
{
  char *f,                              /* forward and reverse pointers into */
       *r;                              /*   test string */
  int palin;                            /* flag: do we have palindrome? */

  /* Remove any blanks from potential palindrome */

  for (r = f = test; *f != '\0'; f++)
    if (*f != ' ')
      *r++ = *f;
  *r = '\0';

  /*
   * Walk pointers through string from both ends;
   * mismatch means not palindrome and testing stops
   */

  palin = TRUE;
  for (f = test, r--; f < r && palin; f++, r--)
    if (*f != *r)
      palin = FALSE;

  return palin;
}
```

FIGURE 5.5. Palindrome checker.

checks to see if its input lines are palindromes. A palindrome is a group of characters that, excluding blanks, reads the same forward or backward. For example, ''able was I ere I saw elba'' is a palindrome.

Most of *Pal* is built from existing functions. get_line (Chapter 4) reads each input line, and strcpy copies it. ispalin is new, however. It determines whether a string is a palindrome, after removing the blanks. main simply calls these functions, echoing each line followed by a message stating whether it is a palindrome.

To simplify the later palindrome checking, the first for in ispalin removes any blanks from the string being checked.

```
for (r = f = test; *f != '\0'; f++)
  if (*f != ' ')
    *r++ = *f;
*r = '\0';
```

As the character pointer f walks through the string test, each nonblank character is copied into the character pointed to by r and r is incremented, as the following shows. Since r starts by pointing to test's first character, this effectively removes all of its blanks. If test contains no blanks, the string is simply copied onto itself.

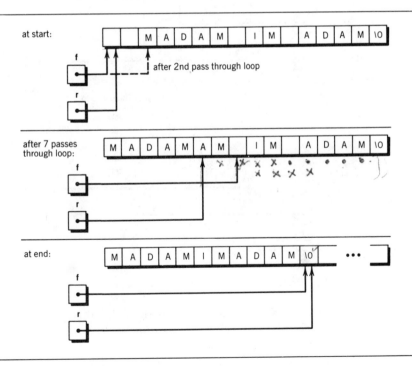

The second **for** checks to see if the string is a palindrome. The comma operator allows multiple initializations and actions within the loop.

```
palin = TRUE;
for (f = test, r--; f < r && palin; f++, r--)
  if (*f != *r)
    palin = FALSE;
```

This **for** works by having a pointer **f** go forward from the start of the string and a pointer **r** go backward from its end, as shown in the following diagram. As these pointers move along, the characters they point to are compared and the loop stops when the characters are different (it is not a palindrome) or the pointers cross (it is a palindrome). Because **r** points at the terminating null after the blanks are removed, it is decremented when the loop is initialized. It is a good idea to initialize index variables (here, pointers) within the loop; whether to initialize related variables in the loop (such as **palin**) is up to you.

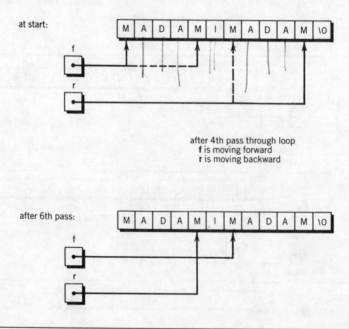

at start:

after 4th pass through loop
f is moving forward
r is moving backward

after 6th pass:

Since the **for** is more general than the **while**, you may be wondering when each is appropriate. **for** is appropriate when the loop control statements are simple and related, and the same values are updated each time the loop is executed. **while** should be used when an equivalent **for** would contain unrelated computations or would omit both *Start* and *Action*. When in doubt, it often helps to write the code for both and use the one that appears to be more readable.

PROGRAMMING PRACTICE

5-10. Modify *Pal* to strip all punctuation, as well as any tabs, from the input string.

5-11. Write a function, `strrev`, that takes its single character string argument and reverses it in place.

5-12. Write a program that prints all the prime numbers between 1 and 1000. A prime number is one that is exactly divisible only by one and itself.

THE NULL STATEMENT

Any semicolon not preceded by an expression is a *null statement*. A null statement does nothing and is used when no action is desired but the language syntax requires a statement. This occurs most frequently when side effects in a loop's control expression obviate any need for the loop's body. Using the null statement makes these loops more compact by allowing expression statements to be moved from the loop's body into its controlling expression. As an example, Figure 5.6 shows the standard

```
/*
 * Find length of string.
 */
int strlen(str_ptr)
char *str_ptr;
{
  char *end_ptr;

  for (end_ptr = str_ptr; *end_ptr != '\0'; end_ptr++)
    ;                                   /* find end of string */
  return end_ptr - str_ptr;
}
```

FIGURE 5.6. Finding the length of a character string.

I/O library function `strlen`, which computes the length of a null-terminated character string. The string's length is computed by running a pointer through the string until the null character is reached and then subtracting a pointer to the string's first character from the pointer. The difference between two pointers to the same array is the number of elements separating them.

A null statement should never be placed on the same line as a `for` or a `while`, because it is easy to ignore a semicolon at the end of the line and mistake the following lines for the loop's body. Whenever the null statement is used, it should be placed on a line by itself, indented slightly, and followed by a comment, as we have done in our examples.

Accidentally inserting a null statement following a loop's control expression is a common mistake with disastrous results. The loop

```
for (sum = i = 0; i < N; i++);  /* sum first "N" scores */
    sum += score[i];            /* (but accidentally null loop body) */
```

was probably meant to add `N` scores together in the variable `sum`. However, the null statement following the loop's control expression forms the loop's body. Thus, the statement

```
sum += score[i];
```

is executed only after the loop is terminated, when i is `N` + 1 and is probably no longer a legal subscript.

PROGRAMMING PRACTICE

5-13. Rewrite `strlen` to use a `while` loop instead of a `for` loop. Which version do you find more readable? Which version is more efficient? (*Hint*: Examine the machine code your compiler generates for both versions.)

5-14. Write the standard I/O library functions `strncat` and `strncpy`, which behave similarly to `strcat` and `strcpy`, except that a maximum of n characters are concatenated or copied.

ALTERING CONTROL FLOW—BREAK, CONTINUE, AND GOTO

Normally, statements are executed sequentially. We now describe statements that can be used to alter the normal sequential flow of control.

Although it is easy to use these statements to violate some of the basic principles of structured programming, and although their use is never absolutely necessary, on occasion they are convenient and help to simplify our programs.

Sometimes leaving a loop from within its body simplifies the loop's control expression by separating tests for special cases or errors. In addition to its already described use in exiting a `switch`, `break` can be used to exit immediately from anywhere within the nearest enclosing `for`, `while`, or `do – while`, as the following illustrates.

```
while (condition)
{
      •
      •
      •
    if (error)
        break;
}
```

break causes control to pass to the statement after the loop

As an example, consider a loop to find the first nonblank on an input line

```
while (c = getchar(), c!=' ' && c!='\t' && c!=EOF && c!='\n')
    ;       /* skip nonblanks */
```

is more readable when written using `break`:

```
while (c = getchar(), c!=' ' && c!='\t') /* blanks and tabs */
    if (c == EOF || c == '\n')
        break;              /* special cases: end of file and end of line */
```

The `break` causes the `while` to exit and control to pass to whatever statement follows it. Using break simplifies the loop's control expression and makes it clearer that end of file and end of line are special cases.

The `continue` statement skips the remaining part of a loop iteration and is most often used to avoid excessive nesting within the loop. After a `continue` within a `for`, the *Action* is evaluated, before the loop's control expression. In a `while` or `do-while`, `continue` causes the control expression to be evaluated immediately.

One common use of `continue` is in checking for error conditions at the beginning of a loop, thus skipping the rest of the loop if an error occurs. As an example, Figure 5.7 shows a function that does some unspecified but complicated processing on a table. Whenever an out-of-range element is encountered, an error message is written and `continue` is used to

```
/*
 * Process table of elements.
 */
process(table, tabentries)
int table[], tabentries;
{
  int i;

  for (i = 0; i < tabentries; i++)
  {
    if (table[i] < MINVAL || table[i] > MAXVAL)
    {
      printf("Element #%d, value %d, is out of range\n", i, table[i]);
      continue;            /* skip processing if element in error */
    }
    processing of valid table elements
  }
}
```

FIGURE 5.7. Using `continue` to avoid the remainder of a loop.

skip any further processing of the element. Since the `continue` is within a `for`, when it is executed, the *Action* (`i++`) is evaluated before the loop termination test occurs. Despite its occasional usefulness, `continue` can usually be avoided by rewriting the complex code as a separate function.

The final way to alter control flow is the `goto` statement. A `goto` can be used to branch to a labeled statement within any statement group enclosing it. A *label* has the same syntax as an identifier and is visible only within the statement group in which it is defined.

```
goto label
...
label: statement
```

A `goto` is executed by transferring control to the statement labeled by *label*. There must be a statement to which control can be transferred; the null statement must be used if control is to be transferred to the end of a compound statement or function body.

A reasonable use of `goto` is to exit from within nested loops when an error condition occurs:

```
while (...)
  for (...)
  {
    ...
    if (error condition)
      goto error;
    ...
  }
```

```
   ...
error:
   printf("Serious error detected...time to go home!\n");
   ...
```

When the error condition occurs, control is transferred to the label error and the error message is printed. Because break and continue exit only a single loop, avoiding a goto in a situation like this requires a boolean variable to note the error condition and additional tests of its value in the expressions controlling the loops. Another way to avoid using a goto is to make the code fragment containing the loops a function; return can then be used to exit the loops when the error condition occurs, and return a value indicating the error condition. (The complete use of functions and return is covered in the next chapter.)

There are many reasons to avoid using gotos. When goto is used, most compilers generate less efficient code than with structured loop constructs. In addition, using many of them quickly renders a program unreadable. Since there are several reasonable ways to avoid using goto, it is a good idea to do so whenever possible and to document any goto whose use is deemed necessary. The goto is used infrequently in most well-written programs, and we have found no need for it in any of the programs in this book.

CONCISE CONTROL EXPRESSIONS

As mentioned earlier, the control expressions of the if, for, while, and do-while statements are evaluated and compared with zero to determine the action to be taken, thus making explicit comparisons with zero in any control expression unnecessary.

if (*expression* != 0)	*is equivalent to*	if (*expression*)
if (*expression* == 0)	*is equivalent to*	if (!*expression*)

Since zero is used both as the end-of-string character and as the null pointer, testing if the end of a string has been reached or if a pointer is null is often done implicitly. As an example, Figure 5.8 shows a more concise version of the standard I/O library function strlen we saw earlier. *end_ptr is the entire control expression for the for. Its value is compared implicitly to zero and the loop stops when end_ptr points to the null character at the end of the string.

```
/*
 * Find length of string.
 */
int strlen(str_ptr)
char *str_ptr;
{
  char *end_ptr;

  for (end_ptr = str_ptr; *end_ptr; end_ptr++)
    ;                                   /* find end of string */
  return end_ptr - str_ptr;
}
```

FIGURE 5.8. Finding the length of a string using implicit test for null character.

The version of strlen shown in Figure 5.8 requires str_ptr to point to a valid character string, as does the strlen in the standard I/O library. If instead str_ptr is NULL, strlen will bomb at run time. We can make strlen verify that str_ptr is not NULL by adding the following before the for:

```
if (!str_ptr)          /* null pointer? */
  return -1;           /*   return impossible legal string length */
```

When str_ptr is the null pointer, !str_ptr evaluates to nonzero and the function returns -1.

Because of the implicit comparison with zero, using the assignment operator when the equality operator was desired can be disastrous. When

```
if (errorcnt = 0)
  printf("No errors");
```

is executed, the printf will never be executed, regardless of errorcnt's value. This happens because every time the if is executed, errorcnt is set to zero, causing the implicit test to fail. Most likely, the correct form is

```
if (errorcnt == 0)
  printf("No errors");
```

Any time an assignment of a constant to a variable forms a control expression, it is likely to be in error.

PROGRAMMING PRACTICE

5-15. Taking advantage of the implicit tests against zero, write a function print_reverse that prints an array of n elements in reverse order.

```
All 78 values in range

  0-  9 |
 10- 19 |***                                                          (3)
 20- 29 |*                                                            (1)
 30- 39 |
 40- 49 |*                                                            (1)
 50- 59 |*****                                                        (5)
 60- 69 |***********                                                  (11)
 70- 79 |*************************************                         (37)
 80- 89 |************                                                 (12)
 90- 99 |***                                                          (3)
100-100 |*****                                                        (5)
```

FIGURE 5.9. Sample histogram output.

CASE STUDY—A HISTOGRAM PROGRAM

We end this chapter with a program (called *Histo*) that produces a histogram of its input. A histogram is a visual representation of a frequency distribution that is composed of bars representing different ranges of values. Each bar's length represents the relative frequency of the group of values represented by that bar. Figure 5.9 shows sample output from *Histo*.

Histo is interesting because it is an example of a useful program, clearly and cleanly written in just under 100 lines of C, that uses many of the control structures discussed in this chapter. The following sections describe its input, internal processing, and output in more detail, followed by a listing of the program.

THE HISTOGRAM PROGRAM—INPUT

Histo's input is a series of free-format integer values to be read using scanf. Figure 5.10 shows the histogram input used to produce the histo-

```
89  87  56  89  67  78  79  80  85  97 100 100  23
45  12  14  87  88  84  84  84  77  77  72  73  68
69  69 100 100  11  75  71  71  72  79  84  71  72
70  74  75  73  71  79  72  55  55  68  65  67  72
71  75  73  71  74  71  71  78  79  80 100  91  92
66  61  61  57  57  65  71  74  78  78  78  78  78
```

FIGURE 5.10. Sample histogram program input.

gram output shown in Figure 5.9. *Histo* terminates with an appropriate error message if there are any input errors, such as a nonnumeric character. Most users would probably prefer it to simply skip over or report all occurrences of bad input, but this is difficult to do with scanf. In Chapter 7 we develop an alternative to scanf that greatly simplifies input error handling.

All input values are checked to verify that they fall within the legal range (defined as constants within the program). After the input has been read, the number of out-of-range values is written.

THE HISTOGRAM PROGRAM—INTERNAL PROCESSING

Each valid data value must be counted into the correct group, or *bucket*. There is an array of these data buckets, one for each range of values. Each bucket counts those values falling within the range of values it represents. Once all input values have been read, these counters are used to print the histogram.

When the program starts, the range of values in each bucket is easily computed from defined constants for the minimum and maximum legal data values and the desired number of buckets. Selecting an appropriate bucket is also straightforward, as illustrated in the following.

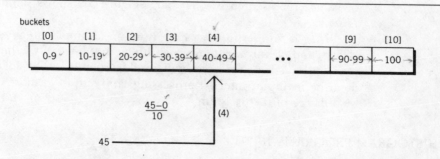

In this example, we assume that the minimum value is 0 and that each bucket holds 10 different values. Then for an input of 45, we can determine the correct bucket by subtracting the minimum value (0) from the data value (45) and dividing the result by the size of a bucket (10). The result (4) is the bucket in which the data value should be counted (remember, we are using integer division here).

THE HISTOGRAM PROGRAM—OUTPUT

Histo's output is a horizontal bar chart like the one shown in Figure 5.9. Each bar is a row of asterisks, and each asterisk represents a single value.

Each row of asterisks is preceded by the range of values the row represents, and is followed by a count of the values falling in that range. If there are no values in the row, the count is suppressed.

If there are many input values, it is possible that more asterisks will be needed than there are columns available on the output device. Should this occur, the output is scaled so that the row with the most asterisks covers the available width and the other rows are proportionally shorter, allowing users to see the relationship between the various groups. To make sure that scaling doesn't make any row with proportionally few values appear to have none at all, at least one asterisk is written for each row that has one or more values. In any case, the exact count is still written at each row's end.

THE HISTOGRAM PROGRAM

The histogram program is broken into two functions other than main. fill_bkts reads input values, checks their legality, and updates the appropriate bucket. It returns an int indicating whether any input errors were encountered. print_histo prints the histogram based on the counts in the buckets. main computes the bucket size, invokes fill_bkts to update them, and then invokes print_histo only if no input errors are detected. Here is a skeletal version of the main program.

```
main()
{
    compute bucket size
    if (we can fill the buckets without error)
        print the histogram
}
```

Histo is shown in Figure 5.11, and at this point should be easily understandable. Glancing through the program, you will notice null statements, considerable use of the comma and conditional operators, and loops manipulating multiple indexes. Although *Histo* is a sizable program, it is worthwhile taking some time to study it in preparation for the larger programs we present in later chapters.

PROGRAMMING PRACTICE

5-16. Modify the constants for the minimum and maximum values and bucket count in *Histo*, and examine the effects on the output.

5-17. Modify *Histo* to read the minimum and maximum values and bucket

```
/*
 *  Produce nice histogram from input values.
 */
#include <stdio.h>


#define  MAXCOLS   50         /* columns available for markers */
#define  MARKER    '*'        /* character used to mark columns */
#define  MAXVAL    100        /* largest legal input value */
#define  MINVAL    0          /* smallest legal input value */
#define  NUMBKTS   11         /* number of buckets */


main()
{
  int buckets[NUMBKTS];       /* buckets to place values in */
  int bktsize;                /* range bucket represents */

  bktsize = (MAXVAL - MINVAL) / (NUMBKTS - 1);
  if (fill_bkts(buckets, bktsize))
    print_histo(buckets, bktsize);
  else
    printf("Illegal data value--no histogram printed\n");
}


/*
 * Read values, updating bucket counts.  Returns nonzero only
 * if EOF was reached without error.
 */
int fill_bkts(buckets, bktsize)
int buckets[];                /* buckets to place values in */
int bktsize;                  /* range of values in bucket */
{
  int badcnt,                 /* count of out-of-range values */
      bkt,                    /* next bucket to initialize */
      inpres,                 /* result of reading in an input line */
      totalcnt,               /* count of values */
      value;                  /* next input value */


  for (bkt = 0; bkt <= NUMBKTS; buckets[bkt++] = 0)
    ;                         /* initialize bucket counts */
  badcnt = totalcnt = 0;
  while (inpres = scanf("%d", &value), inpres == 1)
  {
    if (value >= MINVAL && value <= MAXVAL)
      buckets[(value - MINVAL) / bktsize]++;
    else
      badcnt++;
    totalcnt++;
  }
```

```
  if (!badcnt)
    printf("All %d values in range\n", totalcnt);
  else
    printf("Out of range %d, total %d\n", badcnt, totalcnt);
  return inpres == EOF;        /* did we get all the input? */
}

/*
 * Print a nice histogram, first computing a scaling factor.
 */
print_histo(buckets, bktsize)
int buckets[];                 /* buckets to place values in */
int bktsize;                   /* range of values in bucket */
{
  int bottom,                  /* first value in current bucket */
      bkt,                     /* current bucket */
      markcnt,                 /* number of marks written */
      most,                    /* values in largest bucket */
      values;                  /* number of values to write out */
  float scale;                 /* scaling factor */

  /* compute scaling factor */

  for (bkt = most = 0; bkt < NUMBKTS; bkt++)
    if (most < buckets[bkt])
      most = buckets[bkt];
  scale = (most > MAXCOLS) ? (MAXCOLS / (float) most) : 1.0;

  /* print the histogram */

  putchar('\n');
  for (bkt = 0, bottom = MINVAL; bkt < NUMBKTS; bottom += bktsize, bkt++)
  {
    /* write range */

    printf("%3d-%3d |", bottom,
               (bkt == NUMBKTS - 1) ? MAXVAL : bottom + bktsize - 1);

    /* compute number of MARKERS to write, making sure that at least
       one is written if there are any values in the bucket */

    if (buckets[bkt] && !(values = buckets[bkt] * scale))
      values = 1;

    /* writes MARKERS and count of values */

    for (markcnt = 0; markcnt < MAXCOLS; markcnt++)
      putchar((markcnt < values) ? MARKER : ' ');
    if (buckets[bkt])
      printf(" (%ld)", buckets[bkt]);
    putchar('\n');
  }
}
```

FIGURE 5.11. The histogram program.

count. Obviously, there must be some internal maximum bucket count; the program should verify that the desired bucket count is not too large.

5-18. Our histogram has a horizontal orientation; modify `print_histo` to print a histogram with a vertical orientation instead.

5-19. Modify *Histo* to use pointers where appropriate. Does this have a noticeable effect on the program's speed?

5-20. We have pointed out many of the problems with `scanf`. A simple solution is to write a function `getnum` that uses `scanf` to try to read a number. If `scanf` fails, `getnum` skips characters until a white space character is reached. Write `getnum` and modify *Histo* to use it. What problems are there with `getnum`?

CHAPTER 6

FUNCTIONS

One of C's strengths is that functions are easy to define and use. In this chapter we discuss functions in detail, concentrating on how they communicate with one another through parameter passing and return values. In addition we examine pointers to functions, which are used to pass functions as parameters. We conclude with a discussion of recursive functions (functions that call themselves), presenting an implementation of an interesting and useful recursive algorithm, binary search.

USING POINTERS TO ALTER NONLOCAL VARIABLES

We have seen that in C, all parameters are passed by value; every time a function is called, each parameter has space allocated for it and is then assigned the value of its corresponding argument (the value of the parameters when a function is called are known as its *arguments*). When the function exits, the space is deallocated. In effect, parameters can be treated as previously initialized local variables. Because modifying a parameter does not affect its corresponding argument, *a function cannot change the values it is passed*. This allows the use of arbitrary expressions as function arguments and prevents a function from accidentally modifying its arguments.

There are times, however, when it is useful to have a function alter the value of a variable in its calling function; scanf is one example. Because changes to parameters are local to the function, it cannot directly change the variable's value. Instead, we must use & to pass a pointer to it; the function can then dereference the pointer with * whenever the variable's value is to be accessed or modified.

```
/*
 * Incorrect version of swap.
 */
swap(x,y)
int x,y;
{
  int temp = x;

  x = y, y = temp;
}
```

FIGURE 6.1. Incorrect version of swapping function.

We illustrate this technique with a function **swap** that exchanges the values of two integer variables. Because of call by value, the version of **swap** shown in Figure 6.1 does not do what we want: it swaps the values of its parameters x and y but does not affect the values of its arguments.

For **swap** to exchange the values of variables in its calling function, it must be passed *pointers* to them; the values can then be swapped indirectly through these pointers. A corrected version of **swap** is shown in Figure 6.2a and an example call in Figure 6.2b.

```
/*
 * Corrected version of swap - exchange two values.
 */
swap(x_ptr, y_ptr)
int *x_ptr, *y_ptr;
{
  int temp = *x_ptr;

  *x_ptr = *y_ptr, *y_ptr = temp;
}
```

(a)   Correctly exchange two values using pointers

```
{
  int s, t;
      . . .
  swap(&s,&t);
}
```

(b)   Exchanging the values in s and t

FIGURE 6.2. Corrected version of swap and example call. The values are exchanged through pointers.

The call to swap shown in Figure 6.2*b* is illustrated in the following figure, which assumes that the addresses of s and t are 1000 and 2000, respectively, s is 5, and t is 10. When swap is called, x_ptr becomes 1000 and y_ptr becomes 2000, the addresses of their corresponding arguments. The assignment temp = *x_ptr causes the value in location 1000 (5) to be placed in temp. Similarly, *x_ptr = *y_ptr assigns location 1000 the value in location 2000 (10), and *y_ptr = temp completes the exchange by placing temp's contents (5) in location 2000.

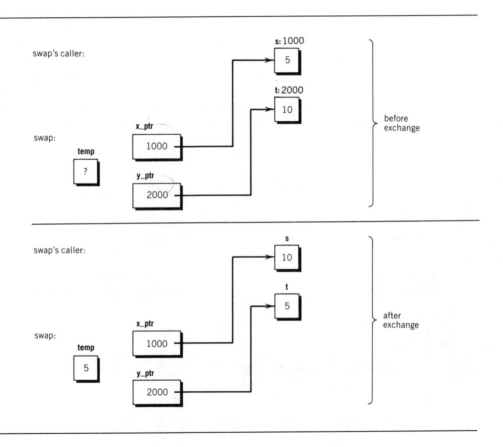

Remember that when we have a pointer parameter, its corresponding argument must also be a pointer. For swap to work correctly, it must be passed the addresses of the variables whose values are to be exchanged. Passing the variables themselves is likely to cause an addressing exception.

Perhaps the most common mistake made when writing functions with pointer parameters is to use the pointers inconsistently. One way to avoid this problem is to first write the function without any pointer parameters, pretending that C has call by reference parameter passing. Once the function has been written this way, the appropriate parameters can be transformed into pointers by modifying their declarations, renaming them to reflect their new use, and replacing all their uses with the appropriate pointer name, preceded by a *. Indeed, this is how we got the correct version of swap from the incorrect one. We replaced the int variables x and y with the pointer variables x_ptr and y_ptr and preceded all uses of these pointers with *. Although it is not necessary for swap, references through pointer variables may have to be parenthesized to guarantee the desired order of evaluation.

Another common mistake is to accidentally pass a pointer's address instead of the pointer itself. An example is shown in Figure 6.3. get_val is supposed to use scanf to read a single value, placing it in the location pointed to by x_ptr and returning whether the value read is between min and max. There is a bug in this implementation, however. Since x_ptr is already a pointer to the location where scanf should place the value read, scanf is reading its value into x_ptr instead of what it points to, invalidating later accesses through x_ptr. Since we already have the pointer we need, we do not want to take its address:

```
    return (scanf("%d", x_ptr) == 1)          /* This is correct */
            && (*x_ptr >= min) && (*x_ptr <= max);
```

```
/*
 * Reads value, places it in "*x_ptr", and returns whether or not it is
 * between "max" and "min".  Warning, the surgeon general has determined
 * that there is a bug in this program!
 */
int get_val(x_ptr, min, max)
int *x_ptr, min, max;
{
  return (scanf("%d", &x_ptr) == 1)          /* BUG ALERT! */
            && (*x_ptr >= min) && (*x_ptr <= max);
}
```

(a) Reading a value and checking that it is in range

```
{
  int x;
  . . .
  if (!get_val(&x, 1, 100))                   /* read legal? value into x */
    printf("Bad value found...\n");
}
```

(b) An example call of get_val

FIGURE 6.3. An example of the incorrect use of pointer parameters.

PROGRAMMING PRACTICE

6-1. Turn Figure 6.3 into a program and run it. What happens? Are there certain values for which the program appears to work? Fix Figure 6.3 so that it works as intended.

6-2. Write a function, maxmin, that returns through its parameters the largest and smallest values in an array of floating point numbers. Use the declaration

```
maxmin(table, n, max_ptr, min_ptr)
float table[], *max_ptr, *min_ptr;
int n;
```

6-3. Write the function str_swap, whose arguments are pointers to strings. The values of these pointers are swapped. When is str_swap useful? (*Hint*: This requires pointers to pointers. It helps to draw a picture in order to see what is going on.)

PARAMETERS AND TYPE CHECKING

C's parameter-passing mechanism only works correctly when the type of each argument in a function's call is the same as the type of its corresponding parameter. To avoid errors resulting from type mismatches, we must use a cast if their types differ.

Unfortunately, type mismatches are not always detected at compile time and can cause strange run-time behavior. We use the function inrange, shown in Figure 6.4a, as an example. inrange verifies that a given floating point value is between two other values, returning zero only if it is out of range.

Consider what happens when inrange is called, as shown in Figure 6.4b. Surprisingly, the error message is never printed, regardless of the value of **result** passed to inrange. This occurs because inrange expects its parameters to be **doubles** (two words in floating point representation) and instead receives **ints** (one word in two's complement representation). As a result, on a VAX-750, regardless of the values passed, **min** and **max** are always zero—clearly, not what was intended. Luckily, we can correct the call shown in Figure 6.4b by making sure that each of its arguments is a **double**:

```
if (!inrange(1.0, 100.0, (double) result))
```

All floating point constants are **doubles**, and the cast guarantees that a

```
/*
 * Return one if "value" is between "min" and "max", zero if it isn't.
 */
int inrange(min,max,value)
double min, max, value;
{
  return value >= min && value <= max;
}
```

    (a) *Function to check if a value is in a given range*

```
int result;
    . . .
if (!inrange(1, 100, result))
  printf("Error: %d is out of range\n", result);
```

    (b) *Example call of* inrange *with a parameter type mismatch*

FIGURE 6.4. Example of parameter type mismatch.

copy of result will be converted to a double before being passed as a parameter.

AUTOMATIC TYPE CONVERSIONS

Some parameter conversions are done automatically. Any char or short argument is implicitly cast to an int before it is passed; similarly, a float argument is cast to a double. In the following call to inrange, it is unnecessary to cast low_val, high_val, or result explicitly, because the necessary conversions are done automatically before they are passed.

```
float low_val, high_val, result;
    . . .
if (!inrange(low_val, high_val, result))
  printf("Error: %f is out of range\n", result)
```

Within functions, short or char *parameters*, but not local variables, are automatically redeclared as int; float parameters become doubles. Appropriate casts are inserted wherever the parameter is used; for example, when the compiler redeclares a short parameter as an int, it implicitly casts its value to short wherever it appears within the function. Thus, the definition of inrange in Figure 6.5a behaves as if it were written as in Figure 6.5b. Since the compiler must insert code to do type conversions wherever char, short, and float parameters are used, it is significantly more efficient to pass int, long, and double parameters instead.

```
int inrange(min,max,value)
short min, max, value;
{
  return value >= min && value <= max;
}
```

(a) A version of inrange *for* short *parameters*

```
int inrange(min,max,value)
int min, max, value;
{
  return (short) value >= (short) min && (short) value <= (short) max;
}
```

(b) inrange *after the compiler's automatic conversions*

FIGURE 6.5. An example of automatic type conversions.

PARAMETERS AND PORTABILITY

C's lack of type checking, combined with programmer carelessness, leads to programs that work on one machine but fail on another. Consider the version of inrange shown in Figure 6.6a as invoked in Figure 6.6b. (We know you are getting a little tired of inrange, but please bear with us; this is the last example using it.) On the VAX-750, int and long happen to be the same size (32 bits), and the code works as expected. However, on the IBM-PC, where int is one word and long is two words, we get bizarre results. It is easy to make this program work correctly on all machines; we simply cast the arguments appropriately or use long constants:

```
if (!inrange(1L, 100L, (long) result))
```

Portability problems can also occur when we pass NULL to a function expecting a pointer. If we do not cast NULL to the correct pointer type, our program will not be portable to machines where pointers and integers are not the same size. For example, suppose we have a function f that takes a single parameter, a pointer to a char. To see why the call

```
f(NULL)
```

is *not* portable, consider an architecture that has two-word pointers and one-word ints. Since NULL is defined as the constant zero, we are passing a one-word integer when a two-word pointer is expected. It is easy to prevent this mistake by casting NULL appropriately. The call

```
f((char *) NULL)
```

```
int inrange(min,max,value)
long min, max, value;
{
  return value >= min && value <= max;
}
```

(a) Defining inrange *with* long *arguments*

```
{
  int result;
  . . .
  if (!inrange(1, 100, result))
    printf("Error: %d is out of range\n", result);
}
```

(b) Calling inrange *incorrectly with* int *arguments*

FIGURE 6.6. Yet another version of our range checking function. The call isn't portable.

is portable.

Not only do we have to be careful that there are no type mismatches, we must also ensure that we pass the correct number of parameters. Functions ignore extra parameters; missing parameters contain undefined values. Although C's lack of type checking can be exploited to write functions that handle variable numbers of arguments such as printf or scanf, these functions are not portable. Indeed, they must contain knowledge about the underlying hardware.

PROGRAMMING PRACTICE

6-4. Try the various versions of inrange on your machine. Can you explain their output by examining the relative sizes of .the data types on your machine? Which version produces the smallest amount of code? The largest?

6-5. Write a function, isvalid, that is similar to inrange, except that it verifies whether a pointer is between two other pointers. Assume the pointers passed to isvalid are pointers to long. A null pointer for either range should disable that range check.

RETURN VALUES—THE TYPE OF A FUNCTION

In addition to communicating through parameter passing, functions can communicate through return values. A function can return a single short, int, long, char, float, double, or pointer. The type of the function's return value is specified when the function is declared and precedes the function's name, defaulting to int if left unspecified.

All of our previous functions have returned an int or nothing at all. We illustrate the use of a non-int return value in Figure 6.7, a program to compute x^y for integers x and y. Since the result can be fractional if y is negative, or large for small values of x and y, we define power to return a double.

When the compiler encounters a function call, if the type of the function's return value has not been declared, it is assumed to be int.

```
/*
 * Compute powers.
 */
main()
{
  int    x,y;            /* user inputs */
  double power();        /* computes x to the y */

  while (printf("Enter x,y: "), scanf("%d %d", &x, &y) == 2)
    printf("%d to the %d is %f\n", x, y, power(x,y));
}

/*
 * Return x to the y, works best for small integers.
 */
double power(x,y)
int x,y;
{
  double p;             /* start off with x to the zero */

  p = 1.0;
  if (y >= 0)
    while (y--)         /* compute positive powers */
      p *= x;
  else
    while (y++)         /* compute negative powers */
      p /= x;
  return p;
}
```

FIGURE 6.7. Computing x^y for integers x and y.

The *declaration*

```
double power();        /* computes x to the y */
```

appears in main, before power is called, to inform the compiler that power returns a double instead of the default int. Parentheses follow power to specify that power is a function instead of a variable. The types of a function's parameters are not specified in a declaration. Without this declaration, the compiler would incorrectly assume that power returns an int, and incorrect code to handle its return value would be generated. This assumption would be contradicted when power's later definition occurs, causing most compilers to report an error. Not all compilers detect this inconsistency, however, particularly when separate compilation (which we will discuss in the next chapter) allows the function to be defined in another file.

Figure 6.8 shows an alternative way to guarantee that power's type is declared before its use in main; we simply define power before we define main. power's type is then known from its definition, so we no longer need its type declaration in main. We prefer explicit declarations to relying on

```
/*
 * Compute powers.
 */
double power(x,y)       /* return x to the y */
int x,y;                /*    (works best for small integers) */
{
  double p;             /* start off with x to the zero */

  p = 1.0;
  if (y >= 0)
    while (y--)         /* compute positive powers */
      p *= x;
  else
    while (y++)         /* compute negative powers */
      p /= x;
  return p;
}

main()
{
  int x,y;              /* user inputs */

  while (printf("Enter x,y: "), scanf("%d %d", &x, &y) == 2)
    printf("%d to the %d is %f\n", x, y, power(x,y));
}
```

FIGURE 6.8. Defining a function before its use.

the default assumptions of the compiler or the order in which the functions appear in the source file, since we can then determine the program's structure easily by scanning declarations.

PROGRAMMING PRACTICE

6-6. Write the function index, which takes a string and a character, and returns a pointer to the character's first occurrence within the string.

6-7. Write the function rindex, which is similar to index, except that it returns a pointer to the character's last occurrence within the string.

FUNCTIONS THAT RETURN A VALUE

As we have seen, return terminates a function, possibly returning a value to its caller. There are two forms of return:

return *expression*;

and

return;

Some compilers require parentheses around *expression* even though the language syntax doesn't require them. return without an expression does not return a value and is similar to simply dropping off the function's end. This form should not be used in a function that is supposed to return a value.

return can appear anywhere within the function body, and a function can contain more than one return. As an example, Figure 6.9*a* shows the function search that searches for a value in an array of integers, returning a pointer to the place where the value is found. Figure 6.9*b* is an example call. search uses a pointer to traverse the array, and return to exit the function immediately when a match is found. If the entire table was searched and the value was not found, the return at the function's end returns a null pointer.

When a value is returned, it is automatically cast to the function's type (when such a cast makes sense). This automatic return value conversion is often useful; in search it means that we do not have to cast the returned NULL to a pointer. In functions that do computations using doubles, yet return ints, any double returned will be truncated into an int before being given to the caller.

```
/*
 * Search "num" element table for "value", returning a pointer to
 * the matching element, or the null pointer if it is not found.
 */
int *search(tab_ptr, num, value)
int *tab_ptr,                    /* pointer to table's first element */
    num,                         /* number of elements in table */
    value;                       /* value we're looking for */
{
  for (; num--; tab_ptr++)
    if (*tab_ptr == value)
      return tab_ptr;            /* found target, return pointer to it */
  return NULL;                   /* failure, return null pointer */
}
```

(a) Function to search an array sequentially

```
int table[MAX],
    *search(),                   /* function doing searching */
    *fnd_ptr,                    /* pointer to found element */
    target;                      /* element searching for */
    . . .
if (fnd_ptr = search(table, MAX, target), fnd_ptr != NULL)
  printf("Found %d as element %d.\n", target, fnd_ptr - table);
else
  printf("Didn't find %d.\n", target);
```

(b) An example call of search

FIGURE 6.9. Sequential search of an array using pointers.

PROGRAMMING PRACTICE

6-8. Improve the sequential search shown in Figure 6.9 by assuming a sorted table.

6-9. Rewrite search to use only one return statement.

6-10. Modify the function insert (Chapter 1) to return a pointer to the place in the table where the value was entered or NULL if the table was full. Rewrite insertion sort using this version of insert.

FUNCTIONS THAT DO NOT RETURN A VALUE

In C, all functions return a value, unlike languages such as Pascal which distinguish between functions that return a value (functions) and those that do not (procedures). C does, however, provide a special type void for functions that do not return a useful value. void can be used only with functions; we cannot declare a variable to be void.

Normally, if a function returns a value, we can use it in an expression. But when we declare a function to return void, we explicitly state that the function's value cannot be used. Thus, a void function should not attempt to return anything.

Of course, as with all types other than int, before a function returning void can be called, its type must be known to the compiler. Figure 6.10 shows a new definition of print_table (Chapter 4). Since print_table does not return a value, we declare its return value as void. If print_table is not defined before it is called, the caller must include the declaration

```
void print_table();
```

to inform the compiler of the function's type.

The value returned by a function returning void is undefined and should not be used. An assignment such as

```
n = print_table(table,MAX)
```

will compile and execute, but print_table's actual return value is arbitrary and system dependent.

In our earlier programs, we left off the function's type on those functions that returned no value. It is better programming practice to declare the type of any function explicitly; declaring functions that do not return a value as void increases readability. Some compilers, however, do not support void.

We can ignore a function's return value by failing to use it in the expression where the function is called. For functions that return a value, the call should be explicitly cast to void if its value is to be ignored. The

```
/*
 * Print table of "num" integers.
 */
void print_table(tab_ptr, num)
int *tab_ptr,                    /* pointer to table's first element */
    num;                         /* number of elements to print */
{
  while (num-- > 0)
    printf("%d\n", *tab_ptr++);
}
```

FIGURE 6.10. Print elements in an array.

cast makes it clear to the program's reader that a conscious choice was made to ignore the return value and that it was not ignored by mistake. For example,

```
(void) scanf("%d", &next);   /* get "next", ignoring return value */
```

explicitly ignores the normal integer status returned by scanf.

POINTERS TO FUNCTIONS

You may have wondered if there is a way to pass functions as parameters. This ability would be useful, for example, in writing a function to evaluate differing mathematical functions, such as sine and cosine, over a range of values, perhaps to generate plots of the functions. Unfortunately, functions cannot be passed as parameters or stored in variables. Instead, we must use *pointers* to functions, which can be thought of as the address of the code executed when a function is called or as a pointer to a block of internal information about the function. A pointer to a function is dereferenced to call the function to which it points.

When declaring a pointer to a function, we specify the pointed-to function's return type, but not its parameters. For example, the declaration

```
type (*func_ptr)();
```

declares func_ptr as a pointer to a function returning *type*. The parentheses around *func_ptr are required; without them we would instead be declaring it as a function returning a pointer to *type*. (We agree that this syntax is gross, but we are stuck with it. We explain the rationale behind C's declaration syntax in Chapter 9. For now, memorize this form.)

We do not apply the address operator (&) to a function to obtain a pointer to it. Instead, we simply use the function name without following it with a parenthesized parameter list. For example, assuming the declaration

```
double (*func_ptr)(), power();
```

we can make func_ptr point to the function power with the assignment

```
func_ptr = power;   /* "funcptr" now points to the "power" function */
```

To call the function pointed to by func_ptr, we simply dereference it as we would any other pointer, following it with a list of parameters. After the previous assignment,

```
(*func_ptr)(2,5)
```

is equivalent to

```
power(2,5)
```

calling **power** to compute 2^5. The parentheses surrounding *func_ptr are necessary to guarantee a correct order of evaluation.

How do we use all this information? We illustrate pointers to functions with the function gen_points, shown in Figure 6.11*a*. gen_points fills a table of points by evaluating the function passed to it over a range of values. A main program that uses gen_points to compute tables of points for the **sin** and **cos** functions and a function to print these tables is shown in Figure 6.11*b*. **sin** and **cos** are defined as part of the math library available in most C implementations. Appendix 4 lists the math library functions and discusses how to compile programs using them.

Within gen_points, we declare the formal parameter func_ptr as a pointer to a function returning a **double**:

```
double (*func_ptr)();
```

When gen_points is called, its first parameter must be a pointer to a function returning a **double**. In the assignment

```
*y_ptr++ = (*funcptr)(nextval)
```

we call the function pointed to by func_ptr, passing it the single parameter nextval. The **double** returned from the function call is stored in the location pointed to by y_ptr and then y_ptr is incremented.

We generate the table of points for **sin** with the call

```
gen_points(sin, xtab, ytab, 0.0, PI, NUMPTS);
```

Because **sin** is not followed by a parameter list, a pointer to it is passed as gen_points's first parameter. Of course, had **sin** been followed by a parameter list, it would have been a function call whose return value was passed to gen_points. Similarly, we generate the table of points for **cos**:

```
gen_points(cos, xtab, ytab, 0.0, PI, NUMPTS);
```

In either case, the compiler must know the type of the function's return value before the function name appears. In this example, the compiler is informed with the declaration

```
double sin(), cos();
```

that appears before either name is used.

```
/*
 * Generate a table of points by evaluating a passed function at
 * different values.
 */
void gen_points(func_ptr, x_ptr, y_ptr, sval, eval, numpts)
double (*func_ptr)(),                    /* function to generate points */
       *x_ptr, *y_ptr,                   /* tables of x,y values */
       sval, eval;                       /* starting and ending points */
int numpts;                              /* number of points to generate */
{
  double  inc = (eval - sval)/(numpts - 1), /* increment between values */
          nextval;                          /* next x value */

  for (nextval = sval; numpts--; nextval += inc)
  {
    *x_ptr++ = nextval;
    *y_ptr++ = (*func_ptr)(nextval);
  }
}
```

(a)   Generating a table of points by evaluating a function

```
#define PI      3.1415926              /* our favorite constant */
#define NUMPTS 100                     /* needed number of points */

main()
{
  double xtab[NUMPTS], ytab[NUMPTS],   /* stores the points */
         sin(), cos();                 /* some functions to plot */
  void gen_points(), pr_points();      /* generate, print points */

  gen_points(sin, xtab, ytab, 0.0, PI, NUMPTS);
  pr_points("sin", xtab, ytab, NUMPTS);
  gen_points(cos, xtab, ytab, 0.0, PI, NUMPTS);
  pr_points("cos", xtab, ytab, NUMPTS);
}

void pr_points(name, nxtx_ptr, nxty_ptr, numpts)
char *name;                            /* name of function to plot */
double *nxtx_ptr, *nxty_ptr;           /* table of points */
int numpts;                            /* number of points */
{
  printf("Points for %s function\n", name);
  while (numpts--)
    printf("%f, %f\n", *nxtx_ptr++, *nxty_ptr++);
}
```

(b) A main program that uses gen_points

FIGURE 6.11. Using pointers to functions.

Using pointers to functions, we have made gen_points general enough to generate points for any single parameter function returning a double. We leave the function to plot the table of values generated by gen_points as a programming practice for the reader.

PROGRAMMING PRACTICE

6-11. Try gen_points on other functions from the math library; good candidates are tan and exp.

6-12. Write a function to plot (horizontally) the table generated by gen_points.

RECURSION

Many algorithms and mathematical definitions are naturally described *recursively*, that is, partially in terms of themselves. One example is the mathematical definition of a factorial. The factorial of n (written $n!$) is the product of all integers between 1 and n and is defined only for non-negative n.

$$n! = \begin{cases} 1 & n = 0 \\ n \times (n-1)! & n \geq 1 \end{cases}$$

Notice that to determine the factorial of any $n \geq 1$, the factorial of $n-1$ must also be determined. As with all recursive definitions, the function's value at one or more points is specified. Some example factorials are $2! = 2$, $3! = 6$, $4! = 24$, and $5! = 120$.

Functions are allowed to call themselves recursively; this makes it easy to translate the mathematical definition of a factorial into the function fact that can compute a factorial, as shown in Figure 6.12*a*. A version of fact that prints additional information allowing us to trace the recursive calls is shown in Figure 6.12*b*, and a trace of the recursive calls to fact done to compute fact(4) is shown in Figure 6.12*c*.

PROGRAMMING PRACTICE

6-13. The Fibonacci numbers are a famous mathematical sequence that can be defined recursively:

```
/*
 * Compute n! for n >= 0.
 */
long fact(n)
int n;
{
  return (n <= 1) ? 1 : n * fact(n-1);
}
```

(a)   Recursively computing n!

```
long fact(n)
int n
{
  long temp;

  printf("Computing %d factorial\n", n);
  temp = (n <= 1) ? 1 : n * fact(n-1);
  printf("Computed %d factorial = %d\n", n, temp);
  return temp;
}
```

(b)   Recursively computing n! *with tracing information*

```
Computing 4 factorial
Computing 3 factorial
Computing 2 factorial
Computing 1 factorial
Computed 1 factorial = 1
Computed 2 factorial = 2
Computed 3 factorial = 6
Computed 4 factorial = 24
```

(c)   Trace of fact(4)

FIGURE 6.12.   Recursive computation of factorials.

$$
fib(n) = \begin{cases} 0 & n = 0 \\ 1 & n = 1 \\ fib(n-1) + fib(n-2) & n \geq 2 \end{cases}
$$

The first 10 Fibonacci numbers are 0, 1, 1, 2, 3, 5, 8, 13, 21, and 34. Write recursive and iterative functions to compute the nth Fibonacci number and print the 100th number in this sequence. Which version is faster? Which would you want to use if you wanted to print the first 100 Fibonacci numbers?

CASE STUDY—BINARY SEARCH

The simplest method to use in searching a table for a target value is simply to compare the value with each table entry until the entire table has been examined or a match is found. This method is known as *sequential search* and, for the average successful search, will examine about half of the table's elements. In an unsuccessful search, every table element must be examined. Although this method is reasonable for searching small unordered tables, for large *sorted* tables we can do much better. Binary search is a much faster (indeed, optimal) algorithm for searching sorted tables that is easily expressed with a recursive algorithm.

In binary search, the target value is compared with the table's middle element. Since the table is sorted, if the target is larger, we know that all values smaller than the middle element (the values in the table's lower half) can be ignored, and we can apply binary search recursively to the table's upper half. Similarly, if the target is smaller, we know that all

```
/*
 * Binary search function (for a sorted table of integers).
 */
int *bsearch(min_ptr, max_ptr, target)
int *min_ptr, *max_ptr;             /* section of table to search */
int target;                         /* value search for */
{
  int *mid_ptr = min_ptr + (max_ptr - min_ptr) / 2;  /* find midpoint */

  if (max_ptr < min_ptr)                    /* value not in table */
    return NULL;
  else if (target < *mid_ptr)               /* adjust upper bound */
    return bsearch(min_ptr, mid_ptr - 1, target);  /*   and search again */
  else if (target > *mid_ptr)               /* adjust lower bound */
    return bsearch(mid_ptr + 1, max_ptr, target);  /*   and search again */
  else
    return mid_ptr;                         /* found it */
}
```

(a)   Binary search

```
{
  int table[MAXVALS], target,     /* table to search and target value */
      n,                          /* elements in table */
      *tar_ptr,                   /* returned pointer to target element */
      *bsearch();                 /* binary searching function */
      . . .
  tar_ptr = bsearch(&table[0], &table[n - 1], target);
      . . .
}
```

(b)   Using binary search

FIGURE 6.13. Binary search function and sample call.

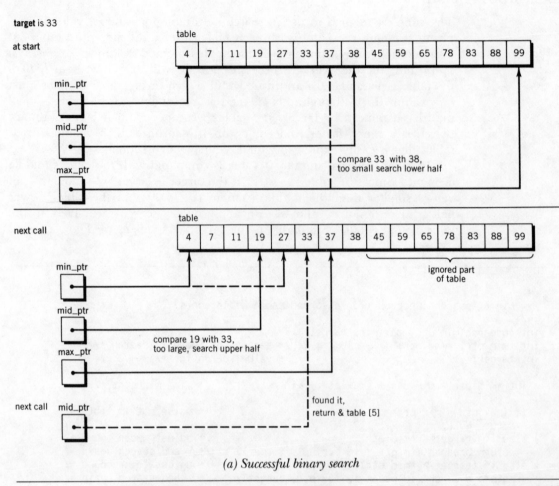

(a) Successful binary search

values larger than the middle element (the values in the table's upper half) can be ignored, and we need only apply binary search recursively to the table's lower half. Lastly, if the target is equal to the middle element, the desired element has been found and the search can stop. When there are no values left to search, we know that the target is not in the table and the search can terminate. Binary search is significantly faster than sequential search because every time we compare the target to a table element, we no longer have to consider half of the remaining values.

The function `bsearch` shown in Figure 6.13a uses binary search to search a sorted table of integers. Figure 6.13b shows a program fragment using `bsearch`. `bsearch` is passed the target value and pointers to the table's first (`min_ptr`) and last (`max_ptr`) elements. For instance, we can search the first n elements of `table` for `target` with the call

```
tar_ptr = bsearch(&table[0], &table[n-1], target);
```

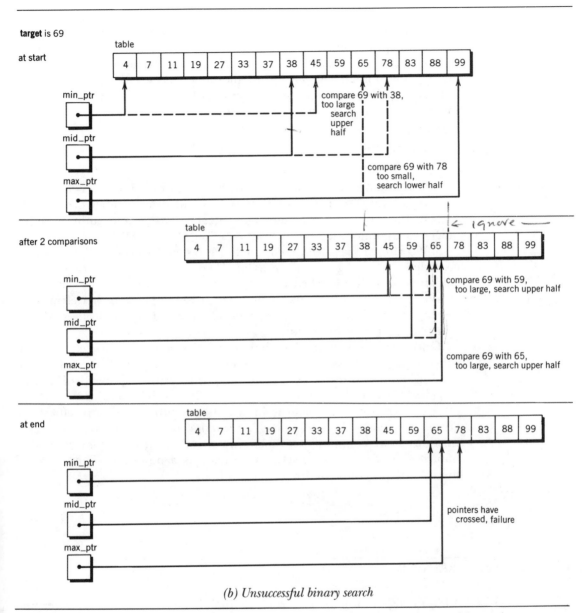

(b) Unsuccessful binary search

FIGURE 6.14. Illustration of binary search during both successful and unsuccessful searches.

bsearch returns a pointer to the matching table element or the null pointer if no such element is found. Any variable saving bsearch's return value must be a pointer to an int.

An illustration of a successful binary search on a 15-element table is shown in Figure 6.14a. Figure 6.14b illustrates an unsuccessful search on the same table. With every recursive call to bsearch, the pointers min_ptr and max_ptr move toward each other. The search and recursive calls terminate when the pointers cross or the target value is found.

When bsearch is called, it first calculates the address of the middle element in the unsearched portion of the table (the whole table when it is first called). Because addition or division of pointer types is not allowed, this calculation is done with the expression

mid_ptr = min_ptr + (max_ptr – min_ptr) / 2

instead of adding the two pointers together and dividing by two. Recall that the subtraction of the two pointers produces the number of elements between them (an integer), and both integer division and addition of an integer to a pointer are legal operations.

After mid_ptr has been computed, we test to determine if the search has failed. The target is not present when the pointers representing the endpoints of the unsearched portion of the table cross (max_ptr < min_ptr). This happens only when one element is left to search, and that element is not the target. If the search fails, the null pointer (automatically cast to a pointer to an int) is returned.

Once we are assured that there are unexamined table elements, we compare the target with the value pointed to by mid_ptr. If the values are equal, a pointer to the desired table entry is returned. Otherwise, bsearch is applied recursively to the appropriate section of the table.

Although functions such as fact and bsearch can be more efficiently written iteratively than recursively, recursion can often be used to make functions more compact or to make them reflect an algorithm or mathematical definition more closely. Recursion is a powerful technique used often in the programs in the rest of this book.

PROGRAMMING PRACTICE

6-14. Add tracing information to bsearch that prints messages whenever the function is entered or exited, noting the values delimiting the area left to be searched.

6-15. Rewrite the binary search algorithm nonrecursively. (*Hint*: It is a little messier than it seems.) Is this version more efficient than the recursive version? Which version is more compact?

6-16. Because of the overhead involved in calculating the midpoint, binary search is often slower than sequential search when searching small tables. Determine the point on your system where both functions take the same amount of time. Then write a single search function, called with the same arguments as **bsearch**, that does a sequential search if the table is small (less than the breakeven point) and otherwise calls **bsearch**.

CHAPTER 7

PROGRAM STRUCTURE AND STORAGE CLASSES

So far, our programs and functions have resided in a single source file and have communicated with each other solely through parameter passing and return values. However, we are not confined to such a simple program structure. We can build an executable program from multiple source files, with each file compiled separately and linked together, and we can write functions that communicate through globally accessible variables. In this chapter, we examine the mechanism (called *storage classes*) that supports these more complex program structures and illustrate the usefulness of separate compilation with the implementation of a "set" data type and its associated operations.

AUTOMATIC VARIABLES

Along with its type, every variable and function has a storage class that specifies its visibility and lifetime. The storage class precedes the type in a declaration and can be any one of **auto**, **register**, **extern**, or **static**. If the storage class is not specified, a default storage class is determined from the declaration's context.

We have already used variables with the storage class **auto**. Variables declared within function bodies are called *automatic* variables and are given the storage class **auto** by default (the name comes from their *automatic* creation and deletion on block entry and exit). Although it is unnecessary and rarely done, the keyword **auto** can be used to make the storage class explicit:

```
{                                           {
    int x,y;                                    auto int x,y;
    . . .         is equivalent to
}                                           }
```

Automatic variables are visible only from the point of their declaration until the block's end and cannot be directly accessed outside it.

An automatic variable exists only from block entry to block exit. Whenever a block is entered, space is allocated for its local (automatic) variables; this space is then deallocated when the block is exited. As a result, the next time the block is entered, its local variables may not even use the same physical memory locations. Unfortunately, automatic variables are not automatically initialized to zero; instead, they start with whatever was previously in the memory space allocated for them—usually garbage. This means that to avoid hard-to-find problems, we have to be careful to initialize all variables before using them.

We can initialize a variable when we declare it by following its name with an equal sign and an arbitrary expression. For example,

```
int i = 0;
```

declares **i** as an integer, and then initializes it to zero. The initializing expression can include previously declared local variables, the function's formal parameters, and function calls. Each time the function is called, the initialization expression is evaluated and assigned to the declared variable. Unfortunately, automatic arrays cannot be initialized when they are declared, although later in the chapter we will see a way to avoid that restriction.

Initializing variables when they are declared leads to more concise functions. As an example, Figure 7.1 contains the function **strrev**, which takes a string and reverses it in place. We use two pointers to reverse the string; **f_ptr** starts out pointing to its first character, **r_ptr** to its last. The string is reversed by moving the pointers toward each other; as they move along, the characters they point to are switched, as shown below. The process stops when the pointers cross or point to the same character.

Both **f_ptr** and **r_ptr** are initialized when they are declared. **f_ptr** is initialized with the formal parameter **to_rev**'s value and **r_ptr** is initialized with its length, computed using both the function **strlen** and the local variable **f_ptr**. The order of the declarations is important; because **f_ptr**'s value is used in initializing **r_ptr**, it must be declared before **r_ptr**.

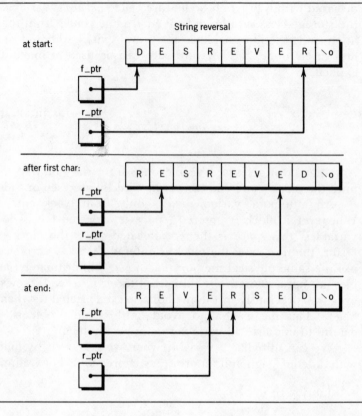

String reversal

at start:

f_ptr

r_ptr

after first char:

f_ptr

r_ptr

at end:

f_ptr

r_ptr

Automatic variables may be declared local to any block, a convenience that aids modularity. As an example, Figure 7.2 contains a short program that first computes the average of its input and then prints any input values less than the average. First, the program reads scores into an array, accumulating the total score in sum. For speed, we use a pointer to traverse the array instead of explicit subscripting. Then, after the scores are read, the average score is computed and any below-average scores are printed. We do this within a nested block that contains two local variables, avg and next_ptr. They are declared there, instead of at the beginning of the function's body, to make it clear that they are needed only for this small section of code.

Attempting to access a variable outside its declaring block causes a compile-time error. For example, placing

```
printf("I told you, the average is: %.2f\n", avg);
```

outside the inner block but before main's end will cause the compiler to generate an "undefined variable" error. Be careful that any variable declared within a block is not needed outside it.

```
/*
 * Reverse a string in place.
 */
strrev(to_rev)
char *to_rev;                           /* string to reverse */
{
  char *f_ptr = to_rev,                 /* pointer to string's first char */
       *r_ptr = f_ptr + strlen(f_ptr) - 1, /* pointer to string's last char */
       tmp;                             /* holds character during switch */

  while(f_ptr < r_ptr)                  /* swap chars */
    tmp = *f_ptr, *f_ptr++ = *r_ptr, *r_ptr-- = tmp;
}
```

FIGURE 7.1. Reversing a string in place.

```
/*
 * Read scores, compute average, and print below average.
 */
#include <stdio.h>
#define  MAX_STUDENTS 1000

main()
{
  int n,                        /* number of scores */
      scores[MAX_STUDENTS],     /* holds scores */
      *end_ptr = scores;        /* pointer to just beyond last score */
  float sum = 0.0;              /* total scores */

  /* Get input data and compute sum -- stop reading if no more room,
     end of file, or bad input data */

  for (n = 0; n < MAX_STUDENTS && scanf("%d", end_ptr) == 1; n++)
    sum += *end_ptr++;

  /* Figure average and print out low scores */

  {
    int *next_ptr = scores;     /* pointer to next array element */
    float avg = sum / n;        /* average of scores */

    printf("Average: %.2f\nBelow Average Scores:\n", avg);
    for (; next_ptr < end_ptr; next_ptr++)
      if (*next_ptr < avg)
        printf("%d\n", *next_ptr);
  }
}
```

FIGURE 7.2. An example of declaring variables in inner blocks—printing below-average scores.

Carelessly chosen variable names can cause confusion when blocks are nested. When a variable is redeclared in an inner block, it becomes inaccessible to the rest of the inner block, and from the point of redeclaration the inner block accesses the locally declared variable. When the inner block exits, the variable's original declaration becomes visible again. Using the same name for variables within nested blocks can adversely affect readability and should be avoided.

PROGRAMMING PRACTICE

7-1. Modify the palindrome checking function in Chapter 6 to initialize its variables within their declarations. Is the function still readable?

REGISTER VARIABLES

We can tell the compiler that an automatic variable or function parameter should be kept in one of the machine's high-speed registers, instead of placed by default in memory, by giving it the storage class register. As an example,

```
register int sum;
```

declares sum as a register variable. Making frequently accessed variables register leads to faster and slightly smaller programs.

There are, however, some restrictions on the use of register variables. Most compilers allow only int, char, or pointer automatic variables and parameters to be placed in registers. Additionally, most machines have few registers available to user programs, usually two or three. If the variable is not the right type or not enough registers are available, the register declaration is ignored and the variable is placed in memory instead. Lastly, and perhaps obviously, since a register variable is not kept in memory, we cannot use & to take its address.

The function to sum the array shown in Figure 7.3 is about 20 percent faster, and contains 7 percent fewer machine language instructions than the same function without the register declarations, (measurements were taken with a program compiled by the standard 4.2bsd UNIX C compiler with the optimizing and profiling options turned on run on a lightly loaded system). Since there are usually few available registers, it is important to carefully select the variables placed in them. You need not

```
/*
 * Return the total of the first "n" elements of table pointed to by "tab_ptr".
 */
int sum(tab_ptr, n)
register int *tab_ptr;                   /* ptr to array's first element */
int n;                                   /* number of elements */
{
   register int *end_ptr = tab_ptr + n - 1,  /* ptr to array's last element */
               sum       = 0;                 /* running total */

   while (tab_ptr <= end_ptr)
     sum += *tab_ptr++;
   return sum;
}
```

FIGURE 7.3. Fast function to sum elements in an array.

declare variables as **register** until the program has been written and timed. Then the most often used variables in the functions that take the most time can be put into registers.

PROGRAMMING PRACTICE

7-2. Profile the histogram program (Chapter 5) to determine where most of its time is spent. Add **register** declarations in those places. Repeat the process until no more performance is gained by additional declarations.

7-3. Make the pointer version of **strcpy** (Chapter 4) into a function with **register** declarations. How much more efficient is it than the version implemented without using **register**?

EXTERNAL VARIABLES AND FUNCTIONS

In addition to declaring variables at the start of blocks, we can declare variables outside any function anywhere in the file. These variables (like the global variables of Pascal or the common variables of FORTRAN) are known as *externals* and can be accessed by other functions without being passed as parameters to them. Any function can access a previously declared external simply by referring to it by name. Besides having

```
/*
 * Character-counting program (assumes seven-bit characters).
 */
#define MAXCHARS      128      /* ASCII character set (7 bits matter) */
#define MASK          0177     /* used to remove any high order bits */

long count[MAXCHARS];          /* external--holds character counters */

main()
{
  int c;                       /* next character */
  void print_totals();         /* to write out totals */

  while (c = getchar(), c != EOF)
    count[c & MASK]++;         /* count character, stripping extra bits */
  print_totals();
}

void print_totals()            /* writes totals */
{
  int i;

  for (i = 0; i < MAXCHARS; i++)
    if (count[i])              /* only write total if nonzero */
      printf("\\%03o: %ld\n", i, count[i]);
}
```

FIGURE 7.4. An example of externals—a character-counting program.

global visibility, externals differ from automatics in that space for externals is allocated once, is initialized to zero when the program starts, and remains allocated throughout the program's execution.

We illustrate one common use of external variables in Figure 7.4, a program that counts occurrences of each unique character in its input. As each character is read, it is used as an index in a table of counters (count) and the appropriate counter is updated. We actually use only the first seven bits of the character as the index; in ASCII the eighth bit is ignored. Since count is declared outside any function, it is an external variable. The definitions of main and print_totals follow count's declaration and can use it by referring to it by name.

The default initialization of externals makes programs more concise because external counters do not have to be explicitly initialized. We did not bother to initialize count in Figure 7.4, since its elements are zero by default. Although this implicit initialization is convenient (and is taken advantage of by countless programs), programs are more readable when variables are explicitly initialized.

When using external variables, consider carefully the tradeoff between readability and convenience. The extra effort involved in using only automatic variables passed as parameters increases modularity, aiding readability. In longer programs, external variables obscure the connections between functions, decreasing readability and modular independence. An external variable's value is also easily changed by any of the program's functions, leading to subtle errors when the change is accidental. The most reasonable uses of external variables are for tables and for variables shared between routines when it is inconvenient to pass them as parameters.

PROGRAMMING PRACTICE

7-4. Rewrite the character-counting program (Figure 7.4) without any external variables. Which version is more readable? Which version is more compact?

7-5. Rewrite the program in the previous exercise so that initialization of the table and its printing are done in-line in **main**. Use blocks to limit the scope of any index variables used.

INITIALIZING EXTERNAL VARIABLES

We initialize external variables in the same way as their automatic counterparts. In addition, external arrays, unlike automatic arrays, can be initialized. We do this by supplying a brace-enclosed, comma-separated list of expressions as the initialization expression. The values in this list become the initial values of the corresponding array elements; missing values default to zero and extra values result in an error. External initializations are done once, conceptually before the program begins execution, so they cannot contain function calls.

As an example, we can initialize **days** to contain the days for each month with the declaration

```
int days[] = {31, 28, 31, 30, 31, 30, 31, 31, 30, 31, 30, 31};
```

If the subscript is omitted, the compiler allocates enough space for all initialized elements. The array's size can be supplied, but it must be large enough to hold the given elements. Unfortunately, there is no convenient way to initialize only selected array elements. Remember, we can initialize external but not automatic arrays.

Letting the compiler calculate the array's size is especially useful when initializing character strings, since it saves us the trouble of computing their length.

```
char message[] = {'h', 'i', ' ', 'm', 'o', 'm', '!', '\0'};
```

declares `message` to be an array of eight characters, initialized with the string "hi mom!". A convenient shorthand for the above,

```
char *message = "hi mom!";
```

automatically places the null at the string's end.

Explicit initialization makes programs more readable. We improve Figure 7.4 by explicitly initializing `count`:

```
long count[MAXCHARS] = {0};
```

Instead of listing many zeros, we explicitly initialize `count[0]` to zero; the other elements are zero by default. Initializing the array's first element to zero is an idiom that makes explicit the expectation that all array elements start with zero.

EXTERNAL DECLARATIONS AND DEFINITIONS

In Figure 7.4 we conveniently defined `count` before the functions using it, allowing them to access it simply by referring to it by name. A function can, however, access any external variable (even those defined after it or in another source file) by *declaring* it with the storage class specifier `extern`. This external declaration specifies the variable's type and informs the compiler that space for the variable is defined somewhere else, but it does not allocate space for the variable. An external variable is *defined* (has space allocated for it) whenever it is declared outside any function without the `extern` storage class specifier. Since an external variable definition also declares the variable's type, an external declaration is not required if the external variable was defined earlier in the source file.

As an illustration, consider Figure 7.5. `count` is defined after the functions using it, so the *external declaration*

```
extern long count[];
```

must appear in each of the functions accessing `count`, as shown in Figure 7.5*a*, or before any of the functions, as shown in Figure 7.5*b*. This declaration informs the compiler that `count` is an array of integers defined somewhere else in the program. In constrast, the *external definition*

```
long count[MAXCHARS] = {0};
```

```
  main()                              extern long count[];
  {
    extern long count[];              main()
    void print_totals();              {
    int c;                              void print_totals();
    ...                                 int c;
  }                                     ...
                                      }
  void print_totals()
  {                                   void print_totals()
    extern long count[];              {
    int i;                              int i;
    ...                                 ...
  }                                   }

  long count[MAXCHARS] = {0};          long count[MAXCHARS] = {0};

  (a) Local external declarations      (b) Global external declarations
```

FIGURE 7.5. Using external declarations and definitions. An external must be declared before it can be referred to.

allocates space for **count**, initializes its elements to zero, and makes its type known to the compiler. Since no space is allocated in external declarations, the number of elements **count** contains is specified only in its definition.

Both external declarations and definitions inform the compiler of the variable's type. However, a definition also allocates storage for the variable, while a declaration does not. Thus, an external variable should be *defined* only once, but should be *declared* by all functions that need to reference it, or before any of the functions.

The distinction between definition and declaration also applies to functions. A function is defined when its parameters and function body are specified and is external by default. Functions are declared in the same way as variables, except that since all functions are external, **extern** can be left off their declarations. In Figure 7.5, since **main**'s call to **print_totals** precedes its definition, **main** must declare **print_totals**'s type, and does so with the declaration

```
void print_totals();
```

Because **print_totals** is a function, this declaration is equivalent to

```
extern void print_totals();
```

As we have observed, the compiler automatically assumes that any function that has not been declared when it is first used returns an int. This means that we do not need to write external declarations for these functions, and almost all C programs take advantage of this option. Nevertheless, including external declarations for all functions, even those returning int, leads to more readable programs.

PROGRAMMING PRACTICE

7-6. Remove count's external *declarations* from Figure 7.5. What happens when you try to compile it? Remove count's external *definition* from Figure 7.5. What happens when you try to compile it? Are the error messages from the compiler or the linker?

SEPARATE COMPILATION

Externals allow the functions and variables composing a C program to be spread out over multiple files. Figure 7.6 shows a diagram of the compilation process when multiple files are compiled. Each source file is compiled into an *object module* containing its machine language code, a list of the names and addresses of all external functions and variables defined in it, and a list of all of its external references to functions and variables defined in other source files. The *linker* resolves these external references, linking the object modules together to create an executable program. The object modules given to the linker do not have to be generated by the C compiler; often the linker can be used to link together object modules generated by compilers for different programming languages. On UNIX, for example, a C program can call functions written in Pascal, FORTRAN, and assembly language.

In effect, any external declaration or definition causes the external's name to be given to the linker. The linker then creates an executable file from the various object modules by turning all external references into the variable's or function's address.

While resolving external references, the linker adds any referenced library functions. A library is a group of object modules that have been compiled in advance and stored in a special format. Some linkers automatically include the entire library; others include only the referenced functions and any functions or variables they require. Usually no special action is required to use certain libraries, such as standard I/O, although to use other libraries the library's name may have to be given to the

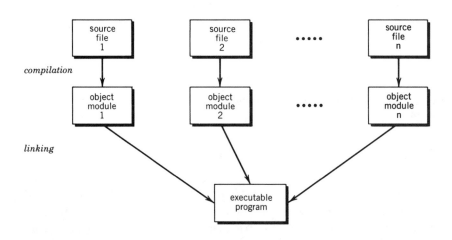

FIGURE 7.6. The process of compilation and linking.

linker. The details of library use and creation vary; you should consult your local reference manual for details.

Both the compiler and the linker can detect errors. Syntax errors and certain semantic errors can be detected by the compiler, and no object module is produced for a source file containing compiler-detectable errors. Errors such as failing to define a referenced external, defining a particular function or variable more than once, or failing to define main can be detected by the linker. Most linkers will not produce an executable program if any errors are detected.

ILLUSTRATING SEPARATE COMPILATION—CHARACTER TESTING

Many programs need to do simple testing to classify characters; for example, to determine if a character is a digit, an upper- or lowercase letter, white space, or printable. The standard libraries provide a set of functions to make these tests; a complete list can be found in Appendix 6. For efficiency, these routines are implemented as macros in most standard I/O library implementations, a topic discussed in the next chapter. These functions are helpful because they are easier to use than the tests they replace, because they increase the readability of the programs that use them, and because they are both machine and character set independent. To illustrate separate compilation, we present an implementation of the character-testing functions listed in Table 7.1. Each function takes a character and returns nonzero only if the tested property holds for it.

TABLE 7.1. Implemented character-testing functions.

Function	Test
isalpha	Upper- or lowercase letter
isdigit	Digit
islower	Lowercase letter
isprint	Printable
isspace	White space (blanks, tabs, and newlines)
isupper	Uppercase letter

We have divided the character-testing package into a header file containing constant definitions (*ctype.h*) and two files that include it. The first (*table.c*) contains a table describing the character set, and the second (*ctype.c*) contains the functions that use it. We chose this organization instead of using a single source file because it separates the portable from the nonportable code. The table is character set dependent, while the functions that use it are not.

Each property (such as printable, white space, and so on) is represented by a constant defined in *ctype.h*, shown in Figure 7.7.

To test if a character has a particular property, each of the functions in *ctype.c* uses the character as an index into a table of unsigned integers (cprop) in *table.c*. Each property is represented by a single bit. If the bit is on, the character has that property, and if it is off, the character does not. For example, if the character is printable, bit 0 is on; if it is a digit, bit 1 is on; and so forth. Because a character can have multiple properties, its description is created by ORing together the constants describing each of its properties. For example, the entry for the letter 'a' is P | L, indicating that it is both printable and a lowercase letter. If a character does not contain any of the properties we test for, its table entry is zero. Figure 7.8 shows *table.c*, which contains the table to describe the ASCII character set.

Given this table, it is easy to write the character-testing functions shown in Figure 7.9. Each function tests whether the bit or bits repre-

```
/*
 *  Character type flags
 */
#define P         001      /* printing */
#define D         002      /* decimal digit */
#define L         010      /* lowercase letter */
#define U         020      /* uppercase letter */
#define S         040      /* white space character */
#define CHRMASK   0177     /* assume only lower seven bits matter */
```

FIGURE 7.7. *ctype.h*—character type header file.

```
/*
 * Character description table.
 */
#include "ctype.h"

unsigned int cprop[] =
{
/* nul */  0,          /* soh */  0,          /* stx */  0,          /* etx */  0,
/* eot */  0,          /* enq */  0,          /* ack */  0,          /* bel */  0,
/* \b  */  P | S,      /* \t  */  P | S,      /* \n  */  P | S,      /* vt  */  P | S,
/* \f  */  P | S,      /* \r  */  P | S,      /* so  */  0,          /* si  */  0,
/* dle */  0,          /* dc1 */  0,          /* dc2 */  0,          /* dc3 */  0,
/* dc4 */  0,          /* nak */  0,          /* syn */  0,          /* etb */  0,
/* can */  0,          /* em  */  0,          /* sub */  0,          /* esc */  0,
/* fs  */  0,          /* gs  */  0,          /* rs  */  0,          /* us  */  0,
/* ' ' */  P | S,      /* '!' */  P,          /* '"' */  P,          /* '#' */  P,
/* '$' */  P,          /* '%' */  P,          /* '&' */  P,          /* ''' */  P,
/* '(' */  P,          /* ')' */  P,          /* '*' */  P,          /* '+' */  P,
/* ',' */  P,          /* '-' */  P,          /* '.' */  P,          /* '/' */  P,
/* '0' */  P | D,      /* '1' */  P | D,      /* '2' */  P | D,      /* '3' */  P | D,
/* '4' */  P | D,      /* '5' */  P | D,      /* '6' */  P | D,      /* '7' */  P | D,
/* '8' */  P | D,      /* '9' */  P,          /* ':' */  P,          /* ';' */  P | D,
/* '<' */  P,          /* '=' */  P,          /* '>' */  P,          /* '?' */  P,
/* '@' */  P,          /* 'A' */  P | U,      /* 'B' */  P | U,      /* 'C' */  P | U,
/* 'D' */  P | U,      /* 'E' */  P | U,      /* 'F' */  P | U,      /* 'G' */  P | U,
/* 'H' */  P | U,      /* 'I' */  P | U,      /* 'J' */  P | U,      /* 'K' */  P | U,
/* 'L' */  P | U,      /* 'M' */  P | U,      /* 'N' */  P | U,      /* 'O' */  P | U,
/* 'P' */  P | U,      /* 'Q' */  P | U,      /* 'R' */  P | U,      /* 'S' */  P | U,
/* 'T' */  P | U,      /* 'U' */  P | U,      /* 'V' */  P | U,      /* 'W' */  P | U,
/* 'X' */  P | U,      /* 'Y' */  P | U,      /* 'Z' */  P | U,      /* '[' */  P,
/* '\' */  P,          /* ']' */  P,          /* '^' */  P,          /* '_' */  P,
/* ''' */  P,          /* 'a' */  P | L,      /* 'b' */  P | L,      /* 'c' */  P | L,
/* 'd' */  P | L,      /* 'e' */  P | L,      /* 'f' */  P | L,      /* 'g' */  P | L,
/* 'h' */  P | L,      /* 'i' */  P | L,      /* 'j' */  P | L,      /* 'k' */  P | L,
/* 'l' */  P | L,      /* 'm' */  P | L,      /* 'n' */  P | L,      /* 'o' */  P | L,
/* 'p' */  P | L,      /* 'q' */  P | L,      /* 'r' */  P | L,      /* 's' */  P | L,
/* 't' */  P | L,      /* 'u' */  P | L,      /* 'v' */  P | L,      /* 'w' */  P | L,
/* 'x' */  P | L,      /* 'y' */  P | L,      /* 'z' */  P | L,      /* '{' */  P,
/* '|' */  P,          /* '}' */  P,          /* '~' */  P,          /* del */  P
};
```

FIGURE 7.8. *table.c*—character description table for the ASCII character set.

senting the desired property are on for the given character. The check is done by ORing together the constants for the properties to check. The result is then ANDed with the character's description in the table. For example, the expression

```
cprop[c & CHRMASK] & (L | U)
```

will be zero unless c is an upper- or lowercase letter. Only the low-order

```
/*
 *  Character type checkers.
 */
#include "ctype.h"

extern unsigned int cprop[];            /* table describing character set */

int isalpha(c)                          /* is 'c' upper- or lowercase? */
int c;
{
return cprop[c & CHRMASK] & (L | U);
}

int isdigit(c)                          /* is 'c' digit? */
int c;
{
return cprop[c & CHRMASK] & D;
}

int islower(c)                          /* is 'c' lowercase? */
int c;
{
return cprop[c & CHRMASK] & L;
}

int isprint(c)                          /* is 'c' printable? */
int c;
{
return cprop[c & CHRMASK] & P;
}

int isspace(c)                          /* is 'c' white space? */
int c;
{
return cprop[c & CHRMASK] & S;
}

int isupper(c)                          /* is 'c' uppercase? */
int c;
{
return cprop[c & CHRMASK] & U;
}
```

FIGURE 7.9. *ctype.c*—character type checking functions.

seven bits of the character are used as the index into the table; the other bits are masked off with CHRMASK.

Both *ctype.c* and *table.c* include *ctype.h* with

```
#include "ctype.h"
```

ctype.h is surrounded by quotation marks instead of by the angle brackets used for previous include files. The quotation marks specify that *ctype. h* is not a system include file and that the preprocessor should not search the standard system locations for it. Recall that including a file causes its contents to be processed as if they were in the file including it, in this case defining the needed constants.

Because `cprop` is defined in a different file from the functions using it, the external declaration

```
extern unsigned int cprop[];
```

precedes any of their definitions. Alternatively, we could have included the external declaration in all functions that need it; however, this increases the program's length without improving its readability.

To illustrate one use of the character-testing functions, Figure 7.10 contains a program (called *Vis*) that makes all characters in its input visi-

```
/*
 *  Make unprintable characters visible
 *   (uses our previously defined testing functions).
 */
#include <stdio.h>

main()
{
  int  c;                                    /* next character */
  char name;                                 /* special character name */

  while (c = getchar(), c != EOF)
    if ((isspace(c) && c != ' '))
      {
        switch(c)                            /* it's a special character */
        {
          case '\b' :  name = 'b';  break;
          case '\f' :  name = 'f';  break;
          case '\n' :  \name = 'n';  break;
          case '\r' :  name = 'r';  break;
          case '\t' :  name = 't';  break;
          case '\v' :  name = 'v';  break;
          default   :  name = '?';  break;   /* should never get here! */
        }
        printf("\\%c%s", name, (c == !\n') ? "\n" : "   ");
      }
    else if (isprint(c))
        printf("%c\t", c);                   /* normal printable character */
    else             \
        printf("\\%03o\t", c);               /* unprintable and not special */
}
```

FIGURE 7.10. *vis. c*—make all characters visible.

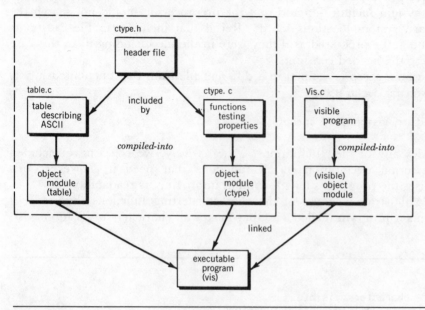

FIGURE 7.11. Compiling *Vis*—using the character test package.

ble even if they are unprintable. We do this by writing the C escape sequence used to specify them, with unprintable characters written as a backslash followed by their octal character code. A newline is output after any newline character in the input.

Even though *Vis* uses some of the character-testing functions, their source and header files are unnecessary. Instead, we can compile *vis.c* separately and then link its object module with the object modules from the character-testing package, a process illustrated in Figure 7.11.

Separate compilation and linking allows us to break large programs into smaller, more manageable pieces that can be developed separately and then, when completed, linked together. This makes libraries easy to use because only their object modules must be available, not their source. It also makes changes easier to implement, because we need only recompile the files affected by those changes, not the entire program.

When we compile files separately, however, we have to keep track of the files that must be recompiled. Forgetting to recompile a particular file can lead to confusing run-time behavior because the source and the executing program are inconsistent. We must also avoid certain errors, such as defining a function to return a particular type in one file and using it as if it returns a different type in another file, because these errors are not caught by either the compiler or the linker. On UNIX and several other systems, the program verifier *lint* and the program maintainer *make* are reasonably successful attempts to correct these disadvantages.

PROGRAMMING PRACTICE

7-7. Add the functions isxdig (is hexadecimal digit), isodig (is octal digit), and ispunct (is punctuation character). If you are not using ASCII, you will have to set up the table appropriately for your own character set.

7-8. Using the character-testing functions, write a program to count the words in its input. (A reasonable definition for a word is a group of upper- or lowercase characters.)

7-9. Using the character-testing functions, write a program that prints out the percentage of its input that is printable. How might such a program be used?

7-10. Using the character-testing functions, write a function dumpmem to dump a specified piece of memory in a readable format, showing the contents of each memory location in octal, followed by its ASCII character if it is printable. Is dumpmem a useful function?

7-11. Add register declarations to *Vis*. Does its performance increase noticeably?

STATIC VARIABLES

The final storage class, static, is used to hide information. static variables and functions are not made available to the linker, so they are visible only in the file in which they are defined. Like externals, all statics are allocated and initialized to zero when the program starts and the space remains allocated throughout the program's execution. This means that static variables retain their values between successive block entries. The rules for initializing static variables are the same as those for externals, so static arrays can be initialized.

LOCAL STATIC VARIABLES

We illustrate the use of static variables with the function out_line, shown in Figure 7.12a. out_line writes a line of output, keeps track of the num-

```
/*
 * Print lines with automatic numbering (uses get_line from Chapter 4).
 */
#define PAGELEN  66                /* length of page */

void out_line(line)
char *line;
{
  static int pageno = 0,          /* current page number */
         int lineno = PAGELEN;    /* lines on page */

  if (lineno == PAGELEN)
  {                               /* start new page, write page number */
    pageno++;
    printf("\fPage Number: %d\n\n", pageno);
    lineno = 0;
  }
  printf("%s", line);
  lineno++;
}
```

(a) Print a line with page numbering

```
main()
{
  char input[MAXLEN];             /* input line */
  void out_line();

  while(get_line(input, MAXLEN) != EOF)
    out_line(input);
}
```

(b) A main program using out_line

FIGURE 7.12. An example of statics—page numbering the input.

ber of lines written, and writes a page number at the top of every new page. The idea behind out_line is to encapsulate all page handling in a single function. Figure 7.12*b* contains a sample call. The page number and line number are kept as static variables (pageno and lineno, respectively), so that their values remain between successive calls to out_line. Their initialization occurs once, the first time out_line is called.

GLOBAL STATIC VARIABLES AND FUNCTIONS

We have noted that by default, external variables are made available to any file making an external reference to them. In contrast, static variables and functions are not made available to the linker and therefore cannot be accessed by other files. In fact, a static external variable or function is visible only to the part of the source file following its declaration.

static external variables are most often used when a file contains functions accessing a common data structure that functions in other files should not be able to access. As an example, Figure 7.13a contains an implementation of an alternative to scanf for input handling. The package contains two globally accessible functions. The first, getnum, skips over white space, reads a long integer from its input a character at a time, and places it in the long pointed to by its parameter. It returns EOF if the end of file is reached, zero if it does not find a number, and one otherwise. The second, skip_garbage, skips over any nonnumeric, non-white-space characters in the input.

With these functions, we can recover easily from input errors. When we need to read an integer, we call getnum. If an error occurs, we write an error message and call skip_garbage to skip over the troublesome characters, as illustrated in Figure 7.13b.

getnum.c also contains two static functions, fetch and unfetch. fetch reads a (possibly pushed-back) character from the input, and unfetch returns a single character to the input. To understand why these functions are useful, consider skip_garbage. We do not know if all unwanted characters have been ignored until a nonblank character has been read. That is, we have to read one character too many. This problem is not unique to skip_garbage; getnum, for instance, does not know if it has finished reading a number until a nondigit has been read. By returning the extra character with unfetch, we simplify our program, since the input processing routines do not have to explicitly pass the character between them.

The static variables savechar and pushed manage push back. savechar holds a pushed-back character, and pushed specifies whether anything has been pushed back. fetch and unfetch are straightforward. If there is no

```
/*
 * Getting a number -- a way around scanf.
 */
#include <stdio.h>
#include "ctype.h"

static int savechar;          /* character pushed back */
static int pushed = 0;        /* is anything pushed back? */

static int fetch()            /* read character with push back */
{
  return pushed ? pushed--, savechar : getchar();
}

static void unfetch(c)        /* push back character */
int c;
{
  pushed++, savechar = c;
}
```

(continued)

```
/* Read a number (ascii only) */

int getnum(num_ptr)
long *num_ptr;                  /* place to put number */
{
  int gotnum,                   /* did we get a number? */
      sign = 1,                 /* number's sign: 1 or -1 */
      c;                        /* next character */

  while (c = fetch(), isspace(c))
    ;                           /* skip over white space */
  if ((gotnum = c) != EOF)
  {
    if (c == '-')               /* set sign */
      sign = -1;
    else if (c != '+')          /* put back if not sign */
      unfetch(c);
    *num_ptr = 0;
    c = fetch();
    if ((gotnum = isdigit(c)) != 0)
      do                        /* build sum */
      {
        *num_ptr = *num_ptr * 10 + c - '0';
        c = fetch();
      } while (isdigit(c));
    unfetch(c);                 /* not digit, put back */
    *num_ptr *= sign;
  }
  return gotnum;                /* number was valid? */
}

void skip_garbage()             /* skip until digit, blank, or EOF */
{
  int c;

  while (c = fetch(), !isspace(c) && !isdigit(c))
    ;           /* skip over junk */
  unfetch(c);
}
```

(a) getnum.c — a partial alternative to scanf

```
long num;
int inpres, getnum();
void skip_garbage();
...
while (inpres = getnum(&num), inpres != EOF)
  if (!inpres)
  {
    printf("Bad input encountered\n");        /* input error found */
    skip_garbage();                           /* skip unwanted characters */
  }
  else                                        /* handle valid input */
    normal_processing();
```

(b) An example use of get_num *and* skip_garbage

FIGURE 7.13. Getting a number from the input—an alternative to scanf for input handling.

pushback, fetch calls getchar to read a character; otherwise, it returns the pushed-back character and remembers that nothing has been pushed back. unfetch simply sets the pushed-back character. Because savechar and pushed are needed by both fetch and unfetch, we declare them outside of these functions. However, we do not want other functions to accidentally modify or use these variables, and we prevent this access by making them static. Similarly, fetch and unfetch are internal to the implementation of getnum and skip_garbage; we make them static so that other functions cannot use them.

PROGRAMMING PRACTICE

7-12. Using fetch and unfetch, write the function get_double that reads in a floating point value, storing it in a double; write the function ignore_line that skips the characters remaining on the current line; and modify get_line (Chapter 4) to work with the package. What other functions would be useful if this package were a complete replacement for scanf? Write them. Are programs written using these functions more compact or more efficient than if they were written using scanf?

7-13. Modify the histogram program in Chapter 5 to use getnum and skip_garbage instead of scanf. Is the program more efficient?

SETS—IMPLEMENTING AN ABSTRACT DATA TYPE

When Pascal and C are compared, a frequent criticism of C is its lack of the "set" data type. A set is an unordered collection of values with certain operations defined on it. Some of the more common operations are adding and deleting values, testing to determine if a value is in a set, and taking the union and intersection of two sets. In this section, we show an implementation of these set operations and present an interesting application of their use.

We implement sets as an *abstract data type* by creating a SET data type and functions for the various set operations. The implementation details of an abstract data type are kept hidden from its users. Programs using sets know only the names of the functions implementing the various operations, certain restrictions on their use, and the order and expected type of parameters. To ensure this, we package the set operations in a single module that is compiled separately. This also allows us to change the implementation or add operations without having to rewrite the programs using them. The concept of an abstract data type should not seem strange. We have been using floats and doubles without knowing either their internal representation or the implementation details of operators such as + or /.

IMPLEMENTING SETS

We implement sets of small positive integers, allowing set elements in the range 0 to 2047. These sets are large enough to be useful without their representation taking up excessive space. As usual, the set size is defined as a constant so that it can be easily changed.

A reasonable representation for sets is a bit array, one bit for each set element. C does not provide bit arrays, but we can simulate them using an array of unsigned ints, with the number of bits in an int determining the number of set elements the array can represent. To access the bit cor-

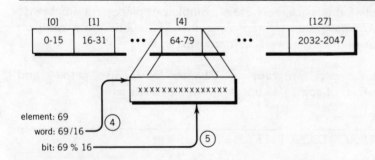

FIGURE 7.14. Locating the bit representing a set element. First we select the array element, then the bit within it. This figure assumes 16 bit ints.

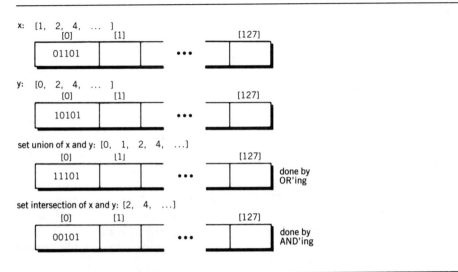

FIGURE 7.15. Illustration of the various set operations.

responding to a given set element, we must determine its location (the array element containing the bit and the bit's position within that array element). We do so by dividing the set element by the number of bits in an `int`; the remainder is the bit's position within the array element. A sample computation is shown in Figure 7.14, assuming 16 bit `int`s.

Given our representation, implementing the various set operations is straightforward. We add an element to the set by turning on the bit it indexes and delete it by turning the bit off. We check membership by examining the bit's value. Lastly, we implement set union by ORing together each of the array elements, and implement set intersection by ANDing. Figure 7.15 illustrates each of these operations on a sample set.

There is no reason for the programs using sets to know that they are implemented as a bit array. In fact, we would like the programs to be able to declare a **SET** type as if the language provided one. To do so, we will use a new C facility, `typedef`, which allows us to define synonyms for existing types. A `typedef` can appear outside any function, and its syntax resembles that of a variable declaration, with the type's name placed where the variable usually occurs. For example,

```
typedef int   ELEMENT;
typedef char *CHARPTR;
```

makes **ELEMENT** a synonym for `int` and **CHARPTR** a synonym for `char *`.

We can use these types as if they were basic types. For instance, the declaration

```
        ELEMENT x;
        CHARPTR y;
```

declares x as an int and y as a pointer to a character. Types created with typedef are in effect from the typedef until the end of the file. We will examine additional examples of typedef's usefulness in later chapters.

The SET type is a typedef to an array of unsigned ints and is defined in the header file *sets.h* (Figure 7.16). *sets.h* also defines constants for the minimum and maximum legal set elements (SET_MIN and SET_MAX), for the number of array elements needed to represent a SET (_SET_WORDS), and for the minimum size int required (_WORD_SIZE). In addition, *sets.h* defines the type ELEMENT (a synonym for int) and includes external declarations for the various set operations. _SET_WORDS and _WORD_SIZE are implementation constants and should not be used by programs using sets; their names begin with an underscore, so they will be less likely to conflict with other defined names. As expected, *sets.h* must be included by all files using sets.

sets.c contains the set operations and is shown in Figure 7.17. It also contains the functions get_bit, set_bit, and get_bit_pos. set_bit and get_bit use get_bit_pos to compute the location of a given set element's bit, and then set or return that bit's value. These functions are internal to the abstract data type SET's implementation, and we keep them hidden by declaring them as static.

set_Add (add an element), set_Del, and set_Mem (test membership) are trivial when built on top of these bit accessing functions. The other oper-

```
/*
 * Definitions to use "sets" of integers.
 */
#define SET_MIN         0           /* smallest set element */
#define SET_MAX         2047        /* largest set element */
#define _WORD_SIZE      16          /* assume at least 16 bit ints */
#define _SET_WORDS      128         /* set elements (2048/16) */

typedef unsigned int  SET[_SET_WORDS];   /* representation of a set */
typedef int ELEMENT;                     /* set elements are ints */

extern void set_Empty(/* SET */),        /* initialize set to empty */
            set_Union(/* SET, SET, SET */), /* union of two sets */
            set_Inter(/* SET, SET, SET */), /* intersection of two sets */
            set_Add(/* SET, ELEMENT */),    /* add element to set */
            set_Del(/* SET, ELEMENT */);    /* delete element from set */
extern int  set_Mem(/* SET, ELEMENT */);    /* is element member of set? */
```

FIGURE 7.16. *sets.h*—header file for sets.

```
/*
 *  Routines to handle sets.
 */
#include "sets.h"

static int get_bit_pos(word_ptr, bit_ptr, elem)   /* find element's position */
int *word_ptr, *bit_ptr;                           /* to be filled with position */
ELEMENT elem;
{
  *word_ptr = elem / _WORD_SIZE;
  *bit_ptr = elem % _WORD_SIZE;
  return elem >= SET_MIN && elem <= SET_MAX;
}

static void set_bit(s, elem, inset)                /* set element's bit */
SET s;
ELEMENT elem;
int inset;
{
  int word, bit;                                   /* element's position */

  if (get_bit_pos(&word, &bit, elem))
    inset ? s[word] |= (01 << bit) : s[word] &= ~(01 << bit);
}

static int get_bit(s, elem)                        /* get element's bit */
SET s;
ELEMENT elem;
{
  int word, bit;                                   /* element's position */

  return get_bit_pos(&word, &bit, elem) ? (s[word] >> bit) & 01 : 0;
}

void set_Add(s, elem)                              /* add element to set */
SET s;
ELEMENT elem;
{ set_bit(s, elem, 1); }

void set_Del(s, elem)                              /* delete element from set */
SET s;
ELEMENT elem;
{ set_bit(s, elem, 0); }

int set_Mem(s, elem)                               /* is element in set? */
SET s;
ELEMENT elem;
{ return get_bit(s, elem); }
```

(continued)

```
void set_Empty(s)                              /* initialize set */
SET s;
{
  int i;

  for (i = 0; i < _SET_WORDS; s[i++] = 0)
    ;
}

void set_Union(x, y, res)                      /* union of two sets */
SET x, y, res;
{
  int i;

  for (i = 0; i < _SET_WORDS; i++)
    res[i] = x[i] | y[i];
}

void set_Inter(x, y, res)                      /* intersect two sets */
SET x, y, res;
{
  int i;

  for (i = 0; i < _SET_WORDS; i++)
    res[i] = x[i] & y[i];
}
```

FIGURE 7.17. *sets.c*—implementing the set operations.

ations, **set_Union** (union of two sets), **set_Inter** (intersection of two sets), and **set_Empty** (initialize a set), deal with sets as a whole and do not use the internal functions. **set_Empty**, for example, initializes a set by setting each of its array elements to zero. We show how these functions are used in the next section.

USING SETS

Figure 7.18 shows a simple example of the use of sets with a program that partitions its input into values that appear once and those that appear many times. This program could be used, for example, to verify that no identification number is used more than once.

The program uses two sets. **unique** contains the values appearing once, **dup** contains the duplicates. When the program starts, **set_Empty** initializes these sets to empty. Values are read using **get_num** and any unexpected characters are skipped with **skip_garbage**. As each value is read, it is checked for membership in **unique**. If it is a member, it is removed from **unique** and added to **dup**. If not, it is added to **unique**. After the

```
/*
 * Identify duplicates in the input.
 */
#include <stdio.h>
#include "sets.h"

main()
{
  SET     unique, dup;                /* unique and duplicate elements */
  ELEMENT elem;                       /* next element */
  long    inpval;                     /* next input value */
  int     inpres;                     /* return value from getnum */
  void    print_set(),                /* to print out sets */
          skip_garbage();             /* to skip over garbage */      Initialize the unique & duplicate sets
  set_Empty(unique), set_Empty(dup);  → Initialize the unique & duplicate sets
  while (inpres = getnum(&inpval), inpres != EOF)
    if (!inpres)
    {
      printf("Bad input, skipping...\n");
      skip_garbage();
    }
    else if (inpval < SET_MIN || inpval > SET_MAX)
      printf("Out of range: %ld\n", inpval);
    else
    {
      elem = inpval;
      if (set_Mem(unique, elem))         /* is element a duplicate? */
        set_Del(unique, elem), set_Add(dup, elem);
      else if (!set_Mem(dup, elem))      /* is element unique? */
        set_Add(unique, elem);
    }
  print_set(unique, "Unique Values");    /* print the sets */
  print_set(dup, "Duplicate Values");
}

void print_set(set, name)              /* print out set and its name */
SET set;
char *name;
{
  ELEMENT i;                           /* next potential element */

  printf("%s\n", name);
  for (i = SET_MIN; i <= SET_MAX; i++)
    if (set_Mem(set, i))
      printf("%d\n", i);
}
```

FIGURE 7.18. A program to check for duplicate input values.

input has been read, we print the input values in unique and then print the members of dup. To print a set, we iterate through all possible values in the set, printing out those values that are set members.

Programs using our SET data type must include the file *sets.h* to obtain the type definition and the definitions of the operations on it. To create an executable program from Figure 7.18, we need to link in the object module containing the implementation of the data type (compiled from *sets.c*). In addition, since we are using getnum, we need to include its object module. The compilation process for our sample program is shown in Figure 7.19.

We are trying to illustrate two important points with this example. The first point is that we should separate the details of a function or data type's implementation from those of its use. The program in Figure 7.18 would be considerably more complex and consequently harder to understand if it also contained the definitions of getnum, skip_garbage, and all the set operations. We can understand how it works without knowing that sets are implemented as bit arrays or that certain characters are pushed back on the input.

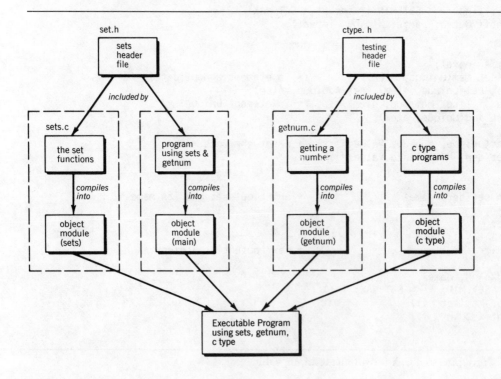

FIGURE 7.19. Compiling the set package.

The second point is that wherever possible, we should build our programs on top of functions we have already written. We should create modules, like our sets, that can easily be used by new programs. Doing so effectively adds features to the language, allowing us to build programs much more quickly than we could if we had to start from scratch each time.

PROGRAMMING PRACTICE

7-14. The difference of two sets is the elements in the first set that are not also present in the second set. Write a function, **set_Diff**, that places the difference of two sets into a third set.

7-15. Write a function, **print_set**, that prints out the elements of a set in traditional set notation. For example, a set containing the elements 3, 7, and 14, should print as ⟨3, 7, 14⟩. Can this be implemented without adding set operations?

7-16. Use **typedef** to define the type **void** if your compiler doesn't support it.

CHAPTER 8

THE PREPROCESSOR

Many useful features of C are not implemented by the compiler, but instead by a program that processes C source files before they are given to the compiler. This program, the C preprocessor, can be used to define constants and macros, include source files, and perform conditional compilation. In this chapter we describe the preprocessor, showing how we can use it to increase the readability, efficiency, and portability of our programs, as well as to make them easier to write and debug.

PREPROCESSOR DIRECTIVES

The preprocessor reads a source file, performs various actions on it, and gives the resulting output to the C compiler. Its actions are determined by directives placed in the source file; source files containing no preprocessor directives are simply passed to the C compiler unchanged. Lines containing a preprocessor directive, called *preprocessor command lines*, are processed by the preprocessor and never seen by the compiler. These lines are differentiated from normal C sources because they begin with a # and start in column 1. Table 8.1 lists the preprocessor directives and their uses. Some of them should be familiar; many of our programs have used #include and #define. The following sections describe the preprocessor directives in detail.

SIMPLE MACRO SUBSTITUTION

We have used #define to define various symbolic constants, such as the number of elements in an array and the end-of-file character. Doing so

TABLE 8.1. C preprocessor directives and their uses.

Directive	Use
#include	Include text from a file.
#define	Define a macro.
#undef	Undefine a macro.
#line	Give a line number for compiler messages.
#if	Test if a compile-time condition holds.
#ifdef	Test if a symbol is defined.
#ifndef.	Test if a symbol is not defined.
#else	Indicate alternatives if a test fails.
#elif	Combination of #if and #else.
#endif	End a preprocessor conditional.

aids readability and modifiability, especially in larger programs. When a numeric value appears in a program, its use is not always easy to determine, especially when the same value means different things in different places. For example, 10 may be an interest rate, the size of an array, or a base for number conversion. A descriptive name for each unique use of a constant makes its use clearer, while making it possible to change the constant's value throughout the program simply by changing the line defining its name.

Although we have not done so, we can use **#define** to give symbolic names to any arbitrary piece of text, not only to numeric constants. We can do this because **#define** is more powerful than we have let on; it is actually a general mechanism for text replacement. The preprocessor command line

    #define NAME   TEXT

instructs the preprocessor to replace all unquoted occurrences of *NAME* with *TEXT* throughout the remainder of the source file. White space is required between **#define** and *NAME* and between *NAME* and *TEXT*. There are no restrictions on *TEXT*. We write defined names in uppercase to distinguish them from variable and function names handled by the compiler. A defined name is often called a *macro*, and the process of substituting its replacement text is called *macro substitution*.

With **#define**, we can give symbolic names to string constants. For example,

    #define DIGITS "0123456789"

causes each occurrence of **DIGITS** to be replaced with the string constant **"0123456789"** throughout the remainder of the source file. We can also give names to arbitrary expressions.

```
#define TWO_PI    (3.1415926 * 2.0)
```

The preprocessor simply substitutes the expression for its defined name *without evaluating it*. For example,

```
circumf = radius * TWO_PI;
```

is replaced with

```
circumf = radius * (3.1415926 * 2.0);
```

No macro substitution takes place when a name is defined; the preprocessor simply remembers the name and its replacement text. Later, when the name is used, the preprocessor substitutes its replacement text and performs macro substitution on any defined names it contains. This allows us to define names in terms of other names and to define them in any order. As an example, Figure 8.1 shows constant definitions that determine the number of array elements needed to hold a bit vector representing a set of values, instead of simply defining precomputed constants for them, as we did in Chapter 7.

The size of the array (_SET_WORDS) is computed from the number of bits needed (_SET_VALUES) and the number of bits in an array element (_WORD_SIZE). _SET_VALUES, in turn, is computed from the largest (MAX_VAL) and smallest (MIN_VAL) values; _WORD_SIZE is computed from the size of an array element and the number of bits in a byte. Figure 8.2 illustrates the replacement process for the expression n < _SET_WORDS.

Whenever the replacement text is an expression, it should be parenthesized to prevent an unexpected order of evaluation when the name it replaces is used. For example, if the expression to compute the number of words needed

```
_SET_VALUES / _WORD_SIZE
```

follows the unparenthesized definitions

```
#define _SET_VALUES   MAX_VAL - MIN_VAL + 1   /* bits we need */
#define _WORD_SIZE    sizeof(int) * 8         /* bits in a long */
```

```
#define MIN_VAL       0                        /* smallest value */
#define MAX_VAL       2047                     /* largest value */
#define _SET_VALUES   (MAX_VAL - MIN_VAL + 1)  /* bits we need */
#define _WORD_SIZE    (sizeof(int) * 8)        /* bits in an int */
#define _SET_WORDS    (_SET_VALUES / _WORD_SIZE) /* words for bit map */
```

FIGURE 8.1. An example of defining constants in terms of other constants.

n < _SET_WORDS

Substituting for **_SET_WORDS**

n < (_SET_VALUES/_WORD_SIZE)

Substituting for **_SET_VALUES** and **_WORD_SIZE**

n < ((MAX_VAL – MIN_VAL + 1)/(sizeof (int) * 8))

Substituting for MAX_VAL and MIN_VAL

n < ((2047 – 0 + 1)/(sizeof (int) * 8))

FIGURE 8.2. Replacing defined names with defined names. All macro replacement takes place when the name is used, not when it is defined.

the result of the preprocessor's substitutions for `_SET_VALUES` and `WORD_SIZE` is:

```
MAX_VAL – MIN_VAL + 1 / sizeof(int) * 8
```

This is certainly different from the desired expression

```
(MAX_VAL – MIN_VAL + 1) / (sizeof(int) * 8)
```

resulting from the parenthesized definitions in Figure 8.1.

To aid debugging, most compilers have an option to show the result of preprocessor substitutions. Since some preprocessors substitute white space along with the replacement text, the resulting output may differ from that shown in our examples. Even though the output differs, the results should be equivalent.

Because the preprocessor simply substitutes expressions without evaluating them, it is reasonable to wonder whether a program is less efficient when an often-used defined name is replaced with an expression. Luckily, most C compilers compute the value of expressions involving only constants at compile time, instead of at run time, allowing us to use defined names freely in the definitions of other names without worrying too much about efficiency. With a compiler that does not evaluate all constant expressions at compile time, an external variable can be initialized with the expression and used in its place.

PROGRAMMING PRACTICE

8-1. Write constant definitions for the maximum and minimum values of the types short, int, and long on your machine. Assuming a two's complement machine, can you write expressions to compute these values? Write similar constant definitions for their unsigned counterparts.

8-2. Reorder the definitions in Figure 8.1. Does this affect subsequent uses of the names?

SYNTACTIC REPLACEMENT

We can use the preprocessor's ability to do arbitrary text replacement in order to hide parts of C's syntax that can be confusing or error prone. For example, we can use the definitions

```
#define   FOREVER       for(;;)      /* infinite loop */
#define   IS            ==           /* equality test */
```

to make infinite loops more explicit:

```
FOREVER
  printf("Reflex test - hit the interrupt key\n");
```

and to prevent the common mistake of using = instead of == for equality tests:

```
if (c IS EOF)
  printf("At the end of file.\n");
```

An interesting use of these definitions is to create an extended syntax for C that resembles another language's syntax. We can use the definitions in Figure 8.3a to write C programs in a Pascal-like syntax, letting the preprocessor translate them into the form the compiler expects. We use these definitions in Figure 8.3b, a function insert that inserts a value into its correct place in a sorted table.

There are some drawbacks to major syntactic replacement. Since defined names have the same syntax as identifiers, operators and other nonalphabetic tokens such as comment delimiters cannot be redefined, limiting the amount of C's syntax that can be hidden. In addition, when the defined names are used incorrectly, the resulting error messages are likely to be less understandable because they correspond to C's syntax instead of the extended syntax. Lastly, maintaining these programs can be difficult for those unfamiliar with the extended syntax used. Despite these limitations, some large programs, including a command interpreter and an object code debugger, have been written in an Algol-like syntax defined using the preprocessor.

Because the replacement text in any definition is arbitrary, no syntax checking can be performed on it by the preprocessor. Syntax errors are

```
/*
 * Definitions for pascal-like syntax.
 */
#define    INTEGER    int
#define    REAL       double
#define    IF         if (
#define    THEN       )
#define    ELSE       else
#define    WHILE      while (
#define    DO         )
#define    BEGIN      {
#define    END        }
#define    PROCEDURE  void
#define    FUNCTION
#define    AND        &&
#define    OR         ||
#define    MOD        %
```

(a) Definitions used to create a Pascal-like syntax

```
PROCEDURE INSERT(table,value)        /* insert value in correct position */
REAL table[], value;

BEGIN
  INTEGER pos;                       /* temporary position in table */

  IF numvals < MAXVALS THEN BEGIN
    pos = numvals - 1;
    WHILE pos >= 0 AND value < table[pos] DO BEGIN
      table[pos + 1] = table[pos];
      pos = pos - 1;
    END
    table[pos] = value;
  END
END
```

(b) Table insertion written using Pascal-like syntax

FIGURE 8.3. Some definitions that allow us to write programs in a Pascal-like syntax, and a function that illustrates their use.

detected when the compiler processes lines where the name is used, not the line where the name is defined. For example, the incorrect definition

```
#define  PI = 3.1415926;   /* incorrect: don't want "=" or ";" */
```

contains the two most common syntax errors: terminating a definition with a semicolon and following the name with an assignment operator. If the definition is followed by

```
circumf = 2 * PI * radius;
```

most compilers will report errors from the two incorrect statements

```
circumf = 2 * = 3.1415926; * radius;
```

that result from the preprocessor's substitutions. When using #define, remember that the preprocessor does not know C; it blindly replaces names with replacement text.

PROGRAMMING PRACTICE

8-3. If the compiler doesn't support void, is it possible to write a macro definition that simulates it? Does it work with your compiler?

8-4. Most preprocessors do syntax checking, such as checking for unusual characters in the source file or unterminated quoted strings. Add some simple syntax errors to an existing source file. Are any errors detected by the preprocessors?

MACRO SUBSTITUTION WITH PARAMETERS

Up to now, once we have defined a name, every occurrence of it has been replaced with identical text. We can vary a name's replacement text by defining a macro with parameters. Subsequent occurrences of the macro name are known as *macro calls*. When a macro is called, the preprocessor performs *macro expansion*, substituting the macro's replacement text for the call and replacing any occurrences of the macro's parameters with its arguments. Macro substitution with parameters is an extension of simple macro substitution, in which the replacement text is a template.

We define a macro with a preprocessor command line of the form

#define *macro-name(parameter-name,* ... *,parameter-name) replacement-text*

There can be no white space between the *macro-name* and the left parenthesis introducing the macro's parameter list. (When white space follows the *macro-name* it is a macro definition with no parameters: the simpler form of #define we encountered earlier.) The parameter list can contain zero or more parameters; these are analogous to the parameters in a function definition. For example,

```
#define CONVRT(temp) ((5.0 / 9.0) * ((temp) - 32))
```

defines a macro named CONVRT with a single parameter temp. CONVRT converts a Fahrenheit temperature into its equivalent Celsius temperature. To prevent order of evaluation problems when CONVRT is expanded, we are careful to parenthesize all occurrences of its parameters in its replacement text, as well as the replacement text itself.

We call a macro with an unquoted expression of the form:

macro-name(*text*, *text*, ... , *text*)

The syntax of a macro call is similar to that of a function call, but its behavior is different. When a macro is called, the preprocessor replaces the call with the replacement text and then replaces every occurrence of a parameter with its corresponding argument. Following CONVRT's definition, for example, the expression CONVRT(x) is a macro call the preprocessor replaces with

```
(5.0 / 9.0) * ((x) - 32))
```

substituting x for temp in CONVRT's replacement text.

A complete program using CONVRT is shown in Figure 8.4. The program reads pairs of Fahrenheit temperatures representing the high and low temperature for various cities, converts them into the corresponding Celsius temperatures, and prints them.

We could have written CONVRT as a function, as in Figure 8.5, but did not simply because it is much less work to write CONVRT as a macro. Of course, we did not have to write either a macro or a function to do the temperature conversion; we could have written the program using the conversion formula directly. However, using the macro CONVRT makes the

---

```
/*
 * Reads in pairs of Fahrenheit temperatures and converts them to Celsius.
 */
#define CONVRT(temp) ((5.0 / 9.0) * ((temp) - 32)) /* Fahrenheit to Celsius */

main()
{
    int minfahr, maxfahr;   /* minimum and maximum temperatures */

    while (scanf("%d %d", &minfahr, &maxfahr) == 2)
        printf("%f\t%f\n", CONVRT(minfahr), CONVRT(maxfahr));
}
```

FIGURE 8.4. Using a macro to do temperature conversion.

```
/*
 * Convert Fahrenheit temperature to Celsius.
 */
double convrt(temp)
int temp;                           /* temperature to convert */
{
   return (5.0 / 9.0) * (temp - 32);
}
```

FIGURE 8.5. Function to do temperature conversion.

program more readable (without decreasing its efficiency), and makes it obvious that the same conversion formula is applied to both input temperatures.

USEFUL MACROS

Macros can do things that functions cannot do. As an example, consider the macro min, which returns the minimum value of its parameters.

```
#define MIN(x,y) ( (x) < (y) ? (x) : (y) )  /* minimum of two values */
```

If the macro call

```
MIN(a + b,c + d)
```

appears after this definition, it is replaced with

```
( (a + b) < (c + d) ? (a + b) : (c + d) )
```

an expression that returns the minimum value of the expressions (a + b) and (c + d). The parameter x has been replaced with a + b, the parameter y with c + d.

Because MIN is a macro and not a function, we can use it to find the minimum of any pair of values of the same data type. If we wrote MIN as a function, we would have to type cast its arguments if their type differed from that of its parameters, or we would have to have different versions of MIN for each data type. We also gain efficiency by writing MIN as a macro, since macro calls are done during preprocessing instead of at run time, and the overhead of a function call (argument passing, variable allocation, calling and returning from the function) is eliminated. There are some problems, however, with using macros; these will be discussed shortly.

Our macros so far have expanded into expressions; however, macros can also expand into arbitrary text, including statements or parts of statements. The macro SWAP, defined by

```
#define SWAP(type,x,y)    /* swap contents of x and y */ \
        { type temp = (x); (x) = (y), (y) = temp; }
```

is useful for many programs, especially those that do sorting. (The definition's first line ends with a backslash to allow it to continue on to the next line.) SWAP expands into a compound statement declaring a temporary variable with the same type as the variable being swapped, using this variable to do the exchange. Whenever a macro expands into more than one statement, a compound statement should be used so that calls to the macro are similar to function calls. The macro call

```
SWAP(double, old, new)
```

is replaced with the statement block

```
{ double temp = old; old = new, new = temp; }
```

that exchanges the values of old and new. Since SWAP is expanded into a compound statement, calls to it should not be terminated by a semicolon. SWAP can exchange values of arbitrary data types. Since there is no way to pass a type specifier to a function, this cannot be done with a function.

Macros can also be used to hide certain idioms of the language, improving the readability of programs with no loss of efficiency. For example, the macros STREQ, STRLT, and STRGT

```
#define STREQ(x,y)  (strcmp((x),(y)) == 0) /* strings equal? */
#define STRLT(x,y)  (strcmp((x),(y)) < 0)  /* is string x < string y? */
#define STRGT(x,y)  (strcmp((x),(y)) > 0)  /* is string x > string y? */
```

test whether one string is lexicographically equal to, less than, or greater than another string. Their names clarify the string equality test strcmp is being used for, hiding the details of its return value. If these macros are not used, the program's reader is forced to remember the meaning of the various return values of strcmp in order to understand the string comparison being performed.

PROGRAMMING PRACTICE

8-5. Write a macro, PRINT_INT, that takes an integer parameter and writes it to the standard output using printf. Can you write a macro to print a value of an arbitrary type appropriately?

8-6. Write a macro, GET_BITS, that takes a value, a starting bit, and the number of bits to return, and returns the value of those bits. What other bit-oriented operations can easily be written as macros?

8-7. Write a macro, INDEX, that expands into a for loop that indexes a variable from a minimum to a maximum. For example,

```
INDEX(i, 1, 100) printf("This is %d\n", i);
```

should expand into

```
for (i = 1; i <= 100; i++) printf("This is %d\n", i);
```

USING MACROS IN MACRO DEFINITIONS

We can also use macros with parameters in defining other macros. Figure 8.6 shows the definition of a macro AREA to compute the area of a circle, along with the definitions from which it is built.

Because PI is a useful constant and SQUARE is a useful macro, we provide definitions for them instead of simply inserting their values in AREA's definition. Following this definition, the preprocessor first replaces a macro call such as AREA(distance) with

```
(PI * SQUARE(distance))
```

Then it expands the defined names PI and SQUARE, resulting in the desired expression:

```
(3.1415926 * ( (distance) * (distance) ))
```

We can also use macros as the arguments of macro calls. For example, given the definition of SQUARE, n^4 can be computed using the expression

```
SQUARE(SQUARE(n))    /* quadruple a value */
```

The preprocessor first expands this expression into

```
((SQUARE(n)) * (SQUARE(n)))
```

replacing SQUARE's parameter x with SQUARE(n). Since there are still defined

```
#define  PI        3.1415926       /* famous friend */
#define  SQUARE(x)  ((x) * (x))      /* square of number */
#define  AREA(r)    (PI * SQUARE(r))  /* area of circle */
```

FIGURE 8.6. Computing a circle's area—defining macros in terms of macros.

names in this expression, the preprocessor applies macro substitution to them, eventually generating the expression

```
((((n) * (n))) * (((n) * (n))))
```

Despite all the parentheses, this correctly computes n^4.

POTENTIAL PROBLEMS

Although macros are useful, there are some pitfalls, most of which can be avoided by remembering that macros are not functions. One drawback is that a macro's code appears in every place the macro is called, while a function's code appears only once, regardless of how many times the function is called. When minimal program size is important, large, often-used macros should be written as functions.

Another drawback is that a macro argument, unlike a function argument, may be evaluated more than once if its corresponding parameter appears in many places in the replacement text. For example:

```
#define CUBE(x) ((x) * (x) * (x))    /* compute x to the third power */
```

defines a macro that computes the cube of its parameter. The call CUBE(x + y) expands to

```
((x + y) * (x + y) * (x + y))
```

causing three evaluations of (x + y).

The possibility of multiple evaluation is particularly troublesome when arguments have side effects. CUBE(a++), a macro call intended to increment a after returning its cube, is expanded into the expression

```
((a++) * (a++) * (a++))
```

which does something different. Expressions appearing as arguments to macros should be used sparingly and should be avoided entirely when they contain side effects.

Forgetting to put parentheses around a macro's parameters within its replacement text can lead to incorrect orders of evaluation. Leaving them off in the following definition of CUBE

```
#define CUBE(x) (x * x * x)    /* sloppily parenthesized definition */
```

causes the call CUBE(a + 2) to expand into the expression

```
(a + 2 * a + 2 * a + 2)
```

which does not return the cube of a + 2.

Lastly, when a macro expands into a compound statement, poorly chosen names can cause scoping problems. For example, the call SWAP(double, old, temp) expands into the compound statement

```
{ double temp = (old); (old) = (temp), (temp) = (temp); }
```

which does not do the expected exchange. When a compound statement is part of a macro's replacement text, its local variables must be chosen so that they do not conflict with any variable name passed as an argument.

PROGRAMMING PRACTICE

8-8. Write the macros DIV and DIV_MOD. DIV(x,y) returns the value of (x / y) for nonzero values of y, otherwise it returns zero. DIV_MOD(d,r,x,y) divides x by y, storing the result in d and the remainder in r.

8-9. Write a macro, MSG(flag,msg), that writes the string msg only if flag is not zero.

8-10. Write a macro, NULL_PTR(type), that returns a null pointer correctly cast to the passed type. When is this macro useful?

8-11. Write a macro, DEREF(ptr, type), that dereferences ptr only if it is not null. If ptr is null the macro prints an error message and returns zero, cast to the appropriate type.

UNDEFINING NAMES

Once a name is defined, all of its later occurrences are replaced with its defined replacement text. Occasionally it is desirable to define a name in only part of the file, either to show that the name is used only in a small section or to allow the name to be redefined. The directive

#undef *NAME*

undefines a defined name, stopping macro substitution for it. We can then use #define to redefine the name. Most preprocessors issue a warning if we try to redefine a name without first undefining it. (Some preprocessors, however, allow multiple definitions of names, storing them in reverse order of definition. Undefining a multiply defined name causes the previous definition to be used as the name's definition. It is best not to rely on this type of preprocessor behavior.)

We can use #undef to define a name for only a single function, giving it the same visibility as a local variable. For example, if we have a function that needs a null pointer to a character, perhaps to pass as a parameter to another function, we can define a constant NIL with

```
#define NIL (char *) 0      /* NULL pointer to character */
```

and use it wherever we need a null pointer, avoiding the explicit casting that would otherwise be required. This definition of NIL can be limited to the function by placing

```
#undef NIL
```

at the function's end. A later function using pointers to doubles can define NIL with

```
#define NIL (double *) 0      /* NULL pointer to double */
```

to define the appropriate null pointer.

FILE INCLUSION

Definitions useful to functions appearing in different source files can be placed in a single file and the file included when needed, preventing unnecessary repetition of definitions. Should it become necessary to change one of these definitions, only the file containing them must be modified and the programs that include it recompiled. The files containing these definitions are called *header files* or *include files*; by convention their names end with the suffix . *h*.

We include a file with the preprocessor directive #include. The preprocessor replaces #include lines with the entire contents of the specified file. If an incompletely specified file name is given, the preprocessor tries to search for the file in various locations determined by the form of #include used. The form

```
#include <filename>
```

instructs the preprocessor to look in only certain system-dependent locations to find *filename* and is usually reserved to include system header files such as *stdio. h*. The alternative form

```
#include "filename"
```

```
/*
 *  Generally useful definitions.
 */
#include <stdio.h>

#define TAB            '\t'                        /* common characters */
#define PAGE           '\f'
#define BELL           '\007'
#define EOS            '\0'
#define CR             '\n'

#define FOREVER        for(;;)                     /* syntactic extensions */
#define IS             ==
#define ISNOT          !=

#define MIN(x,y)       ((x) < (y) ? (x) : (y))     /* minimum of x and y */
#define MAX(x,y)       ((x) < (y) ? (y) : (x))     /* maximum of x and y */
#define ABS(x)         ((x) < 0) ? -(x) : (x))     /* absolute value */
#define INRANGE(x,y,z) ((x) >= (y) && (x) <= (z))  /* is x between y and z? */

#define SWAP(tmp, x, y) (tmp = x, x = y, y = tmp)  /* swap x and y */

#define INDEX(var,start,end)                       /* iterate from start */ \
        for ((var) = (start); (var) <= (end); (var)++)  /* to end */

#define STREQ(x,y)     (strcmp(x,y) == 0)          /* hide strcmp ugliness */
#define STRLT(x,y)     (strcmp(x,y) < 0)
#define STRGT(x,y)     (strcmp(x,y) > 0)
```

FIGURE 8.7. Generally useful definitions found in many programs.

instructs the preprocessor first to look locally for the file and to search the standard locations only if the file is not found locally. This form is used with local include files and files with completely specified names. Some preprocessors have an option whereby additional locations can be specified; check your preprocessor documentation to find out the specific locations that are searched. If an include file cannot be found, an error is reported and preprocessing stops. Included files can include other files; most preprocessors allow at least five levels of nesting. Of course, an included file should not include itself or any file that includes it.

One use of file inclusion, in addition to those we have already reviewed, is that it allows us to create a file of definitions that we find beneficial and to include it in all the programs we write. These definitions can extend C in a useful way while requiring little effort on our part. An example is shown in Figure 8.7. Most of these definitions and macros were explained in earlier sections. We have, however, added the macros **MAX**, which returns the maximum value of its arguments; **ABS**, which returns the absolute value of its argument; and **INRANGE**, which returns nonzero if its first parameter is between its other parameters. We also include a slightly different version of **SWAP** that is passed the temporary variable, along with the variables to be exchanged. This prevents the scoping problem mentioned earlier.

INCLUDING DATA TYPE DEFINITIONS

In addition to holding generally useful macro and constant definitions, include files are often used to provide data type definitions. In the previous chapter, the definitions of the set data type were placed in a file that was included by all functions using the set data type. With our implementation of sets, however, it is necessary to compile and link an additional file containing the functions that implemented the set operations. It is often possible to define a seemingly new data type completely within a header file. As an example, Figure 8.8 shows the include file *boolean.h*, which contains definitions that make it appear as though C has a boolean data type. These definitions are helpful in writing more readable code, as well as making it easier to translate programs written in a language that has a boolean type.

The type **BOOLEAN** is appropriately represented by char because only the values zero and one are needed to represent the two possible states of a boolean variable. For consistency with other languages, the constants **NOT**, **AND**, and **OR** are defined as an alternative to the equivalent C logical operators. Lastly, **BOOL_VAL** returns a string representing the boolean's value and is useful when debugging.

Any program can pretend that C has **BOOLEAN**s by including *boolean.h* and using these definitions. We use them in Figure 8.9, a function,

```
/*
 * Boolean Data Type Definitions.
 */
typedef char            BOOLEAN;             /* the data type */

#define TRUE            1                    /* possible boolean values */
#define FALSE           0                    /*    (TRUE and FALSE)  */

#define NOT             !                    /* boolean operators */
#define AND             &&                   /*    (for readability) */
#define OR              ||

#define BOOL_VAL(x)     ((x) ? "TRUE" : "FALSE")  /* string from boolean value */
```

FIGURE 8.8. *boolean.h*—defining a **BOOLEAN** data type.

```
/*
 *  Is character in string?
 */
#include "boolean.h"

BOOLEAN instr(string,ch)
char *string, ch;
{
  BOOLEAN found = FALSE;        /* have we found it yet? */

  for (; *string != '\0' AND NOT found; string++)
    if (*string == ch)
      found = TRUE;
  return found;
}
```

FIGURE 8.9. Using the boolean definitions.

instr, that determines whether a given character is in a particular string. Using **BOOLEAN** makes instr more readable but less concise.

PROGRAMMING PRACTICE

8-12. Examine some of the C programs you have written. Are there complicated expressions that could be greatly simplified by using macros? Write these macros.

8-13. Define a function and include it in two files that are linked together to form a single object module. What happens? Try the same thing with a variable. Are the results similar?

8-14. Rewrite the character-testing functions from Chapter 7 as macros. Are the macro versions more efficient?

8-15. Define a macro package to do the set operations implemented in Chapter 7 for small sets—sets with no more elements than fit into a long.

CONDITIONAL COMPILATION

Based on the values of various compile-time conditions, such as name definition, the preprocessor can be used to control the source file lines given to the compiler. This process is known as *conditional compilation* and can be used to make our programs more portable and easier to debug. Conditional compilation allows a program's source to compile into different versions depending on our needs.

TESTING NAME DEFINITION

Defined names are often used as flags that control conditional compilation. We can determine the lines to be processed by using the directives #ifdef, #else, and #endif to test if a name is defined. Any set of preprocessor commands of the form

```
#ifdef name
     first-group-of-lines
#else
     second-group-of-lines
#endif
```

causes *first-group-of-lines* to be processed by the preprocessor and compiled if *name* is defined, or *second-group-of-lines* to be processed if it is not. The #else is optional, and if it is omitted and the tested name is undefined, the lines up to the matching #endif are ignored.

As an example of their use, Figure 8.10 shows a new version of the insertion sort program from Chapter 1 that conditionally includes statements that provide debugging output. The debugging statements are included only if the name **DEBUG** is defined when the function is compiled.

```
insert(a, val, n)
int a[], val, n;
{
   int pos;

   for (pos = n; pos > 0 && val < a[pos - 1]; pos = pos - 1)
#ifdef DEBUG
   {
      printf("Moving %d from %d to %d\n", a[pos], pos - 1, pos);
      a[pos] = a[pos - 1];
   }
#else
      a[pos] = a[pos - 1];
#endif
   a[pos] = val;
#ifdef DEBUG
   printf("Inserting %d at %d\n", val, pos);
#endif
}
```

FIGURE 8.10. Insertion routine with debugging statements.

If `DEBUG` has been defined in Figure 8.10, when the preprocessor evaluates the first `#ifdef`, it processes and gives to the compiler only the lines

```
{
    printf("Moving %d from %d to %d\n", a[pos], pos - 1, pos);
    a[pos] = a[pos - 1];
}
```

If `DEBUG` is not defined, the single line

```
a[pos] = val;
```

would be processed and the others ignored.

Rather than adding output statements whenever debugging output is desired and then removing these statements once the program has been debugged, we prefer using the preprocessor to decide if debugging output should be produced. Our programs are more efficient, since the decision is made at compile time instead of run time. Our programs are also smaller, because the debugging statements do not appear in the program's object module when debugging output is not desired. And importantly, our programs are more maintainable, since the debugging statements remain available when later changes are made to the program. There is one disadvantage to this approach, however. Because of the many preprocessor tests, the source is likely to be less readable.

We have been using `#ifdef` to test if a name is defined. A similar preprocessor directive, `#ifndef`, can be used instead to test if a name is undefined. `#ifndef` appears most often in include files to ensure that even if the file has been included more than once, any definitions it contains will not be redefined.

`#ifndef` appears in Figure 8.11, a modified version of *boolean.h* (Figure 8.8) that defines the boolean data type only if it has not already been defined. The file's first line

```
#ifndef BOOL_HDR
```

causes the various names contained in the file to be defined only if `BOOL_HDR` is undefined. We cannot test whether `BOOLEAN` is a defined name because it has been defined using `typedef` instead of `#define`. If `BOOL_HDR` is already defined, we assume that *boolean.h* has already been included and that the header file's definitions can be ignored. Remember that both `#ifdef` and `#ifndef` test only whether the name is defined in the preprocessor; they do not test whether the name of an identifier, function, or type has been declared.

PREDEFINED NAMES

In addition to the names we have explicitly defined and tested with `#ifdef` and `#ifndef`, most preprocessors predefine names such as the name of the

```
/*
 *  Boolean Data Type Definitions.
 */
#ifndef BOOL_HDR
#define BOOL_HDR

typedef char            BOOLEAN;                /* the data type */
#define TRUE            1                       /* possible boolean values */
#define FALSE           0                       /*   (TRUE and FALSE)  */

#define NOT             !                       /* boolean operators */
#define AND             &&                      /*   (for readability) */
#define OR              ||

#define BOOL_VAL(x)     ((x) ? "TRUE" : "FALSE") /* string from boolean value */
#endif
```

FIGURE 8.11. *boolean.h*—a new version of the boolean include file.

machine the program is running on, its host operating system, and the name of the compiler being used. Table 8.2 contains some of the predefined names defined by various C compilers. Not all preprocessors predefine all these names; only those names relevant to the particular preprocessor are defined by it. When a name is defined, however, the program can assume the environment associated with it. For example, the names unix and vax are defined only when the program is being compiled on a VAX running the UNIX operating system.

By testing if various potential predefined names are actually defined, a program can determine its environment and adjust any environmental

TABLE 8.2. Various predefined preprocessor names.
Some systems allow these names to be upper- or lowercase.

Name	Environment
unix	UNIX operating system
os	IBM 360/370 operating system
tss	IBM Time Sharing System
vms	DEC's operating system
cpm	CPM operating system
pdp11	PDP-11 computer
interdata	Interdata computer
vax	VAX computer
decus	Decus C compiler
vax11c	VAX 11 C compiler for VMS
__LINE__	Current line number
__FILE__	Current file name

dependencies, increasing its portability. For example, if we determine the number of bits in an unsigned int with the expression

```
(sizeof(int) * 8)
```

we are assuming that a byte contains eight bits. Unfortunately, many machines have smaller or larger byte sizes, and programs relying on this assumption will either fail or work less efficiently.

A more portable way to determine the machine's byte size is to define a constant BYTESIZ with the number of bits in a byte on the particular machine the program is running on. Figure 8.12 shows how its value is set. During compilation, the program first checks for predefined names representing machines whose byte size is known to be unusual, defining BYTESIZ appropriately for those machines. If none of these names are defined, a default of eight is used for BYTESIZ. Of course, the program still will not behave correctly if it is compiled on a machine with an unusual byte size that has either no name predefined for it or a name for which testing is not done.

Most preprocessors predefine the names __LINE__ and __FILE__ as the current line number and current source file name. We illustrate one use of these definitions in the definition of the macro ASSERT, shown in Figure 8.13. ASSERT's arguments are an expression, representing an assumption of the programmer (something the programmer believes, or *asserts* to be true, which is not otherwise tested), and a string to print if this assumption does not hold when the macro's expansion is executed. Whenever a function makes an assumption whose failure would cause the function to behave incorrectly, a call to ASSERT can be inserted, documenting the assumption and indicating it when it fails. Invariably, our programs fail because an assumption we made turns out not to hold; ASSERT helps us find such assumptions.

The predefined names __LINE__ and __FILE__ are expanded into the

```
#ifdef INTERDATA
#define BYTESIZ  9          /* 9 bit bytes */
#else
#ifdef CYBER
#define BYTESIZ 10          /* 10 bit bytes */
#else
#define BYTESIZ  8          /* 8 bit bytes are the default */
#endif
#endif
```

FIGURE 8.12. Setting up a constant containing the number of bits in a byte. Only those machines that differ from the norm are tested.

```
#define  ASSERT(cond,desc)                  \
         (!(cond) ? printf("Assertion failed: %s (line %d of %s).\n", \
                   (desc), __LINE__, __FILE__), 0 : 1 )
```

FIGURE 8.13. Assertion macro to write an error message if an assumption fails.

line number and file name of the macro call, and their values are included
in the error message written when an assertion fails. **ASSERT** is written as
an expression in order to allow functions to test assertions and exit when
they fail.

To illustrate **ASSERT**'s usefulness, Figure 8.14 contains a new version of
instr in which its assumption that it is passed a non-null string pointer is
made explicit with a call to **ASSERT**. If instr is accidentally passed a null
pointer, the useful error message

Assertion Failed: Null pointer parameter (line 11 of instr.c)

is printed. Although the program will still die with a run-time error when
the pointer is used, with **ASSERT** at least some indication of the problem is
given first. It is certainly more difficult to locate bugs when starting with
a potentially cryptic system message than it is with an error message from
a failed assertion. On some systems, when a program dies abruptly there
may be buffered output that has not been written. To remedy this situation, the appropriate library call to force out the remaining output should
be added to **ASSERT** (Chapter 12 and Appendix 6).

```
/*
 *  Is character in string?
 */
#include "boolean.h"

BOOLEAN instr(string,ch)
char *string, ch;
{
  BOOLEAN found = FALSE;        /* have we found it yet? */

  ASSERT(string, "Null pointer parameter");
  for (; *string != '\0' AND NOT found; string++)
    if (*string == ch)
      found = TRUE;
  return found;
}
```

FIGURE 8.14. Making an assumption explicit with the **ASSERT** macro.

MORE GENERAL COMPILE-TIME TESTS

The preprocessor can test conditions more general than name definition. The directive

    #if constant-expression

causes *constant-expression* to be evaluated and its value to be compared with zero (instead of being tested for definition) to determine the group of lines to process. Unlike testing for name definition, macro substitution can occur in the *constant-expression*.

One use of the simple form of this construction is to "comment out" sections of code that contain comments when the C compiler does not allow nested comments.

```
#if 0                          /* begin ignored section */
    lines-to-be-commented out  /* (lines that can contain comments) */
#endif                         /* end ignored section */
```

The *constant-expression* in this example is always zero, so the *lines-to-be-commented-out* are ignored.

Another common use of #if is to allow for different levels of debugging, with more output at each level. To do this, we define DEBUG as the desired integer level of debugging and use #ifs to test its value in order to choose the particular debugging statements to include. For example,

```
#if DEBUG >= 5
    printf("Debugging level %d: x = %s", DEBUG, x);
#endif
```

causes the printf to be included only if the debugging level is five or higher.

OTHER USEFUL PREPROCESSOR FEATURES

Two other features provided by some preprocessors are likely to become part of the language standard. The first, #elif, transforms preprocessor conditionals of the form shown in Figure 8.15a into the form shown in Figure 8.15b. Any #else immediately followed by an #if can be replaced with #elif and their associated #endif removed.

The other feature is the preprocessor function defined, which takes a *name* and returns a zero only if *name* is undefined. defined is appropriate when a piece of code should be processed if any name in a group of

```
#if constant-expression-1            #if constant-expression-1
  ...                                  ...
#else                                #elif constant-expression-2
#if constant-expression-2             ...
  ...                                #endif
#endif
#endif
```

(a) *Without* elif   (b) *With* elif

FIGURE 8.15. Simplifying conditionals with #elif.

names is defined. Figure 8.16 illustrates how defined and #elif can be combined by defining WORDLEN as the number of bits in a word. Despite their usefulness, only a few preprocessors support #elif and defined, and their use is nonportable.

There is one final preprocessor (actually, the compiler) directive, #line, which is used to tell the preprocessor the file name and line from which a line in its input was derived.

    #line   line-number   "filename"

If the file name is omitted from a #line, the current file name is assumed.

#line appears most frequently in C programs that have been generated or modified by other programs (*pre-preprocessors*) before they are seen by the preprocessor or compiler. Because line numbers referred to in a preprocessor or compiler error message may not correspond exactly to the line where the error occurred in the source file used to generate these programs, the pre-preprocessors use #line to make error messages refer to the correct lines in the original source file.

```
#if defined(PDP11)
#define WORDLEN 16              /* 16 bit words */
#elif defined(VAX) | defined(IBM370)
#define WORDLEN 32              /* 32 bit words */
#elif defined(INTERDATA)
#define WORDLEN 36              /* 36 bit words */
#endif
```

FIGURE 8.16. Defining the number of bits in a word—simplified using #elif and defined.

C H A P T E R   9

ARRAYS
AND POINTERS
REVISITED

So far, our programs have needed only simple, one-dimensional arrays with integer, character, and real elements. In this chapter we introduce two-dimensional arrays and arrays of pointers, concentrating on the use of pointers to gain performance improvements. The chapter concludes with a look at C's declaration syntax—how variables and functions are declared to take advantage of the rich combinations of arrays, pointers, and functions available as data types in the language. This chapter is rather detailed, but careful study will result in program efficiency and a thorough understanding of important fine points of the language.

TWO-DIMENSIONAL ARRAYS

We declare two-dimensional arrays by enclosing the bounds of each dimension separately in brackets. The declaration

```
#define  MAX_STUDENTS    20
#define  MAX_TESTS       10
         . . .
int  scores[MAX_STUDENTS][MAX_TESTS];
```

defines **scores** to be a two-dimensional array of **ints** containing a total of 200 elements. As with one-dimensional arrays, the array name is a pointer to the first element of the array, or, more correctly for two-dimensional arrays, a pointer to the first *row* of the array.

It is conventional to think of the first dimension as representing the rows of a matrix and the second as the columns, so **scores** has been declared to contain 20 rows of 10 columns each. One use of **scores** is to contain the test scores for students in a class, with each row corresponding to the test scores for a particular student and each column corresponding to the scores for a particular test.

Figure 9.1 shows the indexing scheme used to access the elements of **scores**. As might be expected, elements of two-dimensional arrays are accessed using double sets of brackets. As with one-dimensional arrays, each dimension of the array is indexed from zero to its maximum size minus one; the first index selects the row, and the second index selects the column within that row. Thus, the legal indexes for **scores** range from **scores[0][0]** to **scores[19][9]**.

To illustrate conventional two-dimensional array use, Figure 9.2 contains a function, **print_scores**, that prints **scores'** elements, one row per

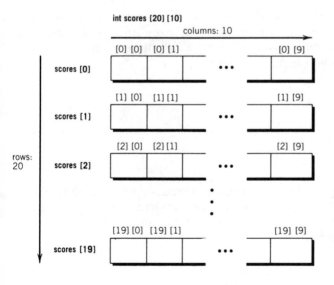

FIGURE 9.1. Elements of a two-dimensional array viewed as a matrix.

```
/*
 * Print scores, one student per line.
 */
void print_scores(s, max)
int  s[][MAX_TESTS],
     max;
{
  int    student, test;

  for (student = 0; student < max ; putchar('\n'), student++)
    for (test = 0; test < MAX_TESTS; test++)
      printf("%d ", s[student][test]);
}
```

FIGURE 9.2. Print test scores using conventional array subscripting.

line. Each output line contains the test scores for a particular student. print_scores assumes that **MAX_TESTS** is defined as the number of tests (or columns). Two variables, student and test, are used to index the array; student selects the row and test selects the element within that row.

Notice in Figure 9.2 that the two-dimensional array parameter is declared in a different way from its one-dimensional counterpart. Because the compiler must know the number of columns in each row to subscript the array's elements correctly, the number of columns (the second dimension) must be specified in the array's parameter declaration. But as with one-dimensional arrays, when a two-dimensional array is passed as a parameter, only a pointer is passed (a pointer to the first *row*). This pointer is used in accessing array elements.

PROGRAMMING PRACTICE

9-1. Write a function, read_scores, that reads in a student identification number, followed by the student's test scores. The student number should be used to select the row in the array. Implement an appropriate error-testing and flagging mechanism.

9-2. Write a function, print_tests, that prints out the elements of scores, one column per line. Each line of output should contain all of the scores for a particular test.

INTERNAL REPRESENTATION OF TWO-DIMENSIONAL ARRAYS

To understand why the second dimension is needed but the first is not when a two-dimensional array is passed to a function, we need to understand the internal representation of two-dimensional arrays (see diagram below). The values of these arrays are stored in "row major" order. That is, the elements of row zero are stored consecutively in memory, then the elements of row one, and so on. In a reference to a two-dimensional array element, such as scores[10][5], the compiler calculates the element's position from the two subscripts and its knowledge of the number of columns in each row. With scores declared as

```
int scores[20][10];
```

we find scores[10][5] at &scores[0][0] plus all the elements in rows zero through nine, plus five; that is, at

```
&scores[0][0] + 10 × 10 × sizeof(int) + 5
```

Therefore, if scores[0][0] is at location 1000 and we are using a four-byte-per-int machine, this is $1000 + 10 \times 10 \times 4 + 5 = 1405$. Generalizing, scores[i][j] is found at

```
&scores[0][0] + i × 10 × sizeof(int) + j = 1000 + 40i + j.
```

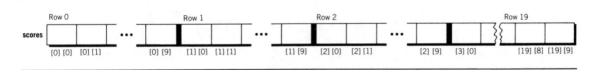

PROGRAMMING PRACTICE

9-3. Since the elements of any two-dimensional array are stored consecutively, how can the sum of scores' elements be computed without using two-dimensional subscripting? (*Hint*: Remember that scores is stored as a one-dimensional array, with &scores[0][0] pointing to its first element and &scores[19][9] pointing to its last one.) Write a function to do this task.

INITIALIZING TWO-DIMENSIONAL ARRAYS

Like their one-dimensional counterparts, static and external multidimensional arrays may be initialized by following their declaration with a list of values enclosed in braces. For example,

```
static int board[3][3] = {1, 1, 1, 2, 2, 2, 3, 3, 3};
```

initializes the elements in **board**'s first row to one, those in its second row to two, and those in its third row to three. By surrounding the elements in the row with braces, two-dimensional arrays can also be initialized row by row, making the declaration

```
static int board[3][3] = {{1,1,1}, {2,2,2}, {3,3,3}};
```

equivalent to the previous one.

Because we often think of two-dimensional arrays as a matrix, we usually format array initializers to show the two-dimensional structure. Also, since the size and structure of the array can be determined from the values in the initializer, the first dimension of the array (that is, the number of rows) need not be specified. The previous declaration and initialization of **board** can also be written as

```
static int  board[][3] =
            {
                {1, 1, 1},
                {2, 2, 2},
                {3, 3, 3}
            };
```

If values are missing in an initializer, they are set to zero, so there is no need to supply values for all elements in the array. The declaration

```
static int board[3][3] = {{1,1}, {1} };
```

initializes the first two elements of the first row and the first element in the second row to one, initializing all other elements to zero. Unfortunately, there is no way to initialize only selected rows. The simplest way to initialize rows that do not require initialization themselves, but precede rows that do, is to initialize their first element to zero.

PROGRAMMING PRACTICE

9-4. Write a function to determine whether a particular square two-dimensional array is a magic square (all rows, columns, and diagonals add up to the same value).

9-5. Write a function to determine whether a particular square two-dimensional array is an identity matrix (ones on the diagonal, zeros everywhere else).

POINTERS AND TWO-DIMENSIONAL ARRAYS

As we discovered in Chapter 4, all array accesses are automatically converted to an equivalent pointer expression. Whenever an element in a two-dimensional array is referenced with two subscripts, C converts the array access into an equivalent pointer expression. The expression scores[i][j], for example, is converted into the equivalent pointer expression

    ((scores + i) + j)

Figure 9.3 illustrates how this somewhat bizarre-looking expression obtains the value of scores[i][j] and the rest of this section should clarify why that expression works and how accessing two-dimensional array elements with pointers can give us increased efficiency.

We will illustrate the relationship between pointers and two-dimensional arrays by rewriting a function **test_avg** to use pointers to traverse the array rather than two-dimensional array subscripting. In Figure

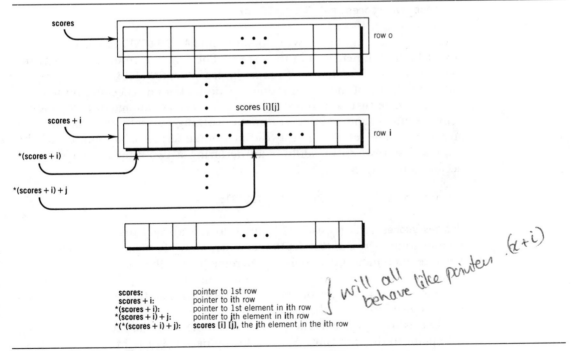

FIGURE 9.3. Using *(*(scores + i) + j) to access scores[i][j].

```
/*
 * Compute the average of the values in a given column of a 2D array.
 */
double test_avg(scores, max, n)
int scores[][MAX_TESTS],              /* 2D array with "MAX_TESTS" columns */
    max,                              /* number of rows in "scores" */
    n;                                /* column we want to average */
{
  double sum = 0.0;                   /* column total */
  int    i;                           /* row index */

  for (i = 0; i < max; i++)
    sum += scores[i][n];
  return sum / max;
}
```

FIGURE 9.4. Computing the average of a given *column* of a two-dimensional array using conventional array subscripting.

9.4 we write it using conventional array subscripting. test_avg computes the average of values in a given column of an array, and is called by

```
test_avg(scores, MAX_STUDENTS, n);
```

where n is the column we wish to sum and MAX_STUDENTS is the number of rows (the first dimension) in the array. The function returns a double, the average of the nth column. (n must be less than MAX_TESTS, but for generality and clarity of the presentation, we do no bounds checking on it.)

To rewrite test_avg to use pointers, we take advantage of array names being pointers, and pointer arithmetic working correctly with pointers to any type. The name of a two-dimensional array is a pointer to the array's first row, so in addition to declaring a two-dimensional array, a declaration such as

```
int scores[MAX_STUDENTS][MAX_TESTS];
```

defines scores as a (constant) pointer to the array's first row; that is, a pointer to an array of MAX_TESTS elements, as we first noted in Figure 9.1. Because incrementing a pointer increments by the size of the thing it points to, we can traverse a two-dimensional array by initializing a pointer to the first row of the array and incrementing the pointer each time we need to get to the next row.

Let us use row_ptr as the pointer to the next row of scores, initializing it to point to the first row. We do this by declaring row_ptr

```
int (*row_ptr)[MAX_TESTS] = scores;  /* pointer to first row of SCORES */
```

That is, `row_ptr` is a pointer to an array of **MAX_TESTS** ints. The parentheses around *`row_ptr` are necessary because * has lower precedence than []. Without the parentheses, as in

        int *row_ptr[MAX_TESTS];

we would be declaring `row_ptr` as an array of **MAX_TESTS** elements, each a pointer to an `int`.

When we increment `row_ptr` (by `row_ptr++`), the incrementing is done in units of the size of each row of `scores`, making `row_ptr` point to the next row. Since `row_ptr` points to a particular row, (*`row_ptr`)[n] chooses the nth element in the row, as shown in Figure 9.5. All we need to do is initialize `row_ptr` to point to the first row, then loop by incrementing `row_ptr`.

The pointer indexing version of **test_avg** is shown in Figure 9.6. We

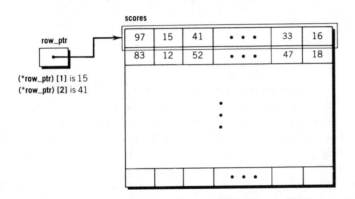

after **row_ptr + +**

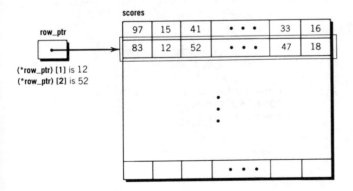

FIGURE 9.5. `row_ptr` initialized to point to the first row of `scores`. Incrementing `row_ptr` causes it to point to the next row of `scores`.

```
/*
 * Compute the average of the scores on a given test — POINTER VERSION.
 */
double test_avg(scores, max, n)
int scores[][MAX_TESTS],                  /* pointer to array's first row */
    max,                                  /* number of rows in array */
    n;                                    /* column to sum */
{
  double sum = 0.0;                       /* column total */
  int    i,                               /* row index */
         (*row_ptr)[MAX_TESTS] = scores;  /* pointer to first row */

  for (i = 0; i < max; i++)
    sum += (*row_ptr++)[n];
  return sum / max;
}
```

FIGURE 9.6. Computing the average of a column of a two-dimensional array using a pointer to access the array elements.

compiled and ran both of these versions on a DEC VAX 11/750 using an array with 10,000 rows. The direct array indexing version took 0.57 seconds and the pointer version took 0.42 seconds, a savings of 26 percent.

We can use pointers to process the rows as well as the columns. Figure 9.7 is a routine that computes the average of each *row* using pointers.

```
/*
 * Compute the average score of a student (row) using a pointer
 * to the given row.
 */
double student_avg (scores, n)
int     scores[][MAX_TESTS],           /* 2D array of student scores */
        n;                             /* the row to average */
{
  int     *col_ptr = &scores[n][0];    /* pointer to first element */
  long    sum = 0;                     /* total so far */
  int     i;                           /* row index */

  for (i = 0; i < MAX_TESTS; i++)
    sum += *col_ptr++;
  return (double) sum / MAX_TESTS;
}
```

FIGURE 9.7. Compute the average of a row using a pointer to access the individual row values.

Its operation is even simpler than that of Figure 9.6. Again we declare the argument scores to be a two-dimensional array, and again we do not need to specify the size of the first dimension. Within the function, we use a pointer (called col_ptr) that points to the individual items (columns) in each *row*. Since it is pointing to individual ints, we declare it as a pointer to int and initialize it to point to the first element in row n of scores:

```
int   *col_ptr = &scores[n][0];
```

Then we march col_ptr through the elements of the given row, summing by adding the pointed-to value to sum:

```
sum += *col_ptr++;
```

PROGRAMMING PRACTICE

9-6. Write a function, print_reverse, that prints the values in an array in reverse order, last row first and first row last. First, write it using the usual array subscripting; then rewrite it so that the rows are indexed with a pointer. Finally, rewrite it so that all elements are indexed with pointers. Which of the three versions is the fastest?

9-7. Write a function, sort_scores, that takes two arguments: scores, a two-dimensional array of ints, and n, the column to sort on. The array should be sorted so that the *n*th column is sorted from low to high.

ARRAYS OF POINTERS—RAGGED ARRAYS

In two-dimensional arrays, the same number of elements is contained in each row. But if we use arrays of pointers, we can create arrays with rows of varying lengths, called *ragged arrays*.

One common and important use of ragged arrays is in defining a table of strings. Instead of making each entry in the table a fixed number of characters, we can make it a pointer to a string of varying length. By supplying a list of character strings, the compiler initializes the elements of an array of pointers. For example,

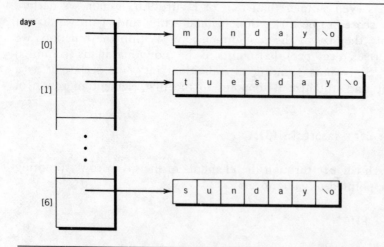

FIGURE 9.8. Compile-time initialization of an array of character strings.

```
static char *days[] =
            {
                    "monday",
                    "tuesday",
                    "wednesday",
                    "thursday",
                    "friday",
                    "saturday",
                    "sunday"
            };
```

declares **days** to be an array of seven pointers to characters, allocates space for each of the listed string constants, and assigns to each element of **days** a pointer to the corresponding string. The result of this declaration is shown in Figure 9.8. The compiler determines the number of elements in **days**, allocating enough space for the required number of pointers and allowing us to omit the subscript from the declaration.

The elements of an array of pointers are accessed in the same way as elements of an array of any other type. Figure 9.9 contains a function that is passed a table of character strings, along with the number of entries in the table, and prints the pointed-to strings, one per line. The printing is done by passing **printf** the next table entry, **table[i]**, a pointer to a character string.

An element in an array of pointers can be used as if it were a pointer to the first element in a row of a two-dimensional array, allowing us to use two-dimensional array subscripting even though **table** was declared to

```
/*
 *  Print a table of character strings, one per line.
 */
void print_tab(table, n)
char *table[];                    /* table of pointers to strings */
int  n;                           /* number of elements in the table */
{
  int   i;

  for (i = 0; i < n; i++)
    printf("%s\n", table[i]);
}
```

FIGURE 9.9. Print a table of n character strings, one per line.

be a one-dimensional array. The type of **table** is "array of pointers to char." **table[0]** is the first character pointer in the array. Adding one to **table[0]** gives a pointer to the second element in the row. More generally, **table[i] + j** is a pointer to the *j*th character in the string pointed to by **table[i]**. To access the *j*th character, we write either ***(table[i] + j)**, or the equivalent, **table[i][j]**, as shown in Figure 9.10. For example, since **table[0]** is a pointer to **monday**, we can access the **'n'** by **table[0][2]**.

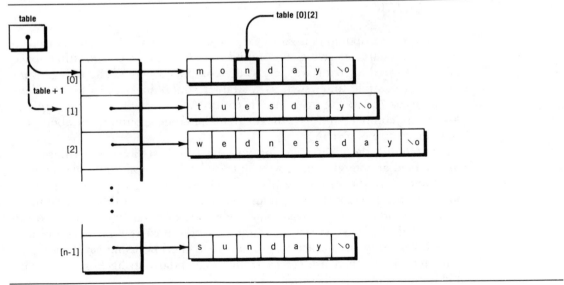

FIGURE 9.10. Accessing an individual character using an array of pointers to character strings.

PROGRAMMING PRACTICE

9-8. Write a function, `print_tab_len`, that prints the length of each character string in a table of character strings.

9-9. Write a function, `reverse_tab`, that reverses each of the strings in a table of character strings. (*Hint*: Use `strrev` from Chapter 7 to reverse the individual strings.)

9-10. Using normal array subscripting, write a function

```
search_tab(char_tab, target)
```

that takes two arguments—a table of character strings, `char_tab`, and a character string, `target`. The function searches `char_tab` for `target` and returns a pointer to the matching string in the table. If `target` is not in the table, `NULL` is returned.

9-11. Write a function, `month_name`, that takes a single-integer argument and returns a pointer to the associated month name. The month names should be kept in a `static` table of character strings local to the function.

DYNAMIC STRING ALLOCATION

In the arrays of pointers used so far, each array element was initialized to point to a character string at compile time. The task of allocating space for the pointed-to string was left to the compiler when all the strings were known at compile time, such as for tables containing strings for the days of the week (as in Figure 9.8). In contrast, if the table's entries are not known at compile time, we have to make some assumptions about the maximum size of a string.

Extending the idea of storing varying length static strings (those that are defined at compile time), we want to write a program that allows us to read and store the strings by placing a pointer to the string into the next location in an array of string pointers. One way to do this is to define a two-dimensional array of `chars` and copy the newly entered string into the next location. If `nxt_string` is a pointer to the next row in the array and `line` is an array of characters, we can read the line using `get_line` (from Chapter 4) and then use `strcpy` from the standard string library to copy the string, somewhat like this:

```
char line[MAXLINE],          /* the input line */
     strtbl[NLINES][MAXLINE], /* array of NLINES by MAXLINE */
     (*nxt_string)[MAXLINE] = strtbl;  /* ptr to an array of MAXLINE chars */
int  nchars;                 /* returned from "get_line" */
     . . .
nchars = get_line(line, MAXLINE);
strcpy (*nxt_string++, line);
     . . .
```

But this is unsatisfactory for one important reason: *each* row of the array is the same length, large enough to hold the maximum-length string. Since most strings are shorter than the maximum, we waste space in each row.

Instead, we use a technique similar to that shown in Figure 9.8. strtbl will be an array of pointers to char, and each string will be the exact length needed. We perform this feat by using a predefined function from the standard library—that is, we ask the operating system to give us a block of storage large enough to hold the string.

The function used to do this is malloc (for memory allocation). malloc takes a single argument, the number of characters of storage needed (type unsigned int), and returns a pointer (type char *) to a block at least as big as requested, with all alignment constraints satisfied. If there is not enough space, malloc returns the NULL pointer, defined in the include file *stdio.h*. We can use malloc because get_line returns the number of characters entered, and this is the amount of space we need (we need to add one because get_line does not count the trailing null). Figure 9.11 shows how malloc returns a pointer to a block of storage.

Using malloc is simple. We read the line, request the needed size, assign the pointer to the newly allocated storage returned by malloc, and

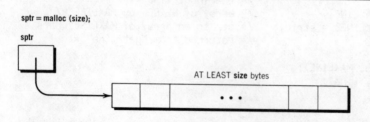

```
sptr = malloc (size);
```

FIGURE 9.11. A call to malloc returns a block of at least the requested size.

```
/*
 * Read strings and keep a pointer to them in a string table.
 */
#include <stdio.h>
#include <strings.h>            /* may be differently named */

#define  MAXLINE     80        /* chars per line */
#define  NLINES      100       /* lines to store */

main()
{
  int   i = 0, j,              /* indexes into "strtbl" array */
        nchars;                /* number of chars read */
  char  line[MAXLINE],         /* current input line */
        *malloc(),             /* always declare malloc */
        *sptr,                 /* pointer to block returned from malloc */
        *strtbl[NLINES];       /* string table — array of pointers to strings */

  while ((nchars = get_line(line, MAXLINE)) != EOF &&      /* get input lines */
         (sptr = malloc((unsigned) nchars + 1)) != NULL)  /* until EOF or no memory */
    {
      strcpy (sptr, line);     /* copy to space pointed to by "sptr" */
      strtbl[i++] = sptr;      /* copy pointer into the array */
    }
  if (sptr == NULL)            /* malloc has failed */
    printf("\nOut of internal storage.  Here's what you've got so far:\n");
  putchar('\n');
  for (j = 0; j < i; j++)      /* print table, one entry per line */
    printf ("%s\n", strtbl[j]);
}
```

FIGURE 9.12. A program that uses dynamically allocated space for arbitrary length strings (up to 80 characters).

then copy the input line to the pointed-to space. We also want to be sure that we declare malloc properly; it is a function returning char *.

```
char *malloc(),                      /* always declare malloc */
      *sptr,                         /* ptr to block returned from malloc */
      *strtbl[NLINES];               /* table of pointers to strings */
int   i=0, nchars;
      . . .
nchars = get_line(line, MAXLINE);    /* get a line, return chars read */
sptr = malloc((unsigned) nchars + 1);
if (sptr != NULL)                    /* test return from malloc */
{
  strcpy(sptr, line);                /* copy to space pointed to by "sptr" */
  strtbl[i++] = sptr;                /* put pointer into the array */
}
      . . .                          /* continue */
```

If malloc fails (which can certainly occur in small microcomputers but is unlikely in large address-space machines), we have to decide what to do on a case-by-case basis. Figure 9.12 is a program that reads strings (until end of file), allocating space using malloc. The string is copied into the newly allocated space, and a pointer to the string is placed in the next location in the string table, building on the program fragment above. In this program, when malloc fails, we stop reading input, print a warning, and then print the contents of the string table. We have coded the test of the return from malloc a little more compactly than in the previous example, doing the malloc within the while loop's condition, but the result is the same: if we run out of dynamic space, we stop what we are doing and print what we have. (malloc is usually written on top of an operating system utility; in UNIX this is sbrk. Managing pools of dynamic memory is an important topic in computer science practice, which we cannot hope to go into detail here.)

PROGRAMMING PRACTICE

9-12. Write a program, *tail*, that prints the last n lines of its input, using the program in Figure 9.12 as a model (n is a program constant). Make reasonable assumptions about the maximum line length and the maximum number of lines in the input (using the constants MAXLINE and NLINES, respectively). Be sure to test the return from malloc and decide on a suitable policy should it fail.

9-13. Write a program, *reverse*, that prints its input in reverse order; the first lines read are the last lines printed. Make sure that *reverse* does something reasonable if there are more lines in the input than were expected or if the program runs out of memory.

TYPE DECLARATIONS

We have introduced several new data types in this chapter (pointers to arrays and arrays of pointers) and have shown how to declare variables of these types. We now conclude this chapter by showing how to declare arbitrarily-complex data types, such as arrays of pointers to functions and pointers to functions returning pointers to functions.

DECLARATORS

Type declarations consist of a basic type followed by a *declarator*, and they specify the type of the identifier contained in the declarator. For example, in the declaration

```
char (*funcptr)();
```

char is the basic type and (*funcptr)() is the declarator. funcptr is the identifier contained in the declarator, and it is declared as a pointer to a function returning a character.

The simplest possible declarator is an identifier and is used to declare a variable of one of the basic types.

```
char x;                    /* a character */
```

Prefacing the identifier with * declares a pointer; following the identifier with () declares a function; and following the identifier with [] declares an array.

```
char *ptr;                 /* pointer to a char */
char tab[MAX];             /* array of chars */
char func();               /* function returning a char */
```

We can declare more complex types, such as pointers to functions and arrays of pointers, by combining the pieces used to form the previous declarators. For example,

```
char *tab[MAX];            /* an array of pointers to char */
char *func();              /* function returning pointer to char */
char (*func_ptr)();        /* pointer to function returning char */
char (*row_ptr)[10];       /* pointer to an array of 10 characters */
```

When declarators are combined, * has lower precedence than either () or

[], so to declare a pointer to an array or function, parentheses must be used to override the normal precedence.

We can declare even more complex types. To do so, it is helpful to think of the English description of an identifier's type as being composed of several pieces. Each piece of the description is either a basic type, "an array of," "a pointer to," or "a function returning." Suppose, for example, that we want to declare a <u>table of pointers to functions</u>. (Such a table could contain pointers to each of the various functions we want gen_points (Chapter 6) to compute points for. The plotting program then becomes a simple loop that accesses each array element and calls gen_points with it.) We break its description into:

an array of   pointers to   functions returning   doubles

The final piece is the base type of the identifier.

To compose the declarator, we work through the description from left to right, examining each piece, and finding the C declarator for a variable with that type. Once we have all of the declarators we again work from left to right, substituting each declarator for the identifier in the declarator to its right, finishing when only a single declarator remains. Figure 9.13

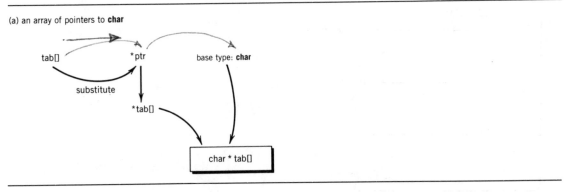

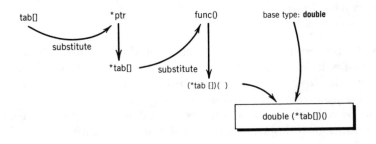

FIGURE 9.13. Composing complex declarations.

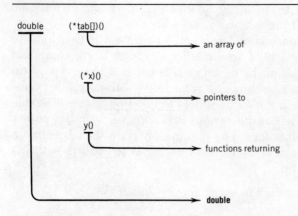

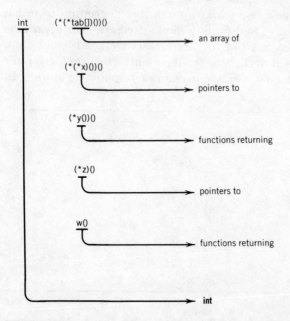

FIGURE 9.14. Understanding complex declarations.

illustrates the process for several different type declarations. Because the precedence of * is less than that of either () or [], pointer declarators must be parenthesized when they are substituted in another declarator.

Since we can compose arbitrarily-complex type declarations, we should also be able to read and understand them. The process used for generating an English description from a declarator is illustrated in Figure 9.14. We determine an identifier's type by finding the type of its innermost declarator, writing it down, substituting a new identifier for the innermost declarator, and repeating the process for the declarator result-ing from the substitution. We have determined the identifier's type when the resulting declarator is a single identifier. The innermost declarator is the identifier and an immediately following [] or (), or, if neither of these is present, an immediately preceding *. Any parentheses around the innermost declarator can be ignored once its type is determined.

Although the compiler can process arbitrarily-complex declarations, most people cannot. To keep declarations readable, it is a good idea to use **typedef** when declaring types more complex than arrays of pointers and pointers to arrays. The following is a more readable way to declare our table of pointers to functions returning **doubles**.

```
typedef double (*PFD)();   /* PFD - ptr to function returning a double */
...
static PFD funcptr[] =     /* A table of pointers to functions */
{
   sin, cos, log, tan
};
```

PROGRAMMING PRACTICE

9-14. Modify the main program for **gen_points** to compute points for each func-tion pointed to in a table of pointers to functions. First, write the pro-gram using simple array indexing for the table of pointers. Then, modify the program to use a pointer to traverse the table. That pointer is a pointer to a pointer to a function returning a **double**.

9-15. Write a function that walks through a table of pointers to functions, exe-cuting each function in turn, until one of them returns zero or all of the functions have been executed.

9-16. How do you declare a pointer to a pointer to a function returning a pointer to an **int**? An array of pointers to pointers to characters? A pointer to an array of 10 integers?

9-17. What are the types of the following identifiers?

```
void (*funcptr[100])();
double *(*funcptr)();
int   (*((*funcptr)()))[10];
```

SPECIFYING TYPES IN CASTS

We have learned that when casting a value from one type to another, the type to cast to must be specified. Specifying a type in a cast is done similarly to specifying a type in a declaration, except that the identifier is omitted. For example,

```
(int *) x;
```

casts x into a pointer to an integer because

```
int *name;
```

declares a pointer to an integer.

As a more complex example, consider passing a null pointer to a function that expects a pointer to a function returning int. For the parameter-passing mechanism to work correctly, the null pointer must be cast to a pointer to a function returning int. The cast is obtained by writing the declaration for a pointer to a function returning int,

```
int (*func_ptr)();
```

removing the identifier, and enclosing the type specifier that is left in parentheses:

```
(int (*)()) NULL
```

Because type specifiers for casts, such as the one shown above, can be difficult to read, it is more understandable to use **typedef**:

```
typedef int (*PFI)();        /* pointer to function returning int */
    . . .
(PFI) NULL;
```

PROGRAMMING PRACTICE

9-18. How would you cast an integer into a pointer to an array of pointers to functions returning int?

CHAPTER 10

CONSTRUCTED DATA TYPES

We have already extensively used one type of programmer-constructed data type—arrays. However, a limitation of arrays is that all elements must be the same underlying type (or at least each must be a type that requires the same amount of storage). In this chapter we examine three new ways of representing collections of values—enumeration types, structures, and unions. We use structures to build a small data base of employee names, numbers, and addresses. We conclude by using all of C's constructed data types in the implementation of a lexical scanner, a collection of functions that can be used to help parse a calculator's input.

ENUMERATION TYPES

When a variable can have only one of a set of values, we may use the *enumeration type* facility to specify the possible values of the variable. We define an enumeration type by giving the keyword **enum** followed by an optional *type designator* and a brace-enclosed list of values.

An enumeration type that allows only the days of the week is defined by

```
enum Days
{
    sunday, monday, tuesday, wednesday, thursday, friday, saturday
};
```

211

Internally, these are defined as constants with an integer value equal to their position in the list: sunday is zero, monday is one, and so on. Of course, these can also be defined with #defines, but enum is an easier, more compact method.

The values of an enumeration type may not be numerical; they follow the rules for identifiers. We can, however, associate a specific integer value with a value of an enumeration type by following the type value with an equal sign and an integer:

```
enum Days
{
    tuesday = 2, wednesday, monday = 1, thursday = 4,
    friday, saturday, sunday
};
```

The associated integer values continue from the assignment. The previous declaration associates tuesday with two, wednesday with three, friday with five, and so on.

This declaration of an enumeration type defines a new programmer-constructed type called enum Days. To declare values of this type, we follow the type designator (enum Days) with the variable names.

```
enum Days day1, day2, all_days[7];
```

After this declaration, day1 and day2 are type enum Days and all_days is an array of seven enum Days. They may take on only the values in the definition of the type. The following assignments are legal:

```
day1 = monday; day2 = tuesday; all_days[0] = sunday;
```

while assignments such as

```
day1 = 1.0; day2 = 5; all_days[0] = 'A';
```

are considered illegal.

Enumerated types are not integers; to use them as integers, we must first cast them to int. Figure 10.1 is a program illustrating the declaration and use of an enumeration type. The main program assigns an initial value to day1, the day after it to day2, and the day before it to day3. We use two functions to determine the day after and the day before. The first function, day_after, takes an argument of type enum Days and returns the day after (modulo the number of days). For example, day_after(saturday) is sunday and day_after(sunday) is monday. We compute the next day by converting the current day to an int and then adding one, modulo the number of days in a week. We then cast this result

```
/*
 * Illustrate use of enumeration types.
 */
#define  NUMDAYS    7

enum Days
{
    sunday, monday, tuesday, wednesday, thursday, friday, saturday
};

main ()
{
  enum Days     day1, day2, day3,
                day_before(), day_after();
  void          print_day();

  day1 = sunday;
  day2 = day_after(day1);
  day3 = day_before(day1);

  printf("The day after "), print_day(day1);
  printf(" is: "), print_day(day2);
  printf("\nAnd the day before is: "), print_day(day3);
  putchar('\n');
}


/*
 *  Return the successor of the given day.
 */
enum Days day_after(day)
enum Days day;
{
    return (enum Days) (((int) day + 1) % NUMDAYS);
}
```

→ Convert *bad* to *day.*

```
/*
 *  Return the predecessor of the given day.
 */
enum Days day_before(day)
enum Days day;
{
  int prev;

  prev = ((int) day — 1) % NUMDAYS;
  return (prev < 0) ? (enum Days) (NUMDAYS — 1) : (enum Days) prev;
}
```

(continued)

```
/*
 *  Print the string corresponding to the day.
 */
void print_day(day)
enum Days    day;
{
  int          day_index = (int) day;
  static char  *days[] =
  {
    "sun", "mon", "tues", "wednes", "thurs", "fri", "satur"
  };

  if (day_index < 0 || day_index >= NUMDAYS)
    printf ("**ERROR**");
  else
    printf ("%sday", days[day_index]);
}
```

FIGURE 10.1. Sample program illustrating enumeration types.

back to the appropriate type, enum Days. The cast converts the integer zero back to sunday, one back to monday, and so on.

The other function, day_before, is similar, returning the day before its argument. We have to be careful, however, that we do not take the modulus of a negative number. The only time a negative number occurs is when we find the predecessor of sunday (zero), in which case we should return the enum Days cast of six, or saturday. We can do this by testing specifically for sunday or by testing the sign of the result of the arithmetic. We chose the latter for no strong reason.

We use enumeration types because they allow for more descriptive names and for even greater separation of functionality from the underlying implementation than defined constants. Although they do not have the full range of uses that enumerated types in other languages have, they are still useful. One useful application of enumeration types is in error returns from functions. A function can return a value that indicates the nature of an error. One specific example is an input validator that can return an enumeration type, indicating such errors as values less than some minimum, values greater than some maximum, and so on, as the following program fragment shows. Another function translates the enumerated value into an error message, as in print_day in Figure 10.1.

```
enum Errors
{
  vallow, valhigh, valok,
};
```

```
      . . .
enum Errors verify(value, min, max)          /* validate "value" */
long  value, min, max;
{
  if (value < min)
    return vallow;
  if (value > max)
    return valhigh;
  else
    return valok;
}
```

PROGRAMMING PRACTICE

10-1. The functions day_after and day_before in Figure 10.1 are quite short. Rewrite them as macros. Extend these macros into more general predecessor and successor macros of any enumerated type (assuming that the values of the enumeration type represent the integers continuously from 0 to $n - 1$).

10-2. Write an input validator for a payroll program. The validator should check for hours and rate of pay within bounds. This requires writing a variation of print_day from Figure 10.1 to print an appropriate message for out-of-range values.

10-3. How can we define a boolean enumerated type? Is an enumerated boolean type preferrable to using typedef or #define?

STRUCTURES

If we need to combine data of different types into a single object, we cannot use an array. Instead, we use the data-packaging mechanisms of structures. We introduce and define structures here, and discuss their use more thoroughly in the next chapter. Structures are one way of making a programming language "extensible"; that is, defining complex data objects by packaging them together and giving them a new type name allows the language to operate on data types other than those originally defined in the language. It is a modern and powerful development in language and program design.

STRUCTURE DEFINITION

If we have different pieces of information that must be kept together as a single data record, we do so with a structure (similar, for example, to Pascal records). A structure consists of the keyword struct and the declarations of the names and data types that are part of the structure. In addition, we can give the structure a name and declare variables to be of the structure type.

As an example, a single data record in a personnel data base might consist of an employee number, name, and address. We can define a structure to hold this information by first declaring a new type, struct p_record, consisting of the three fields emp_number (a long), name, and address (character arrays)

```
struct p_record
{
    long    emp_number;
    char    name[MAX];
    char    address[MAX];
};
```

This looks like the following diagram:

struct	p_record
emp_number	long
name	array of char
address	array of char

Now that the type struct p_record has been defined, we can declare variables that have that type

```
struct p_record   next_person, old_person;
```

The name of the structure, p_record in this case, is called the *structure tag*. Remember, after these declarations, struct p_record is a type and next_person and old_person are variables. The type of next_person and old_person is "struct p_record."

FIELD SELECTION

Variables of a structure type are used as if they were an ordinary type; that is, we can read their values, assign to them, pass them as parameters to functions, and return them as values of a function. (Some compilers do not allow structures to be passed as arguments to functions or as the value of a function. In this case, we can use a pointer to the structure instead.) Since there are multiple fields in a structure, we need a means of selecting the appropriate one. To do this, we use the field selection operator '.'. We access the various fields by giving the variable name, the dot operator, and the appropriate field. Using the earlier declaration of the variable next_person, here is how we would assign values to the fields:

```
next_person.emp_number = 15263;
strcpy (next_person.name, "smallberg, dave");
strcpy (next_person.address, "1449 N. Capri Dr. Surf City, USA 07886");
```

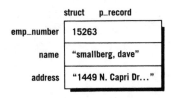

A field of a structure can be any type a variable can, including other structures and arrays. The field names are in a separate "name class" from those of variables, so that a <u>field name</u> can be the same as an existing variable name. The declaration

```
struct point
{
    long x, y;
} x;
```

is valid. We select the x field of **struct point** x in the normal way:

```
x.x = 1234;
```

ASSIGNING, INITIALIZING, AND COMPARING STRUCTURES

For assignment and comparison purposes, structures behave virtually the same as ordinary variables. That is, in addition to assigning to an individual field, we may assign to the entire structure. If **p1** and **p2** have both been declared as variables of the same structure type, the operations in Table 10.1 are valid.

Structures may be initialized at the time they are declared, with the same restrictions as for arrays; automatic structures may not be initialized, but statics and externals can be. If a structure is not specifically initialized, its fields are initialized in the same manner as if they were separately declared variables. That is, they may be initialized to zero (for

TABLE 10.1. Valid operations on structures.

Statement	Meaning
p1 = p2	Assign p2 to p1.
p1 == p2	Compare all fields of p1 and p2. Return one if they are equal, zero otherwise.
p1 != p2	Compare all fields of p1 and p2. Return one if they are not equal, zero otherwise.

statics and externals) or they may contain unknown random values for automatics. As always, we should initialize any variable before it is used.

To initialize the fields of a structure, specify each field's value in brackets after a variable of the structure type is declared. In this example, we have declared next_person to be a static struct p_record.

```
static struct p_record next_person =
{
  1234,                                    /* emp_number */
  "swenson, marcy",                        /* name */
  "7953 Jupiter Ave. L.A., CA. 90035"      /* address */
};
```

The emp_number field is initialized to 1234, the name field to "swenson, marcy," and the address field to "7953 Jupiter Ave. L.A., CA. 90035." Since these are string constants, they are automatically terminated with a null character.

STRUCTURES AS FUNCTION ARGUMENTS

Structures may be passed as arguments to functions. Unlike array names, which are always pointers to the start of the array, structure names are not pointer types. They are passed to functions by the usual parameter-passing mechanism: the entire structure is copied to the function. As a result, changes to a structure argument within a function are not reflected in changes in the actual parameter from the calling routine. This mechanism can be overridden, as with single-value parameters, by passing an address.

Some compilers do not allow us to pass structures as parameters. In this case, a pointer to a structure may always be passed, so that structures may still be used as function arguments or function values. It is faster to pass a pointer (since the structure does not have to be copied), so this is often done even when the compiler supports passing entire structures to functions. Figure 10.2 shows two versions of a small function that prints the fields of a struct p_record. The first version passes an entire structure and is called by

```
void print_struct (person)
struct p_record    person;
{
    printf("Employee:\t%ld\n", person.emp_number);
    printf("Name:\t%s\n",      person.name);
    printf("Address:\t%s\n",  person.address);
}
```

(a) Function `print_struct` *that works on a copy of the structure*

```
void print_struct (person_ptr)
struct p_record    * person_ptr;
{
    printf("Employee:\t%ld\n", (* person_ptr).emp_number);
    printf("Name:\t%s\n",      (* person_ptr).name);
    printf("Address:\t%s\n",  (* person_ptr).address);
}
```

(b) Function `print_struct` *that uses a pointer to a structure*

FIGURE 10.2. Two versions of a function that prints the fields of a structure. *(a)* The structure is copied to the function. *(b)* A pointer to the structure is passed to the function.

```
print_struct(next_record);
```

The second passes a pointer to the structure and is called by passing the address of the structure.

```
print_struct(&next_record);
```

Parentheses are needed when dereferencing the pointer to the structure because the dot field selection operator binds tighter (has higher precedence) than dereferencing.

The three `printf` statements in Figure 10.2*b* dereference the pointer to the structure, and then select the appropriate field. Dereferencing a pointer and then selecting a field of the pointed-to structure is so common that another shorthand notation is provided, a right arrow, made up of a minus sign and a "greater than" symbol: ->. The three `printf` statements in Figure 10.2*b* could also have been written

```
printf("Employee:\t%ld\n", person_ptr->emp_number);
printf("Name:\t%s\n",      person_ptr->name);
printf("Address:\t%s\n",  person_ptr->address);
```

The two forms are equivalent:

```
person_ptr->emp_number   is equivalent to   (* person_ptr).emp_number
```

PROGRAMMING PRACTICE

10-4. Complex numbers are defined as having a real and an imaginary part. Write a structure definition for a type **struct complex**, and write functions for the four mathematical operations add, subtract, multiply, and divide.

10-5. Define a structure type, **struct point**, for two-dimensional space coordinates (consisting of real values of x and y). Write a function, **distance**, that computes the distance between two **struct points**.

10-6. Define a structure type, **struct date**, that describes a date. It should have integer fields for month, day, and year. Write functions to print a date in a nice format, to determine if a date is valid, and to determine the number of days between two **struct dates**.

ARRAYS OF STRUCTURES

From earlier chapters, we know that we can have arrays of any type. Specifically, we can have arrays of structures and use them as we would any other array type. They may be initialized if they are external or static, but not if they are automatic.

We illustrate arrays of structures by defining a table of the personnel records in the previous section. Each element in the array is a **struct p_record** containing an **emp_number**, **name**, and **address** field. The array is declared just as we would any other array. We can declare **p_list** as an array of **SIZE struct p_records** with

```
struct p_record  p_list[SIZE];
```

Since p_list is an array, we use the usual array-accessing methods to reach individual records and then the dot field selection operator to reach fields. For example, to assign to the fields of p_list[2], we write

```
p_list[2].emp_number = 1234;
strcpy (p_list[2].name, "seagull, jonathan livingston");
strcpy (p_list[2].address, "pylon 87a, santa monica pier, california");
```

We can also initialize an array of structures at declaration time. The following declares an array of struct p_records and initializes its values. Because no size is given for the array, it is determined by the compiler based on the number of items in the declaration, six in this case.

```
static struct p_record    strange_people [] =
{
  {111, "bear, smokey",    "rocky mountains, u.s.a."},
  {112, "hood, robin",     "sherwood forest, england"},
  {113, "reagan, ronald",  "washington, d.c."},
  {114, "kay, david g.",   "tokyo, japan"},
  {115, "fairy, tooth",    "san francisco, ca."}
  {116, "quilici, tony",   "davis, ca."}
};
```

We choose an individual element in the array by indexing on the array name, such as strange_people[1], and we select an individual field using the dot selection operator: strange_people[1].name is ''hood, robin.''

If the entire array is passed to a function, we still select individual elements and fields in the usual way. To call a function print_all that prints the name field of the first n elements (indexed from 0 to n − 1) of an array of p_records, we invoke the function by

```
print_all(strange_people, n);
```

with print_all as follows:

```
/*
 *  Print the name field of each element in a structure.
 */
void print_all(parray, n)
struct p_record  parray[];
int  n;
{
  int    i;

  for (i = 0; i < n; i++)
    printf("Name: %s\n", parray[i].name);
}
```

Arrays of structures are commonly used in data base applications. Information is stored on the basis of some key or identification field, but this is only for ease of accessing. Relevant data are stored in other fields of the record. The beginnings of a mini-data base can be created by using the pieces we now develop. In Chapter 12 we will build on these ideas to create a more useful data base that keeps records on external files and uses an index to access individual records. For now, the data base is just an array of records. After it is built, we will query it interactively by entering employee identifications and returning the name and address.

lookup is a function that does just what its name suggests. It takes three arguments: the identification number we are looking for (id), the table (table), and the number of elements in the table (size). lookup returns a pointer to the desired record, or NULL if id is not in table.

We search table sequentially until we either go past the array's end or id matches the emp_number field of the array element. If there is a match, we return a pointer to the record. The complete function is shown in Figure 10.3.

We use lookup by setting its return to an appropriate pointer variable. If we want to look up an i.d. and print the associated name, we do something like:

```
if ((nextptr = lookup(id, personnel, number)) != NULL)
    printf("Name: %s\n", nextptr->name);
```

For more general use of the struct p_record data type, we change the data type definition slightly so that the name and address fields are pointers to char rather than arrays of char (we use malloc to get the space we need). That way we can have arbitrarily long names and addresses.

```
/*
 *  Look up an i.d. in an array of personnel records, returning a pointer
 *  to the record, if found, or NULL if it is not found.
 */
struct p_record *lookup (id, table, size)
long            id,                     /* the i.d. we're looking for */
struct p_record table[];                /* array of records */
int             size;                   /* the number of records in the array */
{
  int   i;                              /* index for searching "table" */

  for (i = 0; i < size && table[i].emp_number != id; i++)
        ;                               /* scan until too many, or a match */

  return (i == size) ? NULL : &table[i];
}
```

FIGURE 10.3. Function lookup that searches a data base for a given i.d.

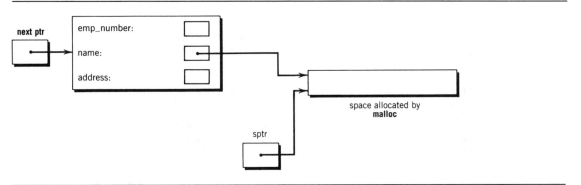

FIGURE 10.4. The name field of a new record points to the space allocated by malloc.

```
struct p_record
{
    long    emp_number;
    char   *name;
    char   *address;
};
```

Figure 10.5 uses earlier pieces, including lookup, to illustrate how such a simple data base is built and how the various array and structure elements are defined. The program is interesting because we are using dynamic storage allocation to get the space we need for the name and address fields of the next record. Using the new definition of a struct p_record, notice that the name and address fields are pointers to char, not fixed-size character arrays. Therefore, when a new name is entered (using get_line from Chapter 4), we copy it into the space allocated by malloc and then place the pointer to this space into the name field of the record. Then we do the same for the address field. Figure 10.4 shows how we place the pointer to the space.

SIZE OF STRUCTURES

A structure is a user-defined data type, but the space allocated when a structure variable is declared is known at compile time. The compile-time function sizeof returns the size in bytes of the structure type or structure variable. The *original* declaration of struct p_record consisted of three fields: a long employee number and two fixed size MAX character arrays. The expression

```
sizeof (struct p_record)
```

```
/*
 *  Program that initializes a data base (an array of structs), then
 *  interactively requests i.d.s, returning the record with the given i.d.
 */
#include <stdio.h>
#include <strings.h>


#define  MAX         80              /* max chars in a string */
#define  SIZE        100             /* max entries in the data base */
#define  ENDOFINPUT  -1              /* indicates end of input */


struct p_record                      /* individual personnel record */
{
    long    emp_number;
    char    *name;
    char    *address;
};


main ()
{
    struct p_record    personnel[SIZE],
                       *lookup(),
                       *nextptr;
    long               id;
    int                inpres, number = 0;
    char               line[MAX];


    while (init_record(&personnel[number++]))     /* get records */
        ;
    while (printf("\nID: "), get_line(line,MAX) != EOF)
        if (sscanf(line, "%ld", &id)
            printf("Bad ID...skipping\n");
        else if ((nextptr=lookup(id, personnel, number)) != NULL)
            printf("\nName: %s\nAddress: %s\n", nextptr->name, nextptr->address);
        else
            printf("\nID %ld not in data base.\n", id);
    }


/*
 * Initialize a record to values from the terminal.
 * Last entry must be -1.
 */
int init_record(rptr)
struct p_record *rptr;
{
    int     inpres;
    long    temp;
    char    *get_field();
    char    line[MAX];
```

```
      printf("Employee Number: ");
      if (get_line(line, MAX) != EOF && sscanf(line, "%ld", &temp) == 1
                && temp != ENDOFINPUT)
      {
        rptr->emp_number = temp;
        rptr->name = get_field("Name: ");
        rptr->address = get_field("Address: ");
        return rptr->name && rptr->address;
      }
      return 0;
}

/*
 *  Get a line of input, first writing out a prompt.
 */
char *get_field(prompt)
char *prompt;
{
    char     line[MAX],               /* next input line */
             *malloc(),
             *sptr;                   /* ptr to block from malloc */
    int      get_line(),
             length;                  /* returned from get_line */

    printf(prompt);
    if ((length = get_line(line, MAX)) != EOF &&
        (sptr = malloc((unsigned) length) + 1)) != NULL)
      strcpy (sptr, line);
    return sptr;
}
```

FIGURE 10.5. Complete mini-data base. The function get_line is from Chapter 4, and lookup is shown in Figure 10.3.

evaluates to a minimum of sizeof(long) plus the number of characters in the two arrays: 2 × MAX. On a four-byte-per-long machine using 80 for MAX, this is at least 168. We say "at least" because the compiler rounds up the space to force alignment as required by the underlying hardware. Alignment requires ints, longs, and other data types on most machines to begin on whole word boundaries rather than on individual byte boundaries.

Since pointers are always incremented in units of the pointed-to type, declaring a pointer to an array of structures and incrementing it to traverse the array works as expected. In Figure 10.6 we use a pointer to print the emp_number field of the first n elements (indexed from 0 to n − 1) of an array of struct p_records. Notice that the function print_emp_number is passed two arguments, an array of structures and the number of elements to print. Earlier we declared a static array of struct p_records called strange_people. If we want to use print_emp_number, we can define a

```
/*
 * Print the "emp_number" field of each record in "people" array.
 */
void print_emp_number (people, n)
struct p_record  people[];
int  n;
{
  struct p_record  *people_ptr = people,      /* ptr to next record */
                   *end_ptr = &people[n-1];   /* ptr to last record */

  for (; people_ptr <= end_ptr; people_ptr++)
    printf("I.D.: %ld\n", people_ptr -> emp_number);
}
```

FIGURE 10.6. A function that prints a single field of an array of structures. people_ptr is incremented in units of the size of each record.

constant that gives the number of elements in the array or we can use sizeof:

```
sizeof(strange_people) / sizeof(struct p_record)
```

This works because the size of strange_people is the total number of bytes the array requires. Each element in the array is sizeof(struct p_record) bytes.

PROGRAMMING PRACTICE

10-7. Modify lookup to use pointers in searching the table. Then modify lookup to do binary search instead of sequential search. Use insertion sort to keep the table sorted.

10-8. Modify gen_points from Chapter 6 to use one array of points rather than two arrays of ints. Write both pointer and array indexing versions.

10-9. Modify the histogram program in Chapter 5 to use a structure to pass its parameters.

10-10. Generalize insertion sort and binary search to work with any data type. (*Hint*: Pass them comparison functions and an offset within the structures to begin comparing.) Make sure to cast pointers appropriately.

UNIONS

Structures allow packaging together different types of values as a single unit. Another similar concept is the ability to store values of different types in a single location. Such a capability is called a *union*. A union may contain one of many different types of values (as long as only one is stored at a time).

We define a union by giving the keyword **union**, an optional union name, and the alternative names and types in the union. For example, we can declare a variable **value** to be a union type, called **Data**, which may contain either an **int** or a **double** with

```
union Data
{
    int      i;
    double   d;
} value;
```

We say that **value** is of type **union Data**. As with structures, we assign to the individual field of **value** by using the dot operator. To assign to the **int** field of **value**, we use **.i** and to the **double** field **.d**.

```
value.i = 1234;
value.d = -123.345;
```

Although a union contains enough storage for the largest type, it may contain only one value (here, either an **int** or a **double**) at a time; it is incorrect to assign to one field and then use another. A series of operations such as

```
value.d = -123.345;           /* assign to "d" field */
printf("%d\n", value.i);      /* print "i" field */
```

will produce anomalous results. Internally, unions are allocated storage to allow room for the largest field in the union. **value**, a **union Data**, will be allocated space sufficient for a **double** at all times.

PROGRAMMING PRACTICE

10-11. Create a **union** with one field for each of C's basic data types. Store various values in the **union** and print each of the fields.

CASE STUDY—A LEXICAL SCANNER FOR A CALCULATOR

We use a combination of structures, enumeration types, and unions in a lexical scanner designed to scan an input line and extract meaningful units (known as lexical units or tokens, hence the name *lexical scanner*). In a text passage, tokens are individual words, punctuation marks, and so on. In a C program, tokens are identifiers, keywords, numbers, operators, and special symbols (**{**, **(**, etc.). In a simple calculator the tokens are operands (numbers), operators, and parentheses.

We want the scanner to pick tokens from an input line and return the token type (either an *operator*, *operand*, *right-parenthesis*, or *left-parenthesis*) and its value (if an operator, the particular one, and if an operand, the numerical value). The scanner should also tell us if the next token is *not* one of the tokens that we expect; that is, it is *illegal*.

A natural representation for a token is a structure with two fields: one describing the token's type, the other giving its value. If the token is an operator, the value should be a character, ' + ', ' — ', '*', or whatever; if it is an operand, it should be a **long**. For parentheses, the token's type is enough and we don't need to store its value. Since a token is only one of these at a time, its value can be contained in a union. The token's type will be an enumerated type, either **operator**, **operand**, **left_paren**, or **right_paren**. In Figure 10.7 we define the data structures. We will assume that these definitions are kept in an include file *token.h* to be included in any program that uses tokens.

We use unions when data could be one of many types. Since we need to know which field of the union has a valid value (to avoid the problem of accessing the wrong union field), we often package a union in a structure, in which another field indicates the currently "active" union member. In this case, our structure is a **struct token**, and it has two fields. The **val** field is a union and may be either a **char** or a **long**. The **type** field is an enumerated type used to determine what field of the **val** field contains a valid value.

get_nxt_token is our tokenizer, and is shown in Figure 10.8, along with a main program that uses it to tokenize its input. Each time **get_nxt_token** is called, it gets a character and examines it to determine the type of token it is processing. If the character is in a table of operators, **get_nxt_token** sets the token's type to **operator** and remembers the character as its value. If the character is a digit, the token's type is **operand** and the character and any digits following it are converted to an integer, which is stored as the token's value. If the character is **EOF** or a right or left parenthesis, the token's type is set appropriately, but is not given a value. Otherwise, the token's type is assumed to be **illegal**.

We have reused pieces of earlier programs in building **get_nxt_token**. **fetch** and **unfetch** (Chapter 7) are used to read and unread characters. For efficiency, they have been rewritten as macros. We have borrowed

```
/*
 *    token.h: Data type definitions for the calculator.
 */
enum token_type                         /* token types */
{
    operator, operand, illegal, endoffile, left_paren, right_paren, semicolon
};

union item                              /* operators are chars, operands are longs */
{
    char        operator;
    long        operand;
};

struct token                            /* token type and its value */
{
    enum token_type     type;           /* "operator", "operand", and so on */
    union item          val;            /* operator: char; operand: long */
};
```

FIGURE 10.7. Data structures for a calculator lexical scanner.

```
/*
 * Main program using lexical scanner.
 */
#include "token.h"

main()
{
  struct token *nxt_token,
               *get_nxt_token();

  while (nxt_token = get_nxt_token(), nxt_token->type != endoffile)
    switch(nxt_token->type)
    {
      case illegal:     printf("Illegal input\n");
                        break;
      case operand:     printf("Operand: %ld\n", nxt_token->val.operand);
                        break;
      case operator:    printf("Operator: %c\n", nxt_token->val.operator);
                        break;
      case left_paren:  printf("Left parenthesis\n");
                        break;
      case right_paren: printf("Right parenthesis\n");
                        break;
    }
}
```

(a) *A main program using the scanner to break its input into tokens*

(*continued*)

```
/*
 *  The tokenizer.
 */
#include <stdio.h>
#include <ctype.h>
#include "token.h"


static int savechar;             /* character pushed back */
static int pushed = 0;           /* is anything pushed back? */


#define fetch()                  (pushed ? pushed--, savechar : getchar())
#define unfetch(c)               (pushed++, savechar = c)


/*
 * Is input an operator?  Uses sequential search.
 */
static int is_op(c)
int c;
{
  char *ptr = "+-*/%";                /* operators */


  while (*ptr && c != *ptr)           /* search for operator */
    ptr++;
  return *ptr;
}


/*
 *  Get the next token from the input.
 */
struct token *get_nxt_token()
{
  char          *malloc();
  struct token  *t = (struct token *) malloc(sizeof(struct token));
  int           c;
  long          num = 0;

  if (t)                              /* if we could allocate a token */
  {
    while ((c = fetch()) != EOF && isspace(c))
      ;                               /* skip over white space */
    if (c == EOF)                     /* end of file */
      t->type = endoffile;
    else if (c == '(')                /* left paren */
      t->type = left_paren;
    else if (c == ')')                /* right paren */
      t->type = right_paren;
    else if (c == ';')                /* semicolon */
      t->type = semicolon;
```

```
    else if (is_op(c))              /* operator */
      t->type = operator, t->val.operator = c;
    else if (isdigit(c))            /* number */
    {
      do
      {
        num = num * 10 + c - '0';
      } while (c = fetch(), isdigit(c));
      unfetch(c);
      t->type = operand, t->val.operand = num;
    }
    else                            /* illegal character */
      t->type = illegal;
  }
  return t;
}
```

(b)   The tokenizer

FIGURE 10.8. The tokenizer and a program that uses it to tokenize its input.

---

code from **getnum** (Chapter 7) to convert characters to integers. Finally, searching for an operator is a simple sequential table search that is similiar to the one in Chapter 6.

PROGRAMMING PRACTICE

10-12. Write a program that takes a text file as input, and produces as output each word of the text on a separate line.

10-13. The lexical scanner (Figure 10.8) can be adapted to the task of reading tokens for purposes other than calculation. Modify or extend the scanner so that it performs a function similar to that of **scanf**. It takes a *single* formatting string, and the address of a variable, and reads the next token on the input corresponding to the type in the format string. If the input cannot be accomplished, the function returns zero, and causes the input pointer to point to the first character *after* the one that caused the input to fail.

10-14. Modify **get_nxt_token** to handle identifier names as tokens, and also floating point numbers.

10-15. Write a simple calculator program that uses **get_nxt_token** in parsing its input.

CHAPTER 11

LINKED DATA STRUCTURES

Arrays are data structures that require a fixed amount of storage to be specified and allocated at compile time, preventing us from increasing their size during run time. In addition, as we observed in the insertion sort in Chapter 1, putting data into the middle of an array or deleting data from the middle requires us to shift values to make room for the new or to close up the space used by the old. In this chapter we examine more dynamic data structures—linked lists—and we finish with a useful case study involving several data structures—a C program cross-referencer.

LINKED LISTS

The diagram in Figure 11.1 shows a linked list of five integers. Each element of the list, called a *node*, has two fields, one containing data, the other a pointer to the next element in the list.

The advantage of the linked list is that we can insert an element with-

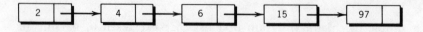

FIGURE 11.1. Diagram of a five-node linked list with values 2, 4, 6, 15, and 97.

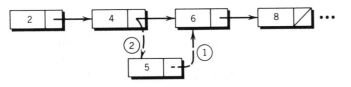

FIGURE 11.2. A linked list with a new node inserted into the middle.

out shifting all of the elements that follow. All we need do is adjust the
pointers appropriately.

To illustrate linked lists, later in this chapter we will write an insertion
sort routine that inserts each new input value into an already sorted list,
as shown in Figure 11.2. To do this, we need a way of representing a
node. Since each node requires at least two fields, we can conveniently
package an entire node as a structure.

```
struct node
{
    long        data;    /* or whatever is needed */
    struct node *next;   /* "next" is a pointer to another node */
};
```

We can clarify the notation and encapsulate the complete data definitions in one place by using a typedef such as

```
typedef struct node  *NODEPTR;
```

This causes NODEPTR to be a new type name, a pointer to a struct node.
Then the earlier structure definition becomes

```
struct node
{
    long    data;
    NODEPTR next;
};
```

To help hide the representation, we put the definitions for struct node
and NODEPTR into a header file called *lists.h* that we can include in programs that manipulate linked lists.

BASIC LINKED LIST OPERATIONS

As we did with sets in Chapter 7, we can treat a list as an abstract data
type, with the following allowable operations: initialize a list to the empty

list (init_list); find a value in a list (search_list); insert a value into a list (insert_list); delete a value from a list (delete_list); and print a list (print_list). By carefully constructing these primitive operations, we hide the underlying representation from other functions that need to use lists but do not care how they are implemented. At some later time, if changes to the representation are required (circular or two-way lists), only the accessing functions need be changed. In this section and the one following we will implement insert_list and print_list. Implementing the others is an exercise for the reader.

Making a Node

The function make_node in Figure 11.3 creates a new node using malloc. We request enough space for a struct node; once we have the space, we insert the value and initialize the next field to NULL (used to indicate the end of the list). Because malloc returns a pointer to char, we must cast it to a NODEPTR. As usual, we declare the type of malloc. The function returns a pointer to the node, or NULL if malloc fails.

Printing the Values in a Linked List

The sorting program in Figure 11.5 calls a function print_list to write the values in the list. This function, shown in Figure 11.4, *traverses* the list, printing the data field in each node, until the list pointer is NULL.

```
/*
 * Make a new node, inserting "value".  Return a pointer to the node.
 * Returns NULL when out of dynamic storage space.
 */
NODEPTR make_node(value)
long  value;
{
  NODEPTR newptr;                 /* pointer to allocated space */
  char    *malloc();

  if ((newptr = (NODEPTR) malloc(sizeof(struct node))) != NULL)
  {
    newptr->data = value;         /* fill in "data" field */
    newptr->next = NULL;          /* "next" field is always NULL */
  }
  return newptr;                  /* returns NULL if malloc fails */
}
```

FIGURE 11.3. A routine that gets a new node, inserting a value. The routine returns a pointer to the node (or NULL if malloc fails).

```
/*
 *  Print a list pointed to by "L".
 */
void print_list(L)
NODEPTR L;
{
  for ( ; L != NULL; L = L->next)
    printf("%ld\n", L->data);
}
```

FIGURE 11.4. The function print_list that prints the **data** fields of the nodes in the list pointed to by L.

Traversing a list means moving through a list in order, "visiting" (or performing some action on) each node in turn. In Figure 11.4 we print the **data** field when we visit the node. We use L itself to go through the list, until L is **NULL**, at which point we are at the end of the list. To get to the next node in the list, we write

L = L->next;

```
/*
 *  Sort integer (long) input using linked lists.
 */
#include <stdio.h>
#include "lists.h"

main()
{
  NODEPTR    L = NULL;                    /* the sorted linked list */
  long       val;                         /* input value */
  void       print_list(), skip_garbage();
  int        inpres;

  while((inpres = getnum(&val)) != EOF)
    if (!inpres)                          /* skip over rest of line */
      skip_garbage();                     /* (from Chapter 7) */
    else
      if (!insert_list(val, &L))          /* insert "val" into "L" */
      {
        printf("\nOut of internal memory space.\n");
        break;                            /* exit the while loop */
      }
  print_list(L);
}
```

FIGURE 11.5. Main program structure for linked list insertion sort.

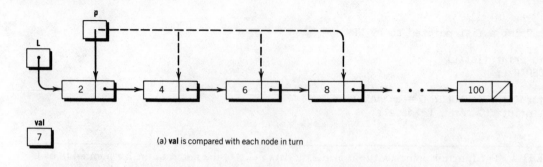

(a) **val** is compared with each node in turn

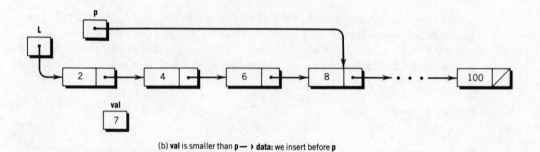

(b) **val** is smaller than **p — › data:** we insert before **p**

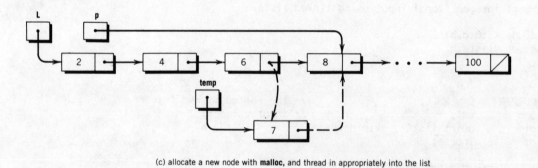

(c) allocate a new node with **malloc,** and thread in appropriately into the list

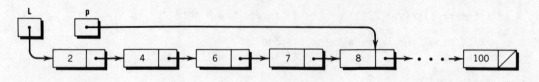

(d) what the list looks like after insertion of new node

FIGURE 11.6. Trace of insertion sort.

INSERTION SORTING USING LINKED LISTS

Now we can combine these ideas to write an insertion sort program using linked lists. The advantage of sorting with a linked list is that we can sort an unlimited number of values (with the array version, we had to predeclare the maximum number of values to be sorted), and we can insert the new value into a linked list without shifting. The insertion sort program is written to read longs and insert them in order into a linked list. On end of input we print the list using print_list. The main program is trivial because we built the list access routines in small, functional pieces. Figure 11.5 shows the complete main program, assuming the data definitions in the include file *lists. h*. We also use getnum from Chapter 7.

Of course, there is still one function to write: insert_list. The function finds the correct place to insert the value so that the list remains sorted, as in Figure 11.6. We write this as a function (Figure 11.7) with two arguments, a value to be inserted and a pointer to a linked list.

```
/*
 * Insert "val" into already sorted linked list "L."  Returns nonzero
 * if space is available, zero otherwise.  Uses make_node to create node.
 */
int insert_list(val, L)
long      val;
NODEPTR   *L;
{
   NODEPTR   curr = *L,               /* current node in list */
             prev = NULL,             /* node before "curr" */
             make_node(),             /* get a new node */
             temp;                    /* pointer to new node */

/* March until correct place, or until end of list. */

   for ( ; curr != NULL && val > curr->data ; curr = curr->next)
     prev = curr;

/* Get new node and insert into proper place (if space is available). */

   if ((temp = make_node(val)) != NULL)
   {
     temp->next = curr;
     if (prev == NULL)                /* insert at start of list */
       *L = temp;
     else
       prev->next = temp;
   }
   return temp != NULL;               /* "temp" is NULL if malloc failed */
}
```

FIGURE 11.7. insert_list function used in the linked list version of insertion sort.

To insert in the list, we must find the place where the node goes, make a node, and hook it into the list. We use two pointers, curr and prev, to do the traversing. We initialize curr to the list's first node and prev to NULL.

curr and prev move down the list, one in trail of the other. This is necessary because we find the correct place to insert by comparing with the value in a node, but we must insert *before* that node. Since our list contains only pointers to the next node we keep this "trailing link pointer" one node behind curr and we always insert after prev. The notion of a trailing pointer, one that points to the predecessor of a node, is a common technique with linked structures. Once we find the place for the new value, we create a new node with make_node and insert it by appropriate manipulation of pointers.

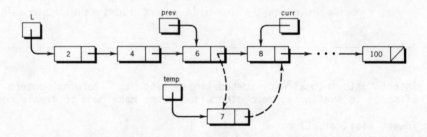

Although linked list insertion sort avoids the time-consuming process of shifting data to make room for a new item, it is still not substantially faster than the array-based insertion sort. For each new value to be inserted, we still have to search the list for the correct place to insert, an operation that takes time proportional to m, if there are m values in the list or array. For all n input values, this takes a total amount of time proportional to n^2. If n doubles, sorting time goes up by a factor of four; if n triples, it goes up nine times. However, the total sorting time for the same n inputs will be about twice as fast for linked lists as for array insertion.

PROGRAMMING PRACTICE

11-1. Write a function that takes a pointer to a linked list, and reverses the order of the nodes. If the list contains nodes with 1, 2, 5, and 7, the list will point to the node with 7, which points to 5, and so on. No data movement should occur, only appropriate alteration of pointers.

11-2. Write a function, `length_list`, that returns the number of elements in a list.

11-3. Write functions that implement the abstract data type *stack* using linked lists. A stack is a restricted access list: insertions and deletions may occur only at one end, the *top* of the stack. The operations are traditionally called *pushing* and *popping*.

11-4. Add the operations `count`, `top`, and `isempty` to the stack data type created in the previous exercise. `count` returns the number of elements on the stack, `top` returns the top element without popping the stack, and `isempty` returns nonzero only if there are elements on the stack.

11-5. Some of the list functions we have written in this chapter can be rewritten more compactly. Do so.

11-6. Write a function, `search_list`, that finds the first location of a given value in a list, and returns a pointer to it. If the value is not in the list, the function should return `NULL`. The function header should be

```
NODEPTR  search_list(val, list);
long     val;
NODEPTR  list;
```

11-7. Write a function, `delete_list`, that removes the first node in a linked list with a given value. If the value is not in the list, the function should do nothing. The function header should be

```
void delete_list(val, list)
long     val;
NODEPTR  *list;
```

`delete_list` should make use of `search_list` of the previous problem. What changes in `search_list` are necessary for this to be reasonable?

RETURNING SPACE TO THE FREE STORAGE POOL

Calls to `malloc` consume space from the storage pool (FSP). If a list is serving a temporary function, we can return space to the FSP by calls to `free`. `free` takes a pointer to a contiguous block of storage (type `char *`) and returns the storage to the FSP. In theory, this storage is no longer accessible to the program. Eventually, the space may be doled out again by `malloc` as part of a larger or smaller block. Since only the space is returned—the name of the pointer is still available in the current block—

```
/*
 * Return each element in "L" to the FSP, then set "L" to the empty list.
 */
void free_list(L)
NODEPTR  *L;
{
  NODEPTR    curr = *L,
             temp;

  for (; curr != NULL ; curr = temp)
  {
    temp = curr->next;
    free ((char *) curr);
  }
  *L = NULL;
}
```

FIGURE 11.8. Function free_list returns the linked list pointed to by L and sets L to the empty list.

problems occur when accessing a freed block of storage through its pointer.

Since free returns only the space pointed to by the pointer argument, it is necessary to traverse an entire list in order to return all its nodes. A slight variant on print_list, whereby "visit the node" becomes a call to free, accomplishes the job, as in Figure 11.8. We cast the argument to free to avoid illegal type combinations. We should avoid accessing a freed node outside the block where it is freed or if a call to malloc intervenes.

PROGRAMMING PRACTICE

11-8. Write functions that implement the abstract data type *queue*. A queue is another restricted list; additions are made to the end and deletions take place from the front. You should have functions to create the queue, to destroy the queue, to add to the queue's end, and to remove from the queue's front.

SORTING STRINGS USING DYNAMICALLY ALLOCATED ARRAYS

We now modify the insertion sort routines slightly so that input consists of character strings (or words), one word per line of input; in the original version, the input was integers. Since integers always take up a fixed amount of storage, each node was always the same size—room for the integer (**data** field) plus room for the pointer to the next node (the **next** field).

Using the technique from Chapter 9, each node will contain a *pointer* to a string rather than the string itself, using **malloc** to allocate the needed space. In this case, the space for each node is a fixed small amount: room for the string pointer plus room for the pointer to the next node.

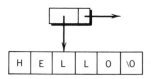

The insertion sort algorithm is identical: compare the new word with each in turn, until it is smaller than the current word, and then insert before the current word. Figure 11.9 shows the situation for the list of words NOW, IS, THE, TIME, FOR, ALL, GOOD, MEN, just before inserting MEN. Figure 11.10 is the new version of **insert_list** for string sorting. We use **strcmp** to compare the strings.

Figure 11.11 shows what is going on. We allocate space for the node with **malloc**. We also need to allocate room for the string S. We do this with another call to **malloc**, using **strlen** to compute the length of S. Since **strlen** does not count the trailing null, we add one to the length in the

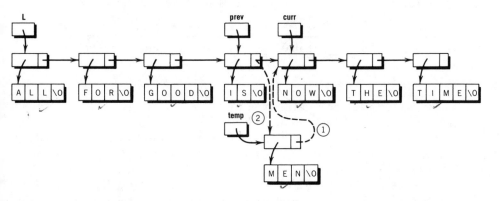

FIGURE 11.9. Linked list of nodes with pointers to a character string. The new word MEN is inserted just before NOW.

```
/*
 *  Insert "S" into already sorted list "L."  Returns nonzero if there is
 *  space and zero otherwise.
 */
#include <strings.h>                 /* declares types of strcpy and strcmp */
#include "lists.h"

int insert_list(S, L)
char     S[];                        /* before, we inserted longs */
NODEPTR  *L;
{
    NODEPTR curr = *L,
            prev = NULL,
            temp;                    /* returned from malloc */
    char    *malloc(),
            *sptr;                   /* pointer from malloc */

/* March until correct place, or end of list. */

    for ( ; curr != NULL && strcmp (S, curr->data) > 0; curr = curr->next)
        prev = curr;

/* Get new node and insert into proper place, if space available. */

    if (temp = (NODEPTR) malloc (sizeof (struct node)) &&
        sptr = malloc ((unsigned) strlen (S) + 1))
    {
        (void) strcpy (sptr, S);        /* copy "S" */
        temp->data = sptr;              /* "data" field points to string */
        temp->next = curr;
        if (prev == NULL)               /* insert at start of list */
            *L = temp;
        else
            prev->next = temp;
    }
    return temp && sptr;                /* one is NULL if malloc failed */
}
```

FIGURE 11.10. Revised version of insert_list that takes a string and inserts it into the proper place in a sorted linked list.

call to malloc. malloc returns type char *, so no cast is needed. sptr is a pointer to the newly allocated block.

Finally, we copy S into the new block pointed to by sptr (using strcpy) and put the pointer (not the string) into the data field of the new node. Then links are adjusted as before.

Since the type of the data field of a node in the list has changed, we also need to change the declarations in *lists.h* and rewrite the function print_list, as well as the driver program from Figure 11.5. These are shown in Figure 11.12.

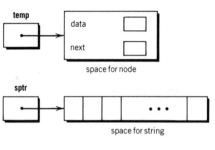

space for node

space for string

(a) allocate space for node and string

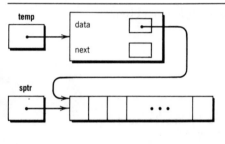

(b) hook string into node

FIGURE 11.11. Diagram showing allocation of new node and allocation of space for the string with malloc.

PROGRAMMING PRACTICE

11-9. Generalize lists so that any data type can be held within the node. (*Hint*: Have the caller provide functions to create a node and to compare two nodes.)

```
typedef  struct node  *NODEPTR;

struct node
{
    char        *data;              /* only change is in "data" field */
    NODEPTR     next;
};
```

(a) *New include file "lists.h" with new type for the* **data** *field*

(*continued*)

```
/*
 *  Print a list pointed to by "L."
 */
void print_list (L)
NODEPTR  L;
{
  for ( ; L != NULL; L = L->next)
    printf("%s\n", L->data);          /* only change is to printf */
}
```

(b) *New version of* print_list. *Note that only the format
     specification in the* printf *statement has changed.*

```
/*
 *  Read strings, one per line, and sort using linked list insertion.
 */
#include <stdio.h>
#include "lists.h"
#define  MAXSTRING     80

main()
{
  NODEPTR   L = NULL;              /* the sorted linked lists */
  char      word[MAXSTRING];       /* input string */
  void      print_list();

  while (get_line(word, MAXSTRING) != EOF)
    if (!insert_list(word, &L))     /* insert "word" into "L" */
    {
      printf("\nOut of internal memory space.\n");
      break;                        /* exit the while loop */
    }
  print_list(L);
}
```

(c) *New main program. The input format now specifies string input.*

FIGURE 11.12. New versions of *lists. h*, print_list, and the main program, showing changes needed
to handle character strings as input. We used get_line from Chapter 4 instead of getnum.

11-10. Write a function, size_list, that determines the total number of bytes
used to store a linked list. When is size_list useful?

LONG STRINGS

In the string-sorting example, we were limited to 80-character strings
because we preallocated an array into which they could then be read.
However, we can combine the notion of a string as a sequence of characters with the notion of arbitrary-length structures if we free ourselves from

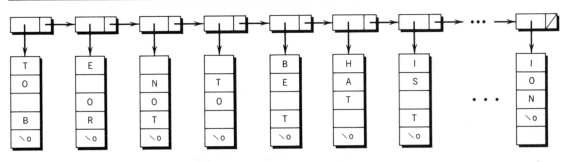

FIGURE 11.13. Arbitrary-length string made up of a linked list of fixed-length strings.

the idea that all characters in a given string must be in a single contiguous array. Instead, we use linked lists of characters, each node containing a pointer to an array of fixed size, and when a string being entered exceeds the maximum size of the array, we link in a new node, as illustrated in Figure 11.13.

Now our linked list is no longer viewed as a collection of separate strings, as was the case with word sorting in Figure 11.12, but rather as one large arbitrary-length string. The changes to the program in Figure 11.12 are small and a complete program is shown in Figure 11.14. This program reads arbitrary-length strings and stores them in a linked list, using **MAX** characters per node (**MAX** is 20 in this version). When we need more space, we get a new node with malloc and use strcpy to copy additional characters to new array space provided by an additional call to malloc. We have also renamed some of the data structures to reflect their use more accurately (**NODEPTR** becomes **STRINGPTR**, for example).

CASE STUDY—A CROSS-REFERENCE PROGRAM

When we write programs, debugging is often aided by having a separate listing of the identifiers in a program and the line numbers where they appear. Such a listing is called a *cross-reference*, and a program to produce it is called a *cross-referencer*. We will build one that can be used for any file of words and, in particular, can be easily adapted for use with C or other programming languages. To give you an idea of what such a program should produce, Figure 11.15a is the first C program (from Chapter 1) and Figure 11.15b is the output of a program cross-referencer run on this program.

```
/*
 * Read and store arbitrary-length strings.
 */
#include <stdio.h>

#define  MAX    20                  /* max chars per node */

typedef  struct node  *STRINGPTR;

struct node                         /* a node in the string */
{
  char       *word;                 /* pointer to the word */
  STRINGPTR  next;                  /* pointer to rest of word */
};


main()
{
  int        c, i;
  STRINGPTR  S, last;               /* long string, pointer to its end */
  char       word[MAX];             /* the input string */
  void       print_string();
  STRINGPTR  insert_string();

  while (c = getchar(), c != EOF)
  {                                 /* get a long string */
    for (S = last = NULL, i = 0; c != '\n' && c != EOF; c=getchar())
    {
      word[i++] = c;
      if (i >= MAX - 1)
      {
        word[i] = '\0';             /* EACH substr ends with '\0' */
        if ((last = insert_string (word, &S, last)) == NULL)
          break;                    /* out of memory - exit loop */
        i = 0;                      /* reset for next node */
      }
    }
    if (last)
    {                               /* make last node */
      word[i++] = '\n';
      word[i] = '\0';
      (void) insert_string (word, &S, last);  /* can't do anything if no memory */
    }
    printf("\nString:\n");          /* print the string */
    print_string(S);
  }
}
```

(a) The main program for reading, storing, and printing long strings

```
/*
 *   Insert string "S" at end of string "L" (possibly empty).
 *   Returns NULL if "malloc" fails.
 */
STRINGPTR insert_string(S, L, last)
char       *S;
STRINGPTR  *L, last;
{
  STRINGPTR   temp;                    /* returned from allocating a node */
  char *malloc(), *strcpy(),
       *sptr;                          /* returned from allocating a string*/

  if ((temp = (STRINGPTR) malloc (sizeof (struct node))) != NULL &&
      (sptr = malloc ((unsigned) strlen (S) + 1)) != NULL)
  {
    (void) strcpy (sptr, S);           /* copy "S" */
    temp->word = sptr;                 /* "word" field points to string */
    temp->next = NULL;
    if (last == NULL)
      *L = temp;                       /* insert at start of string */
    else
      last->next = temp;
    last = temp;                       /* "last" points to last node */
  }
  return temp && sptr;                 /* NULL if malloc failed */
}


/*
 * Print the string pointed to by "S".
 */
void print_string (S)
STRINGPTR S;
{
  for ( ; S != NULL; S = S->next)
    printf ("%s", S->word);
  putchar('\n');
}
```

(b) The routines called from the main program: `insert_string` *and* `print_string`

FIGURE 11.14. Program for reading, storing, and printing arbitrarily long strings.

The top-level structure of a program to do this is simple. The interesting aspects of the program are its data structures and the way the program is organized. For this program, we pay careful attention to selecting a reasonable representation for the <u>table of words</u> and <u>line numbers</u>, but we define the table in such a way that later changes can be made transparent to the rest of the program.

```
/*
 * Generate a table showing interest accumulation.
 */
#define PRINCIPAL     1000.00          /* start with $1000 */
#define IRATE         0.10             /* interest rate of 10% */
#define PERIOD        10               /* over 10-year period */


main()
{
  int     year;                        /* year of period */
  float   sum;                         /* total amount */

  sum = PRINCIPAL;
  year = 0;
  printf("Year\tTotal at %.2f%%\n\n", IRATE * 100.0);
  while (year <= PERIOD)
  {
    printf("%d\t$ %.2f\n", year, sum);
    sum = sum * IRATE + sum;
    year = year + 1;
  }
}
```

(a) A short C program

```
Generate        2
IRATE           5, 15, 19
PERIOD          6, 16
PRINCIPAL       4, 13
Total           15
Year            15
a               2
accumulation    2
amount          11
at              15
d               18
define          4, 5, 6
f               15, 18
float           11
int             10
interest        2, 5
main            8
n               15 (2), 18
of              5, 10
over            6
period          6, 10
printf          15, 18
rate            5
showing         2
```

```
start        4
sum          11, 13, 18, 19 (3)
table        2
total        11
while        16
with         4
year         6, 10 (2), 14, 16, 18, 20 (2)
```

(b) The output of a cross-referencer run on this program

FIGURE 11.15. *(a)* A short C program. *(b)* The output of a cross-referencer run on this program. Numbers in parentheses are repetition counts if a word occurs more than once on the same line.

PROGRAM AND DATA STRUCTURES

A simple data flow model of the program is shown in the following diagram. This model of a program's operation shows the separate functions that we need and the data that flows between them. The functions themselves are viewed as black boxes that take a set of inputs, perform some transformation, and produce a set of outputs.

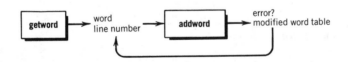

The program reads a word at a time in a function called **getword** and then passes the word and the current line number to a function called **addword**. This function adds the word and the line number to the table of words and line numbers. This table is itself one of the inputs to **addword**. The program's structure is so simple that we can begin designing the program by coding the main program immediately. Then we can add the pieces in a top-down way as they are built. Figure 11.16 is the entire main program. It is just a **while** loop that runs until there are no more words, with a **break** if the word table becomes full. At the end of the program, the word table is printed by the function **writewords**.

The main program includes a header file *xref_tab.h*. This file contains the data structure definitions for the word table and declarations for any globals. Since we have not yet decided on a representation for the word table, we cannot fill in the details of the header file. There are a few assumptions already in the program, however. One is that adding a new word to the table could fail, and we specifically include an error return from **addword** telling us if the table is full. The table might be full because

```
/*
 *  XREF.C - A cross reference program.
 */
#include <stdio.h>
#include "xref_tab.h"

main()
{
  char    word[MAXWORD + 1];          /* next input word */
  int     lineno;                      /* line word is on */
  WORD_TABLE wordtab, init_tab();      /* the word table, function to create it */

  wordtab = init_tab();                /* the word table */
  if (!wordtab)
    printf("Couldn't create word table\n");
  else
  {
    while (getword(word, MAXWORD, &lineno))
      if (!addword(wordtab, word, lineno))
      {
        printf("Out of memory: processing word %s on line %d\n", word, lineno);
        break;                         /* no point in going on */
      }
    writewords(wordtab);            /* write table, even if out of memory */
  }
}
```

FIGURE 11.16. The main cross-referencer program.

it is represented as an array and we have run out of space, or it might fail because it is dynamically allocated and we have no more dynamic memory space. Either way, the underlying table is hidden from the main program. We have defined the table to be a variable called wordtab, of type **WORD_TABLE**, that hints at its type, but the actual definition of the type is in the include file *xref_tab.h*. Any changes in the table representation will require only a change in the data structure definitions in *xref_tab.h* and the access routines in addword, init_tab, and writewords.

How should the word table be represented? We will list the characteristics that the table ought to have, so that we can make a choice in a more informed way. First, the table must be able to contain an arbitrary number of words of arbitrary size. Second, table searches must be fast, since we have to search the table for each word to see if the word is already there. We also need to be able to quickly determine if the word has already occurred on the current line. Finally, and perhaps most importantly, it should be easy to print the table alphabetically by word, and for each word, in line number order.

The first point suggests that the word itself should not be stored in the table. Instead, each table entry should contain a pointer to the (arbitrarily long) word. It also suggests that the table should consist of dynamically allocated records. The second point suggests that there should be a list associated with each entry in the table: the lines on which the word appears. Therefore, each record in the table must contain at least a pointer to the word and a pointer to the line numbers where the word occurs.

Since the words in the table will be printed alphabetically at the end, it seems reasonable to try to keep the table as a sorted list. However, since the table might be large, adding a new entry and searching for an existing entry will be slow, on the average requiring us to examine half the words in the table. An alternative arrangement is to add the new word to the end of the table, along with the current line number, and then sort the table just before printing. With this method, we can add an entry quickly, but sorting the table is costly.

A compromise provides a reasonable solution: we keep separate, sorted lists of the words for each letter of the alphabet (both upper- and lowercase letters). We package these lists into a table of pointers, indexed by the first character of the word. When we read a word, we use its first letter to select the appropriate table entry, and then we use insertion sort to select the correct place for the word in this list. In the worst case (all words begin with the same letter), this method is no better than ordinary insertion sort. On the average, however, we will rarely have to search a long list, and we do not have to sort the table before we print it. Figure 11.17 shows an example of a word table for a few entries.

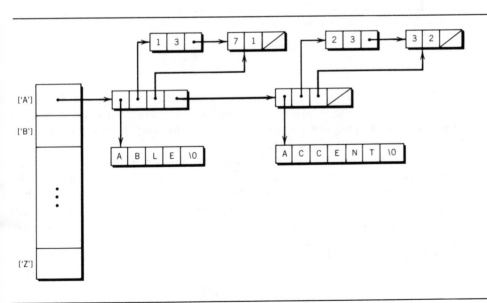

FIGURE 11.17. Our list representation for the cross-referencer word table.

```
/*
 *  XREF_TAB.H - definitions of the word table's internal structure and
 *              of the functions that use it.
 */
#define  MAXWORD    20                  /* longest word */
#define  MAXCHAR   128                  /* number of characters (ASCII) */


typedef struct linenode *LINEPTR;
typedef struct wordnode *WORDPTR;
typedef WORDPTR         *WORD_TABLE;   /* pointer to pointer to struct wordnodes */

struct linenode                        /* node containing a line number */
{
  int      lineno,                     /* line word appears on */
           count;                      /* number of times it appears */
  LINEPTR  next;                       /* next line number for word */
};


struct wordnode                        /* node containing a word */
{
  char     *word;                      /* word (has to be allocated) */
  WORDPTR  next;                       /* next word */
  LINEPTR  first, last;                /* line number pointers */
};


extern char *malloc();                 /* memory allocator */
extern char *strcpy();                 /* string copier */
```

FIGURE 11.18. The include file *xref_tab.h*, where the data structures are defined.

We need a little more information in each node to complete the representation. Rather than use multiple nodes when a word occurs more than once in a single line, we include a count field to hold the number of times a word appears on a given line.

Finally, we perform two actions on the line list in each node: adding new nodes at the end and printing the line list from the front. A list structure with the property that additions are made only at the rear while removals, or traversals, occur only from the front, is called a *queue*. Each node must contain two pointers to be able to maintain the queue in proper order—first, a pointer to the start of the line list, and last, a pointer to the end. Therefore, the word table is an alphabetic table, and the line numbers and counters for each word are simple linked lists organized as queues.

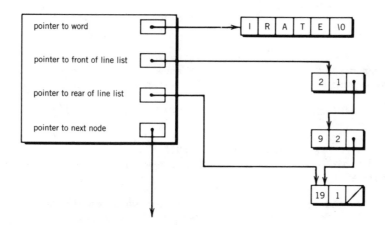

With these representation ideas, we can formally define the data structures for a **struct wordnode** that was used in Figure 11.17. They are defined in the include file *xref_tab.h*, shown in Figure 11.18.

The rest of the program is shown in Figure 11.19. We have broken it into three parts: a routine to parse the input and select individual words; routines to put the words into the word table and update the line numbers; and routines to print the table. These pieces correspond to the files *xref_in.c*, *xref_tab.c*, and *xref_out.c*, respectively. These three files, along with the main program in file *xref.c*, are compiled and linked together to produce the runnable cross-referencer.

```
/*
 *  XREF_IN.C - break the input into words for XREF.  Decisions are
 *            made here about what is a word, and where line breaks go.
 */
#include <stdio.h>
#include <ctype.h>

static int lineno = 1;                    /* current line number */

#define NEXTCHAR(ptr) (((*ptr = getchar()) == '\n') ? (lineno++, 0) : *ptr)

/*
 * Get next word from input.  fill in "linenoptr" with its line number.
 * return NULL when no more words, otherwise length of word.
 */
```

(continued)

```
int getword(word, wordsize, linenoptr)
char *word;                             /* place to store word */
int  wordsize, *linenoptr;              /* size of word, line number to update */
{
  int ch;                               /* next character */
  char *start = word,                   /* save start of word */
       *max = word + wordsize - 1;      /* last possible character */

  while (NEXTCHAR(&ch) != EOF && !isalpha(ch))
    ;                                   /* skip non-letters */
  *linenoptr = lineno;                  /* record line number */
  for (; ch != EOF && isalpha(ch); NEXTCHAR(&ch))
    if (word < max)                     /* save word up to max characters */
      *word++ = ch;
  *word = '\0';
  return word - start;                  /* return word length: zero if no word */
}
```

(a) xref_in.c: The file of routines for handling input

```
/*
 * XREF_TAB.C - handles word table and line number references
 */
#include <stdio.h>
#include "xref_tab.h"

#define  DOALLOC(type)  ((type *) malloc(sizeof(type)))

/*
 * Allocate and intialize table entries to the NULL pointer
 */
WORD_TABLE init_tab()
{
  WORD_TABLE word_tab = (WORD_TABLE) malloc(MAXCHAR * sizeof(WORDPTR));
  WORDPTR *ptr = word_tab,
          *endptr = word_tab + MAXCHAR - 1;

  while (ptr <= endptr)
    *ptr++ = NULL;
  return word_tab;
}
```

```
/*
 * Allocate enough room for the string, and copy it, returning a pointer
 * to the newly allocated string, or NULL if we can't allocate it.
 */
static char *strsave(str)
char *str;
{
  char *newstr = malloc((unsigned) strlen(str) + 1);

  return (newstr != NULL) ? strcpy(newstr, str) : NULL;
}


/*
 * Allocate a new word node, and fill it appropriately.
 */
static WORDPTR makewordnode(word)
char    *word;
{
  WORDPTR wnptr;                                   /* pointer to new word node */

  if ((wnptr = DOALLOC(struct wordnode)) != NULL)
  {
    wnptr->next = NULL;                            /* no following node */
    wnptr->first = wnptr->last = NULL;             /* no lines yet */
    if ((wnptr->word = strsave(word)) == NULL)
      free((char *) wnptr), wnptr = NULL;          /* cannot allocate word, fail */
  }
  return wnptr;
}


/*
 * Allocate new line node, and save line number inside it.
 */
static LINEPTR makelinenode(lineno)
int    lineno;
{
  LINEPTR lnptr;                                   /* newly create line node pointer */

  if ((lnptr = DOALLOC(struct linenode)) != NULL)
  {
    lnptr->lineno = lineno;
    lnptr->count = 1;
    lnptr->next = NULL;
  }
  return lnptr;
}
```

(continued)

```
/*
 * Add a new line number for the given node; check to see if word
 * appears on the same line as the previous one.
 */
static LINEPTR addlineno(wnptr,lineno)
WORDPTR wnptr;                              /* word node pointer to add line to */
int    lineno;                             /* line number */
{
  LINEPTR lnptr = wnptr->last;             /* new line node pointer */

  if (lnptr != NULL && lnptr->lineno == lineno)
    lnptr->count++;                        /* already occurs on this line */
  else
    if ((lnptr = makelinenode(lineno)) != NULL)
    {                                      /* Allocated new node, hook into list */
      if (wnptr->first == NULL)            /* empty list, place at front */
        wnptr->first = lnptr;
      else                                 /* non-empty, place at back */
        wnptr->last->next = lnptr;
      wnptr->last = lnptr;                 /* regardless it's the end of the list */
    }
  return lnptr;                            /* NULL if we can't allocate new node */
}


/*
 * Add new word to table.  We use the word's first letter to index an appropriate
 * list, and then insert the word there.  Return zero if errors, nonzero otherwise.
 */
int addword(word_tab, word, lineno)
WORD_TABLE word_tab;                        /* table of pointers to word lists */
char *word;                                /* word to add */
int    lineno;                             /* line number word appears on */
{
  int   cmpres;                            /* result of comparing words */
  WORDPTR prev = NULL,                     /* pointers for inserting item */
          curr = word_tab[*word],          /* the letter list for this word */
          temp;

  for (; curr != NULL && (cmpres = strcmp(word, curr->word)) > 0; curr=curr->next)
    prev = curr;
  if (!cmpres)
    temp = curr;                           /* word exists */
  else
    if ((temp = makewordnode(word)) != NULL)   /* create word */
    {
      temp->next = curr;
      (prev == NULL) ? (word_tab[*word] = temp) : (prev->next = temp);
    }
  return addlineno(temp, lineno) != NULL;
}
```

(b) xref_tab.c: the file of routines for manipulating the word table

```
/*
 *  XREF_OUT.C - writes the table.  changes to the internal data structure
 *              will force changes here.
 */
#include <stdio.h>
#include "xref_tab.h"

#define  MAXLINENO      7                       /* allow seven line numbers per line */

writewords(word_tab)
WORD_TABLE word_tab;                            /* the table of words */
{
  WORDPTR *endptr = word_tab + MAXCHAR - 1;  /* pointer to last word list */
  WORDPTR curr;                                /* pointer to next node in word list */
  LINEPTR lnptr;                               /* pointer to next line number node */
  int     count;                               /* count of line nos for this word */

  for (; word_tab <= endptr; word_tab++)      /* run through each letter */
    for (curr = *word_tab; curr != NULL; curr = curr->next)
    {                                          /* run through each word w/ that letter */
      count = 0;
      printf("%-*s", MAXWORD, curr->word);
      for (lnptr = curr->first; lnptr != NULL; lnptr = lnptr->next)
      {                                        /* write the line numbers */
        if (count == MAXLINENO)
          printf("\n%-*s", MAXWORD, " "), count = 0;
        printf(" %d" , lnptr->lineno);         /* write line number and count */
        if (lnptr->count > 1)
          printf(" (%d)", lnptr->count);
        if (lnptr->next)                       /* not last */
          putchar(',');
        count++;                               /* next */
      }
    }
  putchar('\n');
}
```

(c) xref_out.c: the file of routines for printing the word table

FIGURE 11.19. The routines called from the main cross-referencer program, and the routines they call.

PROGRAMMING PRACTICE

11-11. Modify the cross-referencer so that it works for C programs. Modify the cross-referencer so that it works for Pascal programs. That is, so the program will *not* print C (or Pascal) reserved words. What is the best form of the reserved word table?

CHAPTER 12

C AND THE OUTSIDE WORLD

Up to this point, our programs have interacted with their environment solely through the standard input and the standard output. In this chapter, we discuss two alternatives: command line arguments and external files. As part of this discussion, we introduce the remaining standard I/O library functions and provide examples of their use. We conclude with the implementation of a small indexed data base for storing names, addresses, and phone numbers, an extension of the version in Chapter 10.

COMMAND LINE ARGUMENTS

We have been hiding something all this time: main is a function that takes arguments. When main is called, it is passed two parameters that together describe the command line that invokes the program. The first is the number of arguments on the command line. The second is an array of pointers to strings containing the various arguments. Traditionally, these are called argc and argv, respectively. We declare main's parameters in the same way as those of any other function.

```
main(argc, argv)
int argc;               /* command line argument count */
char *argv[];           /* command line arguments */
```

By convention, the program's name is accessed through `argv[0]`, so `argc` is always at least one. The other arguments are used most often to specify various program options, as well as the external files the program should process. The precise definition of a command line argument varies from system to system; however, white space is usually used to delimit the arguments. An argument containing white space is placed within quotation marks.

We illustrate command line argument processing with a program (called *echo*) that prints each of its arguments (minus the program name) to the standard output. If, for example, the command line is

```
echo programming in c is fun
```

echo's output is

```
programming in c is fun
```

For this command line, when `main` is called, `argc` is six and `argv` is an array of six pointers to strings, as shown below.

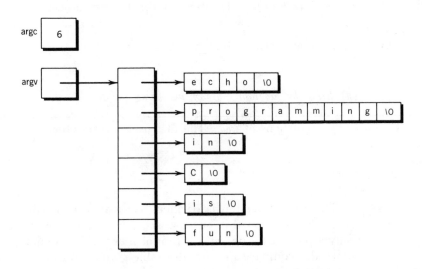

Figure 12.1 contains two implementations of *echo*. The first version is straightforward, using array indexing to traverse `argv` and printing each of the entries except the first (the program name). When written, the arguments are separated by spaces with the last argument followed by a newline.

```
/*
 * Echo arguments (using array indexing).
 */
main(argc, argv)
int argc;                               /* argument count */
char *argv[];                           /* list of arguments */
{
  int next;                             /* index to next argument */

  for (next = 1; next < argc; next++)
    printf("%s%c", argv[next], (next < argc - 1) ? ' ' : '\n');
}
```

(a) Echo the program's arguments using array indexing

```
/*
 * Echo arguments (using pointer indexing).
 */
main(argc, argv)
int argc;                               /* argument count */
char **argv;                            /* list of arguments */
{
  char **last_ptr = argv + argc - 1;    /* pointer to last argument */

  while(++argv <= last_ptr)
    printf("%s%c", *argv, (argv < last_ptr) ? ' ' : '\n');
}
```

(b) Echo the program's arguments using pointers

FIGURE 12.1. Two implementations of *echo*. The first using array subscripting, the second using pointers.

The second version is trickier, using **argv** as a pointer to traverse the array. We can do this because **argv**, like any other array parameter, is really a pointer to the array's first element. Note that **argv** is incremented before the comparison with the table's end, conveniently allowing us to skip over the program's name, which is stored as the table's first entry.

Using a pointer to traverse command line arguments is usually more efficient than using array indexing, but often is harder to read and understand as well. Thus, either method of command line argument processing is acceptable. However, the pointer method should be mastered, even if it is not the method of choice, because it is used frequently in existing programs.

PROGRAMMING PRACTICE

12-1. Rewrite *echo* to print out its arguments in reverse order, first using array indexing, then using pointers.

12-2. Write a program to print only those lines in its input that contain its argument. This is a simplified version of the UNIX *fgrep* utility. Can you easily extend your program to handle multiple arguments?

EXTERNAL FILES

Programs are more useful if they access external files directly, with the file names supplied as the program's arguments. Files are declared using the **FILE** data type defined in <*stdio.h*> and are accessed through standard I/O library functions. **FILE** is not one of C's basic data types. Instead, **FILE** is usually a structure containing information useful to the library routines that process files.

Before we can access a file, we must *open* it, associating the file's name with the file's contents. The standard I/O function **fopen** opens a file, allocating the necessary **FILE** structure and returning a pointer to it. Once a file has been opened, this file pointer refers to the file and is passed to other standard I/O library functions instead of the file's name.

fopen is passed two strings: the name of the file to open and a "mode" specifying how the file will be used. The mode specifies where the initial reads and writes on the file will take place, as well as what to do if the file does not already exist, and can be either "r" (read), "w" (write), or "a" (append). Remember, the mode is a string and not a character. As an example use of **fopen**,

```
#include <stdio.h>              /* defines the FILE data type */
...
FILE *fp;
...
fp = fopen("phone-numbers", "r");  /* open phone number file */
```

opens the file *phone-numbers* for reading.

A file must already exist to be opened for reading, but when it is opened for writing or appending it will be created if it does not already exist. If a file does exist, opening it for writing causes its old contents to be discarded. Opening it for appending causes new writes to take place at the file's end. If there is an error and the file cannot be opened, **fopen** returns **NULL**.

Once a file has been opened, there are a variety of ways to access it. The simplest file-accessing functions are getc and putc, which are analogous to getchar and putchar. getc takes a file pointer, returning the next character in the file, or EOF when end of file is encountered. As with getchar, getc's return value is an integer to allow EOF to be a value outside the character set. putc takes a character and a file pointer, writing the character to the specified file. Both functions return EOF if an error occurs.

When we have finished processing the file, we use fclose to *close* it. Closing a file causes any buffered output to be forced out and frees the file's FILE structure. fclose takes a single file-pointer argument and returns EOF if there is an error in closing the file. Since most systems have a maximum number of files that can be open at any one time (usually about twenty per program), closing a file as soon as it is no longer needed should become a habit.

We now have the pieces to write a useful utility function to copy files. file_copy, shown in Figure 12.2, is passed two file names and copies the contents of one file into another, one character at a time. For example,

```
file_copy("paper.old", "paper");
```

copies the contents of the file *paper* into the file *paper.old*.

Because file_copy is given file names and not file pointers, it has to open the files before accessing them. We are careful to check whether the opening of either file fails, performing the copy only if both opens are successful. Since opening a file for writing destroys the file's contents, we are also careful to do the open for writing only after the open for reading has succeeded. In this way, we destroy the previous contents of the destination file only if there is something to copy.

file_copy's return value indicates whether the files can be opened, with zero indicating a failed open. We have ignored the possibility of other errors and have cast the value returned by fclose to void. (We will soon discuss when it is important to examine its return value.)

COMBINING EXTERNAL FILES AND COMMAND LINE ARGUMENTS

Given the function file_copy, it is easy to write a program to copy one file into another with the names supplied as its arguments. This program (called *cp*) is shown in Figure 12.3. *cp*'s first argument is the file to copy into and its second argument is the file we are copying. For example,

cp datebook.backup datebook

makes the file *datebook.backup* a copy of the file *datebook*. *cp* is a simplified version of the file copying utility found on many operating systems. *cp*

```
/*
 *  Copy "source" to "dest".
 */
#include <stdio.h>

int file_copy(dest, source)
char *dest,                          /* source file name */
     *source;                        /* destination file name */
{
  FILE *sfp, *dfp;                   /* source, destination file pointers */

  if ((sfp = fopen(source,"r")) == NULL)
    printf("Couldn't open %s for reading\n", source);
  else
  {
    if ((dfp = fopen(dest,"w")) == NULL)
      printf("Couldn't open %s for writing\n", dest);
    else
    {
      while ((c = getc(sfp)) != EOF) /* do the copy */
        putc(c, dfp);
      (void) fclose(dfp);
    }
    (void) fclose(sfp);
  }
  return sfp && dfp;
}
```

FIGURE 12.2. Copying one file into another—an example of external files.

```
/*
 * Copy two files.  Usage:  cp dest src.  (Mimics assignment.)
 */
main(argc, argv)
int argc;
char *argv[];
{
  if (argc != 3)                         /* make sure it is: cp dest source */
    printf("Usage is: %s dest source\n", argv[0]);
  else if (!file_copy(argv[1], argv[2]))   /* make sure copy worked */
    printf("Copy failed.\n");
}
```

FIGURE 12.3. Copying one file into another—the arguments provide the file names.

verifies that there are three arguments (the program name and the two file names) and then uses file_copy to do the copying. Any error in invoking the command, such as providing too many or too few arguments, results in an error message. In addition, the user is notified if the copy fails because a file cannot be opened.

FORMATTED I/O TO FILES

As you might have guessed, both printf and scanf have counterparts that do formatted I/O on files. fprintf is like printf, with an additional file pointer argument that specifies the file to which we write. For example,

```
fprintf(fp, "BMW 320i's are great cars!\n");
```

writes a single line onto the file specified by fp. fscanf is like scanf, with an additional file pointer argument that specifies the file from which we read. As an example,

```
inpres = fscanf(fp, "%d", &value);
```

reads a single integer from the file specified by fp, places it in value, and returns the number of values read. Like scanf, fscanf returns EOF when end of file is reached or an error occurs. Because of their similarity to printf and scanf, forgetting to pass a file pointer to fprintf or fscanf is a common mistake.

HANDLING I/O ERRORS

Although it is unlikely, a file read or write can fail. Usually such failures are caused by hardware errors, but write errors can also occur when a device becomes full and there is no room for the newly written characters. All the standard I/O output functions return EOF if a write error occurs, allowing us to check for these errors. We can, for example, make file_copy (Figure 12.2) more robust by checking putc's return value and printing an error message if it is EOF. We should also check fclose's return value, because output is usually buffered and it is possible that the last characters written are not really written to the file until the file is closed.

Detecting read errors is more difficult, since EOF can indicate either an error or end of file. We can use two new library functions, feof and ferror, to distinguish between the two meanings. feof takes a file pointer and returns nonzero only if the end of the file has been reached. ferror is similar, taking a file pointer and returning nonzero only if an error has occurred in processing that file. After any input function has returned

EOF, one of these tests can be made and, if necessary, an appropriate error message printed.

To keep our examples simple, we have avoided the added complication of file I/O error handling. Unfortunately, when we fail to check for read and write errors and an error occurs, our program may behave abnormally, with no indication of any error. An unchecked input error is treated as EOF, prematurely terminating input processing. An unchecked output error can result in incorrect output. Production quality programs should check the values returned by the standard input and output library functions.

THE STANDARD FILES

When a program starts, three files are automatically opened: the standard input, the standard output, and the standard error output. We are familiar with the standard input and standard output; the standard error output is where error messages should be written to distinguish them from normal output. The file pointers corresponding to these files are stdin, stdout and stderr, and are defined in <stdio.h>. These file pointers are constants, and no assignment can be made to them.

Using stdin and stdout, we can define getchar and putchar as macros that expand into calls to getc and putc, as it is done in most standard I/O library implementations.

```
#define getchar()    getc(stdin)       /* next char from std input */
#define putchar(c)   putc(c, stdout)   /* next char from std output */
```

Although printf and scanf cannot be defined as macros because they can be passed a variable number of arguments, using fprintf with stdout is equivalent to using printf:

```
printf("Hi dad!\n");            /* both write to */
fprintf(stdout, "Hi dad!\n");   /*    stdout */
```

Similarly, using fscanf with stdin is equivalent to using scanf:

```
scanf("%d", &value)            /* both read from */
fscanf(stdin, "%d", &value)    /*    stdin */
```

Error messages are usually written to stderr so that they will show up on the terminal even if the standard output has been redirected. We illustrate the use of stderr in the function our_fopen, shown in Figure 12.4. our_fopen's parameters are a file name and a mode, which are passed to fopen to open the file. If the open fails, an error message is printed on the standard error; otherwise, our_fopen returns the file pointer returned by

```
/*
 *  Open a file, writing an error message if it fails.
 */
#include <stdio.h>

FILE *our_fopen(file_name, mode)
char *file_name,                           /* file to open */
     *mode;                                /* "r", "w" or "a" */
{
  FILE *fp = fopen(file_name, mode);       /* open the file */

  if (!fp)                                 /* did open fail */
    fprintf(stderr, "Can't open file \"%s\" for %s\n"", file_name,
                    (*mode == 'r')
                    ? "reading"
                    : ((*mode == 'w') ? "writing" : "appending"));
  return fp;
}
```

FIGURE 12.4. A function to open a file, printing any necessary error message onto the standard error.

fopen. Since our_fopen handles the errors, the functions that use it are simpler because they no longer have this responsibility.

PROGRAMMING PRACTICE

12-3. Write a function, file_append, that appends one file to the end of another. Can file_copy and file_append be combined into one function? Is this a good idea?

12-4. Write a function, fget_line, to read a line of input from a file. This can be done easily by modifying get_line (Chapter 4). Use fget_line to write a function, tail_file, that prints the last n lines of a file.

12-5. Write a function (or macro), our_fclose, that takes a file pointer and closes the file only if the file pointer it is passed is not NULL. Modify file_copy to use our_fopen to open files and our_fclose to close them. Does this simplify the function significantly?

12-6. Many errors are caused by passing an incorrect mode. Make our_fopen verify that it has been given a reasonable mode.

12-7. Modify the histogram program (Chapter 5) to read its data values from a file passed on the command line, while getting the histogram's parameters from the standard input.

12-8. Make `file_copy` check for both read and write errors.

FILES, COMMAND LINE ARGUMENTS, AND OPTIONS

To illustrate the full power of command line arguments, we write a small program (called *wc*) that counts the number of lines, words, and characters in the files specified by its arguments. In addition to file names, we allow the user to specify the desired counts in optional arguments appearing before the names of the files to be processed. It has become traditional for these optional arguments to begin with a dash ("−"), so *wc*'s options will be "−c" to count characters, "−w" to count words, and "−l" to count lines. For ease of use, we allow these options to be specified as either a single argument or separate arguments. Here are some example uses of *wc*:

wc -l datebook termpaper	lines only
wc -c -w datebook termpaper	characters and words only
wc -cw datebook termpaper	characters and words only
wc datebook termpaper	characters, words, and lines

It seems natural to break *wc* into two pieces, the first handling argument processing and file opening and closing, and the second counting the characters, words, and lines in the file. The first part, the main program, is shown in Figure 12.5.

wc's design is typical of most programs that have options. First, the optional arguments are processed and their values recorded. The first argument that does not begin with a dash signals the end of the options. When an argument does begin with a dash, each character of the argument is examined and a flag is set with its value. Any unrecognized options cause an error message describing the program's normal usage to be written to `stderr`. Figure 12.6 shows the relationships between the various pointers used to process the arguments.

Once the options have been processed, each subsequent argument is assumed to be a file name and is opened using `our_fopen` (Figure 12.4). Following a successful file open, the file pointer and option flags are passed to `file_count`, which does the counting. We are careful to close each file after it is printed to avoid running out of file pointers when there are many arguments.

```
/*
 *  Count words, lines and characters in file.
 */
#include <stdio.h>
#include "boolean.h"

main(argc, argv)
int argc;                              /* argument count */
char **argv;                           /* list of arguments */
{
  FILE    *fp, *our_fopen();           /* next file to process */
  BOOLEAN bad_opt, chars, lines, words; /* option flags */
  char    **last_ptr = &argv[argc - 1]; /* pointer to last argument */
  int     i;                           /* index to option */
  void    file_count();                /* does the counting */

  /* Process optional arguments */

  bad_opt = chars = lines = words = FALSE;
  while (++argv <= last_ptr && (*argv)[0] == '-')
    for(i = 1; (*argv)[i] != '\0'; i++)
      switch ((*argv)[i])              /* in row of options */
      {
        case 'c':  chars = TRUE;   break;
        case 'w':  words = TRUE;   break;
        case 'l':  lines = TRUE;   break;
        default:   fprintf(stderr,"wc: bad option %c\n", (*argv)[i]);
                   bad_opt = TRUE;
      }
  if (!chars && !words && !lines)      /* no options means all of them */
    chars = words = lines = TRUE;

  /* Process other arguments */

  if (bad_opt)
    fprintf(stderr,"usage: wc [-c][-w][-l] [files...]\n");
  else if (argv > last_ptr)            /* use stdin if no args */
    file_count(stdin, "Standard Input", chars, words, lines);
  else                                 /* otherwise arg specifies file */
    for( ; argv <= last_ptr; argv++)
      if (fp = our_fopen(*argv,"r"), fp != NULL)
      {
        file_count(fp, *argv, chars, words, lines);
        fclose(fp);
      }
}
```

FIGURE 12.5. *wc.c*—main program of our character-, word-, and linecounter.

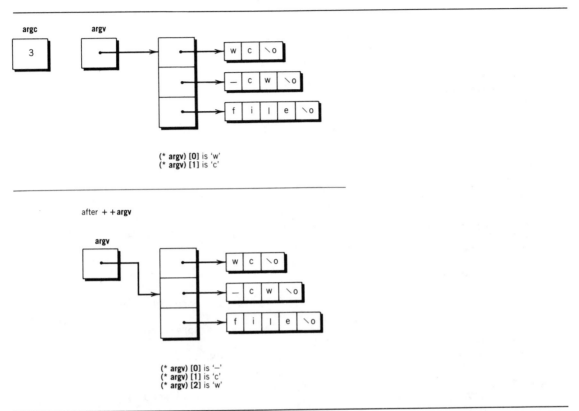

FIGURE 12.6. Processing the optional arguments. `argv` points to the argument, `(*argv)[i]` is the next character in the argument.

An interesting case occurs when there are no arguments. Instead of printing an error message the program assumes that the user wants to use the standard input, and `file_count` is called with `stdin` as its file pointer.

Going through a file and counting the words is simple and is shown in Figure 12.7. The only tricky part consists of defining a word. We have defined a word as a sequence of alphanumeric or punctuation characters. To do this, we use the library functions `isalnum` and `ispunct`, part of the set of character-testing functions discussed in Chapter 7 and listed in Appendix 6.

Command line options to control a program's functioning are a powerful and useful idea. Unfortunately, many programs use them to provide different and often unrelated features. These extra features are used infrequently, if at all, but they make the program significantly harder to read and debug. To avoid falling into this trap, first write a simple version of the program that performs its main task correctly. Options should

```
/*
 * Count words, characters and lines.
 */
#include <stdio.h>
#include <ctype.h>
#include "boolean.h"

#define PRINT(flg,cntl,thing) ((flg) ? printf(cntl, thing) : 0)

void file_count(fp, fname, chars, words, lines)
FILE *fp;                                        /* file pointer */
char *fname;                                     /* file name */
BOOLEAN chars, words, lines;                     /* flags */
{
  long    c_cnt = 0, w_cnt = 0, l_cnt = 0;       /* counters */
  int     c;                                     /* next character */
  BOOLEAN inword = FALSE;                        /* are we in a word */

  while ((c = getc(fp)) != EOF)
  {
    c_cnt++;                                     /* one more character */
    if (c == '\n')
      l_cnt++;                                   /* one more word */
    if (!isalnum(c) && !ispunct(c))
      inword = FALSE;                            /* end of word */
    else if (!inword)
    {
      inword = TRUE;                             /* start of word */
      w_cnt++;
    }
  }
  PRINT(chars, "%10d", c_cnt);                   /* print counters */
  PRINT(words, "%10d", w_cnt);
  PRINT(lines, "%10d", l_cnt);
  PRINT(fname, " %s", fname);                     /* and file name */
  putchar('\n');
}
```

FIGURE 12.7. Function to count characters, words, and lines in a file.

be added only after the program has been used for a while, and adding certain features will clearly make the program more useful.

PROGRAMMING PRACTICE

12-9. Have *wc* print a grand total line if it is given more than one file argument. Add an option to suppress this new default action.

12-10. Many of the programs written in earlier chapters should be extended to process external files. Among these are *insertion sort* (Chapter 1), *uniq* (Chapter 4), *Histo* (Chapter 5), and the *cross-referencer* (Chapter 11). Modify these programs to use external files.

12-11. Add three new options to the *uniq* program of Chapter 4. The first, -c, causes a count of the number of occurrences of any line of output to be printed before the line. The second, -u, causes only those lines that appear uniquely to be output. The last, -d, causes only those lines that are duplicated to appear in the output. What should *uniq* do when combinations of these options are specified?

12-12. Write a program, *sort*, that sorts the files specified as arguments, using any of the sorting methods we have discussed. Note that *sort* simply prints the sorted files onto **stdout** without changing the files. Add a new option to *sort*, -r, that reverses the sense of the sort.

LINE ORIENTED INPUT/OUTPUT

For many programs (such as *uniq*), it is more natural to process the input a line at a time instead of a character at a time. The standard I/O library provides four functions that do line-at-a-time I/O. The most general of these functions are **fputs** and **fgets**. **fputs** takes a string and a file pointer and writes the string to the file. For example,

```
fputs("For a good time, call 555-1212\n", fp);
```

writes a single line to the file specified by **fp**. **fputs** provides a convenient and more efficient way to print a string than **printf**. One drawback, however, is that the file pointer is its last argument instead of its first argument, as with **fprintf**.

fgets reads a line of input from a file and is somewhat similar to **get_line** (Chapter 4). **fgets** takes three parameters: a character array, its size, and a file pointer. It reads characters until a newline is read or the array is full. The array is terminated with a null, and to accommodate the null, the number of characters read will be, at most, one less than the number of characters in the array. The line's trailing newline is included in the array.

```
char buffer[MAXLINE];
    . . .
fgets(buffer, MAXLINE, fp)
```

reads up to **MAXLINE** − 1 characters, placing them into **buffer**.

fgets and get_line differ in their handling of longer than expected input lines. If the line (including the trailing newline) is too long, more calls to fgets can be used to read the rest of the line; get_line ignores the rest of the line. fgets returns NULL when the end of file is reached; otherwise it returns its first argument, a pointer to a character.

As an example, Figure 12.8 shows a version of file_copy written using fgets and fputs instead of getc and putc. The line-copying version produces the same result as the character-copying version, albeit a little slower, since fgets and fputs are usually written using getc and putc.

A problem with fgets is that there is no way to determine if the entire input line was read without examining the returned string, making fgets significantly less useful than it would be if it returned the line length, as get_line does.

The functions gets and puts are closely related to fgets and fputs, and are just different enough to cause confusion. gets takes a character array, reading a line from stdin and placing it into the array, terminating the

```
/*
 * Copy "source" into "dest".
 */
#include <stdio.h>

#define MAX_LINE  256                       /* longest input line */

int file_copy(dest, source)
char *dest,                                 /* source file name */
     *source;                               /* destination file name */
{
  FILE *sfp,                                /* source file pointer */
       *dfp,                                /* destination file pointer */
       *our_fopen();                        /* our file opener */
  char line[MAX_LINE];

  if ((sfp = our_fopen(source,"r")) != NULL)
  {
    if ((dfp = our_fopen(dest,"w")) != NULL)
    {
      while (fgets(line, sizeof(line), sfp)) /* copy source into */
        fputs(line, dfp);                    /* destination */
      fclose(dfp);
    }
    fclose(sfp);
  }
  return sfp && dfp;
}
```

FIGURE 12.8. Copy files line by line. Surprisingly, this is slower than character by character.

array with a null character. **gets** returns a pointer to the array's first character, or **NULL** when the end of file is reached. Unlike **fgets**, **gets** does not place the terminating newline into the array. **puts** is simpler and more useful, taking a string and writing it and a trailing newline onto the standard output.

The most common uses of **puts** and **gets** are to prompt the user for input and to read the response, as shown below.

```
char response[MAX_LINE];
    . . .
puts("What's your name?");
if (gets(response) != NULL)
   printf("Hi %s!  Are you free Friday night?\n", response);
```

The usefulness of **gets** is limited because there is no way to limit the number of characters it reads, which causes the program to "bomb" if more characters are read than the array can accommodate. We prefer **get_line**.

PROGRAMMING PRACTICE

12-13. Write **fgets**, **fputs**, **puts**, and **gets**, using **getc** and **putc**. How can these functions be changed to make them more useful? Make these changes.

RANDOM FILE ACCESS

So far, all file processing has been sequential. There are times, however, when we are interested only in a particular part of a file and want to access that part without having to read all the preceding data. In effect, we want to treat a file like an array, indexing any byte in the file as we would an array element. There are three standard I/O functions to support this random file access: **rewind**, **ftell**, and **fseek**.

rewind takes a file pointer and resets the current position to the beginning of the file. A **rewind** is done implicitly whenever a file is opened with **fopen** for reading or writing, but is of course not done when a file is opened for appending. Any input function immediately following a **rewind** will start reading the file's first character. **rewind** allows a program to read through a file more than once without having to open and close the file.

ftell takes a file pointer and returns a **long** containing the current offset in the file, the position of the next byte to be read or written. An ftell at the beginning of the file returns the position of the file's first byte. Using ftell, a program can save its current position in the file in order to return to it later without having to read all the intervening data.

fseek moves the current file position to a given location within the file. It takes three arguments—a file pointer, a long offset, and an int specifier—and resets the current byte position within the file. The new position is computed by adding the offset to the part of the file specified by the specifier, which can have one of three values: 0 means the beginning of the file, 1 means the current position, and 2 means the end of the file. Here are some example fseek's:

```
long n;
...
fseek(fp, 0L, 0);      /* go to the start: same as rewind(fp) */
fseek(fp, 0L, 1);      /* stay where we are (not too useful!) */
fseek(fp, 0L, 2);      /* go to the end of the file */
fseek(fp, n, 0);       /* go to the nth byte in the file */
fseek(fp, n, 1);       /* skip ahead n bytes */
fseek(fp, -n, 1);      /* go backwards n bytes */
fseek(fp, -n, 2);      /* go to n bytes before the file's end */
```

It is a common mistake to forget that fseek's second parameter is a long; passing any other type will produce unpredictable results. On some systems the offset to fseek must be a value returned by ftell and is not simply the desired byte number. For these examples, however, we are assuming that this is not the case.

fseek returns zero if the file pointer can be moved to the desired position and minus one if there is an error such as attempting to seek past the file's boundaries. We have ignored fseek's return value in these examples; however, by checking it, we can verify that the file position was changed.

Using these functions, we can write the function read_bytes (Figure 12.9), which allows us to read a group of bytes starting from any byte in the file. read_bytes takes a file pointer, a position, a number of bytes to read, and a place to put those bytes. It moves to the desired position and then uses getc to read the requested number of bytes into the specified place. read_bytes returns the number of bytes read, which may be fewer than the number requested if we start reading too far into the file. If there is an error, −1 is returned. We are careful to test fseek's return value, because the file pointer's position will not change if we specify an invalid location to which to move.

INDEXED FILES

When we do not process files in a sequential fashion, we can use fseek to speed processing. As an example, we will write a program (called *view*) that allows a user to examine the contents of a file in any order. To view a line, the user specifies the line number. For instance, specifying 50 causes the 50th line in the file to be printed.

If we assume that many different line numbers will be specified during a run of the program, doing a sequential search for each line will be time-consuming. And in general, since the file's line lengths can vary, we cannot use a formula to determine where each line starts. However, by reading through the file once, we can create a table (called an *index* table) that contains the starting position of each line in the file. Once this table is created, when we are given a line number we can access the desired line in the file by moving to the file position contained in its corresponding table entry, as the following figure shows.

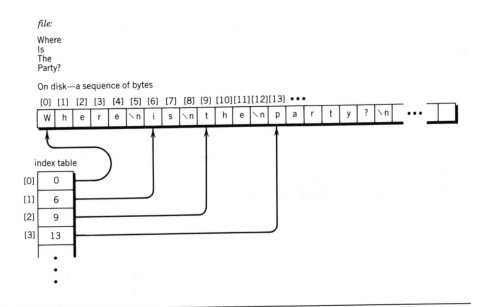

Figure 12.10*a* contains `make_index`, a function that builds an index table. `make_index` builds the table by opening the file to be indexed and, reading through it sequentially, recording the current file position with `ftell` each time a newline is read. Once we have the index, it is easy to write the function `print_line`, shown in Figure 12.10*b*, that prints the desired line. `print_line` uses the line number to index the table, and then uses `fseek` to set the file's current position to the position indexed in the table.

Given `make_index` and `print_line`, it is easy to write *view*, shown in Figure 12.11. `main` opens the file (the name is the program's argument) and calls `make_index` to build the index table. Then `main` reads in line

```
/*
 * Read a group of bytes, given position in file.
 */
long read_bytes(fp, pos, num, place)
FILE *fp;                               /* file to read from */
long pos, num;                          /* position and number */
char place[];                           /* place to put them */
{
  long nread = -1L;                     /* bytes actually read */
  int c;

  if (fseek(fp, pos, 0) == 0)
    for (nread = 0; nread < num && (c = getc(fp)) != EOF; nread++)
      place[nread] = c;
  return nread;
}
```

FIGURE 12.9. Reading a group of bytes from a specified location in a file. This allows us to treat a file as if it were an array.

```
/*
 * Create index and print indexed lines.
 */
#include <stdio.h>

int make_index(fp, index_tab, max_ind)    /* build the index table */
FILE *fp;                                  /* file to index */
long index_tab[];                          /* table of indices */
int max_ind;                               /* maximum number of indices */
{
  long *next_ptr = index_tab,              /* ptr to next index */
       *last_ptr = index_tab + max_ind - 1; /* ptr to end of index table */
  int  c, lastch;                          /* next and last character */

  for (lastch = '\n'; c = getc(fp), c != EOF; lastch = c)
    if (lastch == '\n')                    /* save position of line */
      if (next_ptr <= last_ptr)            /* as long as room */
        *next_ptr++ = ftell(fp) - 1;
      else                                 /* no room in table, give up */
        break;
  return next_ptr - index_tab;             /* number of indices in table */
}
```

(a) make_index: *build an index table*

```
void print_line(fp, index_tab, lineno)     /* print a line */
FILE *fp;                                    /* file we're looking at */
long index_tab[];                            /* index table */
int lineno;                                  /* line number to print */
{
  int c;                                     /* next character */

  if (fseek(fp, index_tab[lineno], 0) != 0) /* get to line */
    fprintf(stderr, "Can't read line %d at %ld\n", lineno, index_tab[lineno]);
  else
  {
    while(c = getc(fp), c != EOF && c != '\n') /* print the line */
      putchar(c);
    putchar('\n');
  }
}
```

(b) print_line: *print a line given its line number*

FIGURE 12.10. Building and using an index table.

numbers from the user, displaying the line using print_line or printing an error message if the line cannot be found. As usual, we use getnum and skip_garbage to handle the reading of input values and our_fopen to open files.

If we know that we want to frequently examine a file that rarely changes, we can store the index table in a file. Then the program that lets us examine the file can use the positions in the index file to access the requested lines. In this way, the overhead of building the table occurs only when the file changes, instead of each time the *view* program is run. We will use this idea in the data base case study at the end of the chapter.

PROGRAMMING PRACTICE

12-14. Extend *view* (Figure 12.11) to handle more than one file. *view* should go on to the next file if it is given a negative line number.

12-15. We can make *view* more efficient by building the index table as we read. That is, the first time we are asked for a line, if the line does not already have an index, we build the part of the index table corresponding to the part of the file preceding that line. Well, don't just sit there—make this change!

```
/*
 * View: a program to allow random display of lines.
 */
#define MAX_INDEX 2000

main(argc, argv)
int argc;
char *argv[];
{
  long index_tab[MAX_INDEX], next;   /* index table, next number */
  int  lines,                        /* lines in table */
       inpres;                       /* result of reading number */
  FILE *fp, *our_fopen();            /* file */
  void print_line(), skip_garbage();

  if (argc != 2)
    fprintf(stderr,"Usage: %s file-name\n", argv[0]);
  else if ((fp = our_fopen(argv[1], "r")) != NULL)
  {
    if ((lines = make_index(fp, index_tab, MAX_INDEX)) != 0)
      while (printf("Line? "), (inpres = getnum(&next)) != EOF)
        if (!inpres)
        {
          fprintf(stderr,"Skipping bad line number...\n");
          skip_garbage();
        }
        else if (next < lines)
          print_line(fp, index_tab, (int) next);
        else
          fprintf(stderr,"Line %ld not found\n", next);
    (void) fclose(fp);
  }
}
```

FIGURE 12.11. A program to display selected lines within a file.

12-16. Use the index table approach to print a file in reverse order.

12-17. *view* behaves badly if the file has more lines than anticipated. Improve it by making the index table a doubly-linked list. That is, make each node in the index table have pointers to both the preceding and following table entries.

12-18. Write a function, file_len, that computes the number of characters in a file without reading any characters. Is this function portable?

12-19. Write a function, tail, that prints out the last n bytes of a file without reading through the file. Extend tail to print out the last n lines.

BINARY INPUT/OUTPUT

The functions from the standard I/O library that we have used so far are designed to read and write characters or character arrays. C also provides two functions that can be used to read and write arbitrary types: fread reads an array from a file and fwrite writes an array to a file. Both are passed four parameters: a pointer to the array's first element (char *), the size (in bytes) of an element, the number of elements in the array, and a file pointer. Both return the number of elements successfully read or written; zero indicates the end of file or an error. Notice that the file pointer is their last argument. (Isn't consistency wonderful?)

We can use fwrite to write an array, x, containing 10 integers to a file as follows:

```
int x[10], n;
. . .
n = fwrite((char *) x, sizeof(int), 10, fp);
```

Because fwrite expects its first parameter to be a pointer to a character and x points to an integer, we must cast x as shown. After the call to fwrite, n will contain the number of elements that were written. Note that all this example fwrite does is to write sizeof(int) × 10 bytes to the file, the first byte coming from &x[0].

We can read the file back into x in a similar way:

```
int x[10], n;
. . .
n = fread((char *) x, sizeof(int), 10, fp);
```

After the call to fread, n contains the number of elements that were read. Like the previous call to fwrite, this call to fread simply reads sizeof(int) × 10 bytes from the file, placing them into x.

fread and fwrite provide a convenient and efficient way to save internal tables between program runs. We can use fwrite to save an internal table when the program finishes and fread to read it the next time the program starts. This method is much more efficient than using fprintf and fscanf but has the disadvantage that the saved table is not text and cannot be easily examined.

While the use of fread and fwrite is portable, the files read and written by them are not. To see why, let us look at a file containing 10 ints written using fwrite. If ints are 4 bytes, this file takes 40 bytes. Now suppose the file is transported to a machine with 2-byte ints, and we try to read it using fread, telling fread to read 10 ints. fread will read only the first 20 bytes of the file. The moral: files that are transferred between machines should not be written with fwrite.

```
/*
 *  Score file management.
 */
#include <stdio.h>

/*
 * Get scores from SCORES file.
 */
int read_scores(scores, table, n)
char scores[];                          /* scores file name */
struct score_rec table[];               /* scores table */
int n;                                  /* scores to read */
{
  FILE *fp = our_fopen(scores, "r");    /* reading scores file */
  int  nread = 0;                       /* scores read */

  if (fp)
  {
    nread = fread((char *) table, sizeof(struct score_rec), n, fp);
    fclose(fp);
  }
  return nread;
}

/*
 * Put scores to SCORES file.
 */
int write_scores(scores, table, n)
char scores[];                          /* scores file name*/
struct score_rec table[];               /* score table */
int n;                                  /* scores to write */
{
  FILE *fp = our_fopen(scores, "w");    /* writing scores file */
  int  nwrite = 0;                      /* scores written */

  if (fp)
  {
    nwrite = fwrite((char *) table, sizeof(struct score_rec), n, fp);
    fclose(fp);
  }
  return nwrite;
}
```

FIGURE 12.12. Module to manage a score file for a game. The score file is kept as a binary file.

RECORD INPUT/OUTPUT

The arrays read and written by **fread** and **fwrite** can contain elements of any type, including structures. As an example, suppose we are writing a game and wish to maintain a table of the game's top 10 scores and their scorers, perhaps so that this list can be updated and printed when the game finishes. The program can store this table internally as an array of structures:

```
struct score_rec
{
  int  score;                   /* score */
  char scorer[40];              /* scorer's name */
};
          . . .
score_rec scoretab[MAX_SCORES];   /* score table */
```

The table is read from the file when the program starts, updated after the game is played, and written to the file before the program finishes.

The module used to manage the scores file is shown in Figure 12.12. read_scores reads from the scores file into the table, returning the number of table entries. write_scores writes the table to the scores file. A single fwrite creates the table, and a single fread reads it. The major difference between these functions and those in our previous example is that each table element is now a struct score_rec instead of an int.

PROGRAMMING PRACTICE

12-20. Extend read_scores and write_scores to manage a score file in which the table of scores is preceded by a single integer containing the number of entries in the table. Why might this be a good idea?

12-21. Write a program that can create an indexed file, using fwrite to write the table of indices. (*Hint*: Use make_index as a starting point.) Then rewrite the view program of Figure 12.11 to use fread to input the index table. How will your program know the number of table entries to read?

12-22. Implement fread and fwrite using getc and putc.

CASE STUDY—AN INDEXED DATA BASE

We bring together many of the concepts covered in this text with the implementation of a small indexed data base containing names, addresses, and phone numbers—a computerized little black book. We will write two programs to manage the data base: *make-index* and *lookup*. *make-index* creates an index file that is used by *lookup* to quickly find the address and phone number associated with a particular name.

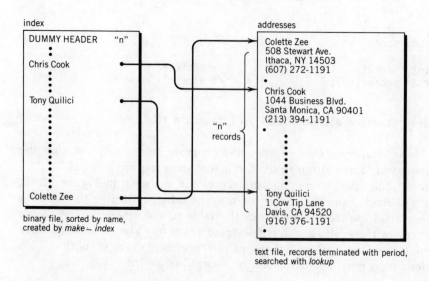

FIGURE 12.13. The organization of the data base.

The data base is made up of a text file, *addresses*, and an index file, *index*, as illustrated in Figure 12.13. *addresses* is divided into records, with the first line of each record containing a name and the following lines containing the corresponding address and phone number. A record ends with a line containing only a period ("."). To make it easy to create and maintain this file using a text editor, there are no restrictions on the number of lines per record or the order of the records in the file.

index is a binary file, with records that contain a name and the starting position of the corresponding record in *addresses*. *make-index* must be run whenever *addresses* is edited to create an up-to-date index file; *index* is not a text file and should not be edited.

make-index creates the index file by reading through *addresses* and building a table of names and record positions. When all records have been processed, *make-index* writes the table into the file *index*, sorted by name. When *lookup* needs to find the address and phone number corresponding to a given name, it can use binary search to look up the name in *index*, and can use the position found there to access the record in *addresses*. This makes the searching for an address reasonably efficient.

We keep the index table as a sorted linked list, with each node pointing to a structure containing a name and a position. As *make-index* reads each record in *addresses*, its name and starting position are placed in one of these structures and inserted into the correct place in the list. When

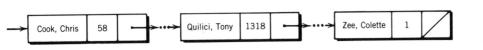

FIGURE 12.14. A sample index table for the file in the previous figure.

addresses has been completely processed, we run through the list, using fwrite to write the index structures into *index*. Before we write any records, however, we write a dummy record containing the number of names that are indexed, so that this information will be available when we search *index*. A sample index table and linked list is shown in Figure 12.14.

Since both programs need the definition of an index structure, it is placed in the header file *index.h*, shown in Figure 12.15. *index.h* also contains constants for the data base file names, the input line length, and the end-of-record delimiter.

make-index (Figure 12.16) is straightforward despite its long length. It opens *addresses*, uses make_table to build the list of indexes, and then writes this list to *index*. make_table reads records from *addresses*. It allocates a new node for each record, saves the record's key and starting position, and inserts the new node into the correct place in the index table. We saw how to maintain sorted lists in Chapter 11; the difference here is that we are keeping structures sorted instead of strings.

```
/*
 * Definitions to use indexes.
 */
#define MAX_LINE   256           /* maximum line length */
#define MAX_KEY    40            /* maximum key size */
#define ADDR_FILE  "addresses"   /* the data base */
#define INDEX_FILE "index"       /* the index file */
#define END_REC    ".\n"         /* end of a record */

struct index_rec                 /* index record */
{
  char key[MAX_KEY];             /*    name */
  long pos;                      /*    position */
};

typedef struct index_rec INDEX;
```

FIGURE 12.15. *index.h*—the data base header file.

```
/*
 *  Creating the index table.
 */
#include <stdio.h>
#include "index.h"                                  /* definition of INDEX */
#include "boolean.h"                                 /* from Chapter 8 */

struct node {                                        /* definition of a list node */
  INDEX data;                                        /*    index record + */
  struct node *next;                                 /*    pointer to next node */
};


#define INDEX_WRITE(fp, val)                         /* handle writing index record */ \
        (fwrite((char *) &(val), sizeof(val), 1, fp) != 1 ? \
            fprintf(stderr, "Couldn't write %s to %s\n", \
            (val).key, INDEX_FILE), exit(1) : 1)


main()
{
  FILE *afp, *ifp, *our_fopen();                     /* the files and file opener */
  struct node *list, *ptr, *make_table();            /* sorted list of records */
  static INDEX header = {"DUMMY HEADER", 0};         /* header record */

  afp = our_fopen(ADDR_FILE, "r");                   /* open up "addresses" file */
  list = make_table(afp, &header.pos);               /* read file into index table */
  (void) fclose(afp);
  ifp = our_fopen(INDEX_FILE, "w");                  /* open up "index file" */
  INDEX_WRITE(ifp, header);                          /* write header record */
  for (ptr = list; ptr != NULL; ptr = ptr->next)     /* write list records */
      INDEX_WRITE(ifp, ptr->data);
  printf("%ld records\n", header.pos);               /* how many did we write? */
  (void) fclose(ifp);
  exit(0);
}


/*
 * Build sorted index table by reading records and recording their position.
 */
struct node *make_table(fp, cnt_ptr)
FILE *fp;
int *cnt_ptr;
{
  struct node *list = NULL,                          /* table is a list */
              *prev, *curr, *temp;                    /* previous/current/new pointers */
  char line[MAX_LINE], *malloc();                    /* next line */
  long pos = 0;                                       /* record's position in file */
  BOOLEAN new_record = TRUE,                         /* starting with new record */
          have_mem = TRUE;                            /* not out of memory */
```

```
*cnt_ptr = 0;
while (pos = ftell(fp), have_mem && fgets(line,sizeof(line), fp) != NULL)
{
  if (new_record && (temp = (struct node *) malloc(sizeof(struct node))) != NULL)
  {
    strncpy(temp->data.key, line, MAX_KEY);      /* build a node */
    temp->data.pos = pos;
    curr = list, prev = NULL;
    for ( ;  curr != NULL && strcmp(temp->data.key, curr->data.key) > 0;
         curr=curr->next)
      prev = curr;                              /* search list to find place */
    temp->next = curr;                          /* insert node */
    (prev == NULL) ? (list = temp) : (prev->next = temp);
    (*cnt_ptr)++;                               /* update node count */
  }
  new_record = strcmp(line, END_REC) == 0;
  have_mem = temp != NULL;
}
if (!have_mem)                                  /* out of memory? */
  fprintf(stderr,"Out of memory.  Key: %s\n", line);
return list;
}
```

FIGURE 12.16. *make-index.c*—creates an indexed data base.

To simplify the program's control structure we use a new version of our_fopen, shown in Figure 12.17, to open files. The new version is similar to the old version, except that if it cannot open the file it terminates the program instead of returning a null pointer. To do this, our_fopen uses another library function, exit. exit stops a program, closing any open files. It takes a single integer parameter that is returned to the operating system as the program's exit status. Traditionally, only successful programs return zero.

We also use exit in the macro INDEX_WRITE that writes a record to the index file and, if there is an error, prints an error messages and exits.

```
#define INDEX_WRITE(fp, val)  /* handle writing index record */ \
        (fwrite((char *) &(val), sizeof(val), 1, fp) != 1 ? \
            fprintf(stderr, "Couldn't write %s to %s\n", \
            (val).key, INDEX_FILE), exit(1) : 1)
```

INDEX_WRITE expands into an expression rather than a statement so we can use it in other expressions. Like our_fopen, INDEX_WRITE encapsulates a common task, and its use simplifies the functions that call it.

Once we have run *index* to build the sorted index table, we can run

```
/*
 * Open a file, writing error message if it fails.
 */
#include <stdio.h>

FILE *our_fopen(file_name, mode)
char *file_name,                        /* file to open */
     *mode;                             /* "r", "w" or "a" */
{
  FILE *fp = fopen(file_name, mode);    /* open the file */

  if (!fp)                              /* did open fail */
  {
    fprintf(stderr, "Can't open file \"%s\" for %s\n", file_name,
                (*mode == 'r')
                    ? "reading"
                    : ((*mode == 'w') ? "writing" : "appending"));
    exit(1);        /* quit early */
  }
  return fp;
}
```

FIGURE 12.17. Using exit to end a program if an error occurs.

```
/*
 * Lookup addresses/phone numbers given name.
 */
#include <stdio.h>
#include "index.h"

main()
{
  FILE  *afp, *ifp, *our_fopen();       /* address and index files */
  char  line[MAX_LINE];                 /* holds user input, record output */
  INDEX header;                         /* header containing cnt */
  long  pos, bsearch();                 /* position of record, search function */
  int   c;

  afp = our_fopen(ADDR_FILE, "r");      /* open "address" and "index" files */
  ifp = our_fopen(INDEX_FILE, "r");
  if (fread((char *) &header, sizeof(header), 1, ifp) == 0)      /* get header record */
    fprintf(stderr, "Can't read header of \"%s\"\n", INDEX_FILE);
```

```
  else
  {
    printf("There are %ld entries\n", header.pos);
    while (printf("Name? "), fgets(line, sizeof(line), stdin))     /* get a name */
      if ((pos = bsearch(ifp, (long) 1, header.pos, line)) == -1) /* look it up in index */
        printf("Couldn't find: %s\n", line);
      else if (fseek(afp, pos, 0) != 0)                           /* get to it in addresses */
        fprintf(stderr,"Can't read record at position %ld\n", pos);
      else
        while (fgets(line, sizeof(line), afp) && strcmp(line,END_REC) != 0)
          fputs(line,stdout);                                     /* print its record */
  }
  (void) (fclose(ifp), fclose(afp));
  exit(0);
}


/*
 * Search index file for name.
 */
long bsearch(ifp, first, last, target)
FILE *ifp;                              /* file to index */
long first, last;                       /* range to search */
char *target;                           /* what we're looking for */
{
  long  pos, mid = (first + last) / 2;  /* next and mid positions */
  INDEX next;                           /* to hold record */
  int   cmp;                            /* holds comparison result */

  if (mid < first || fseek(ifp, mid * sizeof(INDEX), 0) != 0 ||
      fread((char *) &next, sizeof(next), 1, ifp) != 1)
    pos = -1;                           /* couldn't find, or error */
  else
    pos = ((cmp = strncmp(target, next.key, MAX_KEY)) == 0)
              ? next.pos
              : ((cmp < 0) ? bsearch(ifp, first, mid - 1, target)
                           : bsearch(ifp, mid + 1, last, target));
  return pos;
}
```

FIGURE 12.18. *lookup*—searching an indexed data base.

lookup, shown in Figure 12.18, to search entries. The main program
prompts for user names, using **bsearch** to do a binary search of *index* for
the position of the name's record in *addresses*. **bsearch** searches the file for
the name, using **fseek** to access the next index record to examine. Once
we have the position of the name's record in *addresses*, we use **fseek** to
move to that position, and print the name, address, and phone number
found there.

PROGRAMMING PRACTICE

12-23. Modify *make-index* and *lookup* to allow the data base files to be specified as optional arguments.

12-24. The entire name must be specified in order to find its address. Modify *lookup* to allow partial matches and to print all records matching the given name.

12-25. Modify *lookup* to get names to look up from command line arguments.

12-26. Modify *make-index* to allow duplicate names.

12-27. Write a program, *print-labels*, that prints the entire data base in a format suitable for mailing labels.

C H A P T E R 13

PORTABILITY
AND EFFICIENCY

By now you have been exposed to all of C's features and should feel comfortable with the language. We will now discuss portability and efficiency—two issues that are important when writing real programs and that are, unfortunately, often thought to work against each other. When we write programs to be easily transported to different computers, we often eschew constructs that are fast and save storage on the development machine. Conversely, techniques that speed up programs or save storage space are often peculiar to a particular machine. However, the two concerns can be complementary; we often achieve faster, more compact programs through careful algorithm and data structure design, not through code diddling and machine-dependent tricks. In this chapter we show how to write programs that are both portable and efficient. First, we present a series of problems and solutions to writing portable programs and conclude with a series of case studies in which we reduce their running times substantially without hurting their portability.

PORTABILITY

What do we mean by portability? Ideally, a portable program would not need any changes to run with different input or output devices, to run under a different operating system, to run on a different computer, or any combination of these factors. In other words, a portable program can run

TABLE 13.1. Ranges of capabilities found on typical machines.

Characteristic	Values
Word size	32 bits versus 16 bits.
Memory size	Virtual addressing (16M bytes) versus fixed memory space (64K bytes).
Hardware capabilities	Floating point accelerator versus floating point in software.
External storage	200M byte disk versus two 360K byte floppies.
Operating system calls	Highly flexible operating system versus small set of operating system calls.
Displays	Full color versus black and white. Mouse input versus cursor movement keys.
Compiler/linker differences	Long names versus short names.
Character set	ASCII versus EBCDIC.

unmodified in different environments. Unfortunately, the ideal is almost always impossible to attain. To understand why, consider the common computer differences listed in Table 13.1. There are so many differences that it is clear that careful program design and coding are required to achieve any degree of portability between systems that differ as widely as these.

Since writing portable programs requires extra effort, you might wonder why we care about portability. If you always develop and run your code on the same machine, you probably do not care. However, it is rare for a program to spend its entire lifetime on a single machine. A great deal of software, such as most applications programs that run on Apple Macintoshs, IBM PCs, and in fact virtually all micros, is developed— written, tested, and debugged—on larger and faster development machines. Many compilers (since writing a complete, *correct* compiler for a given programming language is a major task) are written in an elaborate verification mode on one machine, and then ported to other target machines. And, because highly interactive or graphics-based programs take so much effort to write, such programs should be able to run on many output devices—from low-resolution character CRTs to high-resolution, full-color devices.

SOME SOLUTIONS TO THE PROBLEMS OF PORTABILITY ACROSS MACHINES

Once we have even a simple set of descriptions of alternative computers and displays, suggestions for portability quickly come to mind. Most of them have already been pointed out. Our suggestion is to use the following guidelines as a checklist for all code where portability is of concern.

Do not assume that `ints` are 32 bits. Use `longs` instead of `ints` whenever the range of an integral variable may be a problem.

This assures that the representation for most integral values will be the same, at least 32 bits. If code is being developed on 36- or 60-bit machines (such as PDP-10s or CDC machines), it is best to assume that an integral type may not be larger than 32 bits on another machine. On both 16- and 32-bit machines, there is no integral type that is larger than 32 bits.

If an integer is being used to represent a quantity that is always constrained in some small range (such as a boolean value or the number of values in a small array), an `int` will port safely to all machines. The proposed C standard requires `ints` to be at least 16 bits. Avoid using `shorts` to represent small values unless space is at a premium. Do not use `chars` to hold small integers, since their size (and whether they are signed) varies among machines.

The problem of overflow does not disappear just because we use `longs` instead of `ints`. When integer overflow is possible, the programmer is responsible for guarding code and devising suitable schemes for protecting against overflow, including using `floats` or `doubles` instead.

We can use the preprocessor to help solve some of the problems involved with different word sizes, as illustrated in Figure 13.1. We define variable type names that reflect their use with `#define` or `typedef`, tailoring their definition to the machine used. Thus, a `SMALL_COUNTER` (used to count from 0 to 255) can be an `unsigned char` on one machine and an `unsigned short` on another.

Do not assume that all pointers are the same size. Cast from one pointer type to another.

We have been consistent in always casting the type of the pointer returned from `malloc`:

```
temp = (NODEPTR) malloc(sizeof(struct node));
```

We do this for two reasons. The first is that `malloc` is defined to return a type pointer to `char`, and pointers to different types may be different sizes. If this is the case, the automatic type conversion between the pointer to `char` and the pointer to `struct node` (in the above example) may use different bits in the word from the explicit cast. The assumption is that the compiler does the right thing on casting between pointer types. The other reason is more theoretical: strong typing. When all variables are typed

```
#ifdef vax
   typedef  unsigned char    SMALL_COUNTER       /* 0..255 */
#endif

#ifdef tops20
   typedef  unsigned short   SMALL_COUNTER       /* 7-bit chars, must use short */
#endif
     . . .
```

(a) *Data definitions in an include file "TYPES.h"*

```
#include "TYPES.h"

main ()
{
  SMALL_COUNTER    n = 0;
     . . .
```

(b) *Using the defined type* SMALL_COUNTER *in a program*

FIGURE 13.1. Use of defined types to isolate the underlying actual type.

and all conversions between types are specified in the program, program correctness is enhanced and program verification is made easier.

Do not assume dynamic allocation will never fail.

All our programs that use dynamic storage allocation (via calls to malloc) test the return from the storage allocation functions. At the least, a program should terminate gracefully when out of storage. Because there is such a wide variety of heap storage space (our sample machines in Table 13.1 varied from 64K- to 16M-bytes per program), the need for error handling or recovery is clear.

Do not assume that pointers are integers.

As an example, it is occasionally necessary to print the address of a variable. However, address types are not well defined in the language; they may be ints or longs, and they may be both on the same machine. Instead of worrying about the issue, simply print addresses as if they were longs, casting so that the types match:

```
printf("Address of x: %ld\n", (long) &x);
```

Do not assume file opens and file writes cannot fail.

When a disk is full, it is possible for a write to fail. As with dynamic storage allocation, we must test the return from the various standard I/O library routines. It might be suspected that on a machine with a large disk, this would be unlikely to happen, but because disk space is like Murphy's law (files expand to fill up all available space), large systems are as likely to run out of space as small ones.

Attempting to write to disk when the file system is full is always a serious problem. A familiar situation is that of a text editor. At the end of a long session of editing, we give a write command to copy out the incore copy of the file, only to find that the file system is full. If we immediately exit with the message, "Too bad, file system full. Cannot write your file. All your work is lost," users are understandably upset. Often it is best to wait for a while and then try again. Full file systems are often temporary, and the file write will succeed at some later time. On floppy disk systems, all that may be needed is a message requesting the user to insert a new disk!

Floating point speed varies enormously. For efficiency, use integer arithmetic whenever possible.

There are rarely representation problems with floating point numbers, but portable code implies that response characteristics are similar across environments. Such is not the case when floating point operations are used, however. When arithmetic can be done with integers, performance is often improved, as we shall see later in the chapter. But that brings up the problem of ints versus longs. You win some, you lose some.

All machines use more space for a **double** than for a **float** (typically, 32 bits for **float**s, 64 for **double**s). There are no inherent portability problems with floating point numbers, since the sizes are more clearly specified and since there are no "unsigned" floating point types.

PROGRAMMING PRACTICE

13-1. If you have access to more than one machine, take a sizeable program that you have written and used on one machine and port it to another. Where were your portability problems? Does the program have identical run-time behavior on both machines?

13-2. Suppose you have to write a program that requires a 100,000 element array of integers and that, in addition, it must be able to run on a machine with 16M bytes of virtual memory and on a machine where arrays are limited to 64,000 bytes. Assume that the only operations on the table are to access an element and to store a value in an array element. Write functions for these operations that use an in-memory array if there is enough room or store the array in an external file if there is not. Should the callers of these functions be aware of how the array is actually accessed?

SOME SOLUTIONS TO THE PROBLEMS OF PORTABILITY ACROSS DISPLAYS

Just as we can present guidelines that solve most machine problems, once we indicate the kinds of differences we are likely to find in displays, it is simple to generate guidelines for dealing with those differences. The most important point is that displays should be viewed as virtual devices. We should not write code that is specific to one particular device. Rather, we should write programs or routines that are generic to the functions that need to be performed. These routines make use of lower-level device-specific routines that are interpreted by a *device driver*.

Even with basic CRTs, virtually every terminal maker has his or her own ideas about the codes needed to perform these functions. Obviously we do not want to include specific direct cursor movement codes in a `printf` statement such as

```
printf("%cY%d[%d;", ESC, row, col);      /* move to "row" and "col" */
```

which is the code for one particular terminal. Instead, we want to call a function, `move_cursor(row, col)`, and then have that function determine the correct action for the terminal.

A function like `move_cursor` can be written portably using two different techniques. If the program can determine the terminal type it will run on at compile time, we can use the preprocessor to define `move_cursor` appropriately. If not, we could write it as shown in Figure 13.2*a*. The terminal type is an enumeration type and is used to select the appropriate action in a `switch` statement. To add another terminal, we add an entry to the enumeration type and another case to the `switch` statement in `move_cursor`. No other code needs to be changed. Another method is to put all terminal information into a file and then read that file when the program starts. Whichever technique is used, we want to keep the details of terminal control hidden from all other parts of the program.

How does the program find out the terminal type? If this information is available through the operating system (as it is in UNIX), an operating system call can be made. If not, it is necessary to ask the user for the terminal. A program that uses direct cursor positioning can begin with a function, `get_term_type`, that returns an enumeration type (the user's terminal) which becomes global to the entire program. Functions such as `move_cursor` are written to use this type. Figure 13.2*b* shows how `get_term_type` can be written to accommodate an operating system function, if available, or a direct request for the terminal type, and how `move_cursor` uses the terminal enumeration type.

```
/*
 *  Move the cursor to the indicated row and column.
 */
void move_cursor(row, col)
int  row, col;
{
   extern enum TERMTYPE  terminal;      /* access the global "terminal" */

   switch (terminal)
   {
   case vt100:   printf(. . .);
                 break;

   case wyse:    printf(. . .);
                 break;

   case gt101:   printf(. . .);
                 break;
      . . .
   }
}
```

(a) *Moving the cursor in a terminal independent manner*

```
/*
 *  Get the terminal type from the operating system, if possible;
 *  otherwise, ask the user for the type.
 */
void get_term_type(terminal)
enum TERMTYPE *terminal;
{
   char *term;
#ifdef unix
   {
     term = getenv("TERM");
       . . .
   }
#else
```

Ask for terminal type

```
#endif
      . . .
}
```

(b) *Getting the terminal type appropriately*

FIGURE 13.2. Two functions, `move_cursor` and `get_term_type`, written to be portable across operating systems.

As with output displays, input device drivers can be written so that their workings are portable and hidden from main programs. In graphics programs, certain devices have a generic capability. Equipment used for pointing, such as mice, tablets, and joysticks, are called *locators*. These devices return two values, an *x* and a *y* screen coordinate. Programs that need locator input should use a generic call like

```
read_locator(&x, &y);
```

rather than placing the locator-accessing code (which can be quite messy) in-line. If a new device is installed or if the code is ported to a machine with a locator different from the one for which it was written, the `read_locator` function can be rewritten.

PROGRAMMING PRACTICE

13-3. Provide versions of the functions `get_term_type` and `move_cursor` that work in the environment your programs are running under. What other terminal accessing functions (such as "clear screen" or "clean to end of line") should be provided?

SPECIFIC C PROBLEMS RELATED TO PORTABILITY

When code is written to be ported to machines and compilers that are different from the ones on which the program was written, we need to be aware of the way C is connected to the rest of the world. Many limitations (such as short identifier names) are not caused by lack of support within the compiler, but instead are restrictions imposed by linking loaders and by historical association between C and certain computers and operating systems. In this section we look at the restrictions that are most troublesome.

Identifier Names and Length

Almost all C compilers allow variables to be mixed case, and most allow long identifier names (31 or more characters). However, if a program includes separately compiled modules or modules written in another programming language, the pieces must be combined using a linking loader. Loaders themselves are programs that may not have been written with the specific needs of C programs in mind. Historically, languages such as FORTRAN have required identifiers to be single case, with six or fewer characters. Consequently, it is necessary to limit external variable and function names to six or fewer characters, mono case, to ensure portability. It is often possible to use longer names, though, as long as they differ within the first six characters.

Short names may conflict with the goal of writing readable programs. When two names are identical in the first six characters, we should rename them slightly so that they vary. For example, two variables used for screen manipulation

```
int   screenlocx, screenlocy;
```

could be renamed to be different in their first character instead of their last:

```
int   xscreenloc, yscreenloc;
```

Another way to provide readable identifier names is to use **#defines** to cause longer variable names to be converted by the preprocessor to shorter names. Using an existing program with a large number of variables such as

```
int   screenlocx, screenlocy, screenlocz, . . .;
```

a header file can be created to redefine them to shorter names, and the file can be included at the start of the program to be ported. A similar technique can be used with mixed-case identifiers.

```
/* Header file "names.h" */

#define   screenlocx          sclx
#define   screenlocy          scly
#define   screenlocz          sclz
           . . .
#define   GetInputData        gtdata
           . . .
```

The only problem with this practice is that error messages from the loader or from a run-time debugger will be related to the externally visible names, so that a redefinition like

```
#define  longstackpush  _X17
```

will cause all references to **longstackpush** to be reported as **_X17** by the loader.

Operating System Dependencies

Because of the historic association between the language and the PDP-11s, VAXs, and the UNIX operating system, code is often written that makes

```
/*
 *  Print the size of file "junk".
 */
#include <stdio.h>
#define  UNKNOWNSIZE    -1L
main()
{
  long file_size(), fs;

  if ((fs = file_size("junk")) == UNKNOWNSIZE)
    puts("Can't get size of junk\n");
  else
    printf("Size of junk: %ld\n", fs);
}


/*
 * Determine the size of the given file.  Makes use of specific
 * operating system calls.  Returns UNKNOWNSIZE if the file doesn't
 * exist or if its size cannot be determined.
 */
long file_size(file)
char *file;                          /* name of file to size */
{
#ifdef unix

#include <sys/types.h>              /* UNIX specific include file */
#include "stat.h"                   /* UNIX specific include file */
{
  struct stat     statbuf;

  return (stat(file, &statbuf) == -1) ? UNKNOWNSIZE : (long) (statbuf.st_size);
}
#endif

#ifdef tops30                       /* a mythical operating system */

#define FILESIZEJSYS    197

  return  (long) jsys(FILESIZEJSYS, file);
#endif

  return UNKNOWNSIZE;               /* unknown o.s. - unknown file size */
}
```

FIGURE 13.3. A program that prints the size of a file. The main program makes a generic call to file_size, which in turn calls specific operating system routines.

subtle use of low-level machine details or that makes operating system calls as if they were part of the C language. Using UNIX operating system calls is easy to do because they are simply library calls. However, UNIX system calls are *not* part of the C language or its standard libraries and are not portable.

To aid portability, we should place all system calls in generically named routines instead of threading specific calls throughout the code. By *generic*, we mean that routines should be named to indicate the function they perform. The generically named function can be written to take into account all machines and operating systems the code will be ported to by protecting the routines with appropriate #ifdefs. A simple example is shown in Figure 13.3, a program to print the size of a file named *junk*.

Note that in Figure 13.3 including all the operating system-specific code, guarded by #ifdefs, makes the code within the function difficult to read. However, the main program itself is more readable, since the purpose of the unusually named system calls is now clear.

Machine Dependencies

Machine dependencies crop up in at least three places: sign conversions, right shifts, and byte ordering. We pointed out in Chapter 2 that conversions between unsigned and signed types, particularly when there is a change in the length of the data type, are not specified in the language. Some machines sign extend, and others zero extend. When converting from a longer to a shorter type, truncation occurs. Are the most or least significant bits retained? The result is machine or compiler dependent.

On right shifts, zeros are *always* shifted in if the variable is an unsigned type. If it is a signed type, zeros are always shifted in if the value is positive. If the value is negative, the shifted-in bits are machine dependent. Left shifts always shift in zeros, so the problem does not occur.

Unfortunately, the order of bytes in a word is different on different machines. A correct compiler will always extract the bytes in a consistent order, but programmer assumptions about where bytes are stored in a word leads to portability problems. For example, in one (rather bizarre) 32-bit, byte-addressable machine, strings are arranged so that characters are packed in a word with the first character in the right-most byte of the first word, the second character in the next byte to the left, and so on. The fifth through the eighth characters are in the next higher word, and so on, until all characters are stored, as in Figure 13.4a. However, in another 36-bit, word-addressed machine, the characters are stored left to right in a word, with the first character in the lowest address. This machine uses seven bits per character, storing five characters in a word (with one bit unused), as in Figure 13.4b.

```
static char message[] = "Rate of pay out of bounds.";
```

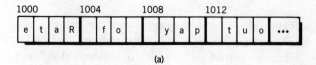

(a)   Arrangement of characters in one 32-bit machine

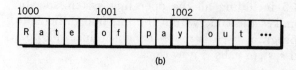

(b)   Arrangement of characters in one 36-bit machine

FIGURE 13.4. Byte ordering and word ordering of strings in 32-bit and 36-bit machines.

Using the Standard Libraries

Although some programmers may use minus one for EOF, or use the values of other constants instead of their defined names, this practice is not advisable, since their specific values may be different across machines or compilers. Instead, use the symbolic constants and the other standard input and output routines in *stdio.h*.

The standard string library defines the functions strcmp, strlen, strcpy, and others. These functions are presumably written to be efficient, and their use is portable across virtually all C compilers. Even though it is fun and tempting to write our own versions, it is good practice to use these standard routines.

Programming is easier and portability is enhanced by using the *ctype.h* include file. This file declares various standard character comparison functions. It is clearer and portable across character sets to use

```
#include <ctype.h>
    . . .
while (islower(c))
    . . .
```

rather than the specific character comparisons in

```
while (c >= 'a' && c <= 'z')
```

The comparison in the second `while` loop implies that the lowercase letters are contiguous, with no intervening non-lowercase characters, but such is not the case with all character sets (although it is true with ASCII). In theory, `islower` is portable across all character sets, since a table lookup is used, as in the version we wrote in Chapter 7.

PROGRAMMING PRACTICE

13-4. `file_size` currently gives up if there is no library function that returns the length of a file. Can the length of a file be computed without using a library function? Modify `file_size` to do so.

13-5. Write a program to search for identifier names in a file or program that are similar in the first *n* characters. *n* should be provided as an optional command-line argument that defaults to eight.

13-6. Find out what the machine-dependent operations (such as right shifts of negative integers) actually do on your machine. Do any of your programs take advantage of them? If any do, can you rewrite your programs to avoid these operations?

PORTABILITY—CONCLUSIONS

You should now understand the difficulties involved in writing portable programs. However, many of these problems can be overcome by careful design and good coding style. Isolate the nonportable, machine-, operating system-, and device-dependent code in as small an area as possible. Use the standard libraries for input and output, for string handling, and for character manipulations, since the use of these functions is portable. Test returns from functions that give error indications, such as file routines and dynamic storage routines, so that a failure on a different machine does not cause your program to bomb. From the start be aware of machine dependencies in operations and word sizes and try to avoid them wherever possible. If you follow these suggestions and keep portability in mind when writing your programs, they will be much easier to port to other machines or operating systems.

PROGRAMMING PRACTICE

13-7. How portable are the programs in this book? Try compiling and running some on different machines.

PROGRAM EFFICIENCY

Throughout the book we have pointed out constructs and uses of the language that either aid or detract from program efficiency. We have tried to show that good program design, careful selection of algorithms, use of appropriate data structures, all packaged together with appropriate access routines, lead to efficient, easily modified programs. In almost any programming situation, using the simplest, most direct methods of solving a problem will also be the most efficient way, particularly when programmer time is included.

There are times, however, when reducing the running time or memory usage of a program or routine is necessary. There are many areas that we can attack to make programs more efficient. Before we do so, however, we need an idea of what we mean by program efficiency, and how we might go about measuring it. One common measure is the time a program takes to run as a function of the size of its inputs. We used this measure back in Chapter 1 when we looked at insertion sorting. That routine takes time proportional to the *square* of the number of input values. If we double the number of values to be sorted, computing time goes up by a factor of four; if we triple the input size, time goes up by a factor of nine, and so forth. This says little, however, about how a particular implementation of insertion sort will do on a particular computer, with its particular operating system and compiler. Nor does it account for any special properties of the input set. For example, what happens if the values are already sorted? Or if they are sorted in reverse order? This idea of "asymptotic performance" needs to be made more definitive. In general, we discuss performance by looking at a routine's performance with average data. If there are special conditions that make it particularly good with a special set of values, or particularly bad, we need to note that also.

Once we have selected an algorithm for a particular job, regardless of its time complexity, we still would like to make it run as fast as possible in our own environment. Here is a collection of hints, tips, and insights into the C programming language and its libraries that should help make any program run faster.

> **Avoid scanf for reading numerical values. Instead, use your own input scanner, such as getnum from Chapter 7.**

Of course scanf is much more sophisticated than getnum. This one function can be used to read an arbitrary number of values, mixing data types in any order. Such an input scanner is powerful, flexible, and convenient. Unfortunately, it is less often useful than we would like, particularly when the input can have errors. In almost every case, we know in advance the number and types of data in the input, whether it comes from a preformatted file, or is entered by an interactive user. Often we can modify getnum to read just the number of values we need.

To compare the efficiency of scanf, we modified getnum slightly so that it reads floats, and added a little driver to call it. The input came from a 5000-line file, with one floating point value per line. We compared its running time with a similar program that calls scanf instead. The running time for the version with our own scanner (time to read the data, but not time to print it, since both versions used printf) was about 4.0 seconds. The execution time for the scanf version was about 11.5 seconds, almost three times as long. In addition, the version with scanf compiled into 12,300 bytes of code, while the version with getnum compiled into 8200 bytes, a reduction of almost one third. Not only do we gain substantially in performance, we save space in the bargain.

PROGRAMMING PRACTICE

13-8. printf is a complex, general purpose output formatting routine. Write an output converter that prints a single floating point number. That is, it takes a float as input and writes its value a character at a time to the output. Compare its running time with that of printf in writing 5000 floats.

> **Avoid conversions (doubles versus floats, for example) in arithmetic expressions, and avoid conversions when passing parameters to functions.**

In C, all arithmetic involving floating point values is conducted with doubles, even if all operands are floats. An expression as simple as

```
a = a + 1;
```

(that is, incrementing a by one, where a is a float) involves several time consuming steps: convert a to a double, add the double 1.0, then reconvert

TABLE 13.2. Automatic conversions in expressions and function argument lists.

Original Type	Converted Type
char, short	int
unsigned char, unsigned short	unsigned int
float	double
array of type	pointer to type
function returning type	pointer to function returning type

back to a float. When there are several floating point variables in an expression, each must be converted to a double for the purposes of the arithmetic. If the result goes to a floating point variable, it must be reconverted back to a float, with possible loss of precision.

There are several of these automatic conversions that occur in arithmetic expressions. Each variable or expression with type listed in the left side of Table 13.2 is converted to the type of the right. These conversions occur in two places: expressions, and function arguments.

The consequences of these conversions are that variables other than type int, long, double, or pointer, extract a performance overhead whenever they are used in expressions, and whenever they are used as parameters in functions. Table 13.2 can be summarized succinctly: whenever possible, use variables and function parameters that are ints, longs, doubles, or pointers. If they are not, time consuming conversions will occur.

Replace array accesses with pointers whenever large arrays are being processed in a loop.

We looked at the advantages of pointer accessing versus two-dimensional array accessing in Chapter 9. It is an easy point to forget because the normal array accessing methods are the obvious way to deal with these structures. However, when arrays are large, it is important to keep both methods in mind.

One important example is in putting images on the screen with a graphics system. Graphical data bases can be extremely large. For example, a typical (small) world map that outlines the continents contains over 8000 vectors. In a dynamic system, one where the world is to rotate, the points that make up the image need to be rotated around the earth's axis, as in Figure 13.5. This corresponds to a rotation about the Y-axis. To calculate the new x, y, and z coordinates of the points, *each* vector in the original data must be multiplied by a rotation matrix. The new values of x, y, and z, given by x', y', and z', are

$$x' = x \cdot cos(\theta) + z \cdot sin(\theta)$$

$$y' = y$$

$$z' = x \cdot cos(\theta) - x \cdot sin(\theta)$$

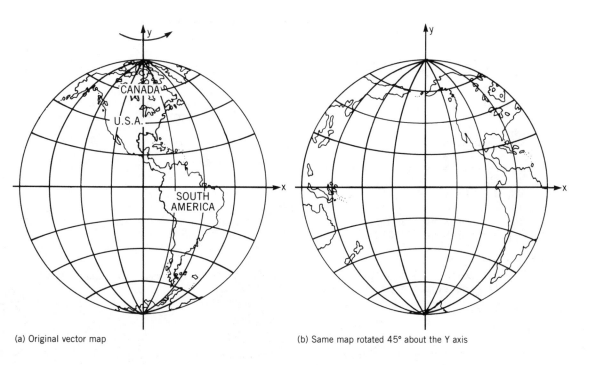

(a) Original vector map   (b) Same map rotated 45° about the Y axis

FIGURE 13.5. Vector map of the world rotated around the Y-axis.

Figure 13.6*a* shows the usual two-dimensional array method for calculating the rotation. Figure 13.6*b* shows the pointer accessing method. We ran both versions on a special-purpose graphics processor, an IRIS 1400, as part of a larger mapping and satellite tracking program. The time for the first version was about 8.0 seconds; for the second, about 3.5, saving over 55 percent. Since this was time the user was waiting for a new view, this time savings was important in the perception of speed in interacting with the system.

Use your own free storage management routines rather than `malloc` and `free` whenever dynamic structures are called for and the size of nodes is known in advance.

In Chapter 11 we built a linked list version of insertion sort. The work was done in a routine called `insert_list`. That routine took a value and a

```
/*
 * Rotate an array of map data by an angle theta around the Y axis.
 * TWO-DIMENSIONAL ARRAY ACCESSING VERSION.
 */
void rot_y(earth_pts, earth_post, theta, npts)
double earth_pts[][3],
       earth_post[][3];
int    theta;                          /* rotation angle in radians */
int    npts;                           /* size of arrays */
{
  double pix, piz;
         ctheta  = cos(theta),
         stheta  = sin(theta);

  for (i = 0; i < npts; i++)
  {
    pix = earth_pts[i][0];
    piz = earth_pts[i][2];

    earth_post[i][0] = pix * ctheta + piz * stheta;
    earth_post[i][1] = earth_pts[i][1];     /* y value unchanged in rotation */
    earth_post[i][2] = piz * ctheta - pix * stheta;

  }
}
```

(a)   Rotation routine written using two-dimensional array accessing

```
/*
 * Rotate an array of map data by an angle theta around the Y axis.
 */
void rot_y(earth_pts, earth_post, theta, npts)
double earth_pts[][3],
       earth_post[][3];
int    theta;                          /* rotation angle in radians */
int    npts;                           /* size of arrays */
{
  double (*pts)[3],                    /* ptr to an array of 3 doubles */
         (*pts_post)[3],
         (*end_pts)[3],                /* ptr to end of array */
         pix, piz;
         ctheta  = cos(theta),
         stheta  = sin(theta);

  pts = earth_pts;                     /* point to first row */
  pts_post = earth_post;               /* point to first row */
  end_pts = earth_pts+npts;            /* point to last row */
```

```
while (pts < end_pts)
{
  pix = (*pts)[0];
  piz = (*pts)[2];

  (*pts_post)[0] = pix * ctheta + piz * stheta;
  (*pts_post)[1] = (*pts)[1];     /* y value unchanged in rotation */
  (*pts_post)[2] = piz * ctheta - pix * stheta;

  pts++;
  pts_post++;
  }
}
```

(b) Rotation routine recoded using pointers

FIGURE 13.6. Routines to perform a rotation of map data around the polar axis. *(a)* Normal two-dimensional array version. *(b)* Pointer version.

pointer to an already-sorted list, and installed the value in its correct place. We wrote **insert_list** to call on another routine, **make_node**, to install the value into a newly allocated node, and to hook up the links in an appropriate way. **make_node** was written as a separate routine because doing so makes it simpler to change the representation and allocation should we decide to do that. And now we have decided to do just that. What we will do is build our own free storage pool by calling **malloc** a fixed number of times at the start of our program (a routine called **fsp_init**). Then in **make_node**, we'll call our own storage allocation routine, **fsp_alloc**, when we need a new node. The rewritten version of **make_node** is shown in Figure 13.7.

Initially, our free storage pool will be a linked list of nodes, pointed to by a global pointer **fsp**.

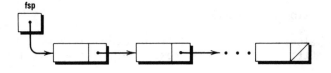

When we need a new node, we simply remove the first node from the free storage pool linked list, and adjust **fsp** appropriately.

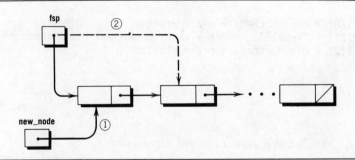

Figure 13.7 shows the declaration and call of **fsp_alloc**. Rather than returning a pointer to a **char**, it returns a **NODEPTR** (a type defined in the include file *lists. h*). The two routines, **fsp_init** and **fsp_alloc**, are shown in Figure 13.8.

The routines in Figure 13.8 are faster than using the system-supplied routines **malloc** and **free** because they are written to be used with nodes of a single type (**struct node**, defined in the include file *lists. h*). Both **malloc** and **free** are general purpose storage allocation routines that must be able

```
/*
 * Make a new node, inserting "value".  Return a pointer to the node.
 * Returns NULL when out of dynamic storage space.  Assume the
 * definitions in "lists.h".
 */
#include "lists.h"
NODEPTR make_node(value)
long value;
{
  NODEPTR fsp_alloc(),               /* allocate from free storage pool */
          newptr;                    /* pointer to allocated space */

  if ((newptr = fsp_alloc()) != NULL)
  {
    newptr->data = value;            /* fill in "data" field */
    newptr->next = NULL;             /* "next" field is always NULL */
  }
  return newptr;                     /* returns NULL if out of space */
```

FIGURE 13.7. Routine to install a value into a new node, calling on our own free storage allocation routine.

to handle requests for blocks of arbitrary size and require complex searching and storage manipulation whenever a call is made. On the other hand, they handle arbitrary storage requests, whereas our own free storage handler requires that we preallocate all the nodes we think we will need. In essence, our version is a compromise between fixed size arrays and the arbitrary allocation and size of dynamic structures. For insertion sorting, linked lists give us the advantage that we can sort with no data shifting, so linked list insertion sorting is likely to be faster than array-based insertion sort.

We ran a version of insertion sort using our own storage allocation functions on a file of 1000 longs. (The routines were compiled and executed on a VAX 11/780 using the Berkeley UNIX C compiler.) The sorting time was about 5.4 seconds, compared to about 6.2 seconds using malloc, a savings of about 13 percent. In linked list operations where there is substantial freeing and reallocating, the savings are greater. Our experience has been that savings of around 13 to 15 percent or more are typical.

```
#include  <stdio.h>
#include  "lists.h"

static NODEPTR  fsp;                    /* pointer to start of free storage pool */

/*
 *  Create a free storage pool of "N" nodes.  Returns the actual number of
 *  nodes created, which may be less than the requested number if malloc fails.
 */
long fsp_init(N)
long N;                                 /* number of nodes requested */
{
  char      *malloc();
  NODEPTR   temp;                       /* ptr to space returned by malloc */
  long      i;                          /* loop index */

  fsp = NULL;
  for (i = 0; i < N && (temp = (NODEPTR) malloc(sizeof(struct node))); i++)
  {
    temp->next = fsp;
    fsp = temp;
  }
  return i;                             /* number of nodes allocated */
}
```

   (a)   Initialize the free storage pool

(continued)

```
/*
 *  Allocate a node from our own free storage pool.
 */
NODEPTR fsp_alloc()
{
   NODEPTR new_node = fsp;

   if (fsp != NULL)
      fsp = fsp->next;

   return new_node;
}
```

(b)   Allocate a node from the free storage pool

```
/*
 *  Return a node to our own fsp.
 */
void fsp_free(nptr)
NODEPTR nptr;
{
   if (nptr != NULL)
   {
      nptr->next = fsp;
      fsp = nptr;
   }
}
```

(c)   Return a node to the free storage pool

FIGURE 13.8. Routines to manage our own free storage pool. *(a)* `fsp_init` initializes the free storage pool. *(b)* `fsp_alloc` allocates a new node. *(c)* `fsp_free` returns a node to the free storage pool.

> **Use efficient algorithms to start with. Use library routines whenever possible (they're written to be efficient). Do not diddle inefficient code.**

The examples we have provided on sorting are important because they illustrate several topics in using C, and in data and control structures. No matter what we do to insertion sort, though, its execution time is proportional to the square of the number of inputs— double the number of values to be sorted and execution time goes up by a factor of four; triple the number and time goes up by nine. We can cut its time by careful coding, by using pointers rather than array indexing, and by using linked lists rather than arrays, but the quadratic time property still holds.

Since sorting is a common operation, the standard C library includes a sort routine called **qsort**, with computing times that are much better than quadratic. **qsort** takes four parameters: a pointer to the array of elements to be sorted (type **char ***, so it usually needs to be cast), the number of elements in the array, the size of each element in bytes, and the name of a comparison function that is used to compare elements in the array. The comparison function must return an integer: less than zero if the first value is less than the second, zero if they are equal, and greater than zero if the first is greater than the second. If this sounds familiar, it is because **strcmp** returns the same values, so **qsort** can be used to sort any data type, numerical or string. Figure 13.9 is a main program that reads **long**s (using **get_data**, not shown), then sorts them via a call to **qsort** and prints them out. The sorting times are shown in Table 13.3. When structures are being sorted, the comparison function can be written

```
/*
 *  A driver program for sorting using "qsort".
 */
#include <stdio.h>

#define MAX    5000                 /* max nbr. of values to sort */

main()
{
  int    comp(),                    /* comparison function for qsort */
         get_data(),                /* read input data */
         i,                         /* loop index for printing */
         nvals;                     /* number of values read */
  long   vals[MAX];                 /* the values to be sorted--in place */

  nvals = get_data(vals, MAX);

  qsort((char *) vals, nvals, sizeof(long), comp);

  puts("\nValues in sorted order:\n");
  for (i = 0; i < nvals; i++)
    printf("%ld\n", vals[i]);
}

/*
 *  Comparison function required for qsort.
 */
int comp(a, b)
long *a, *b;
{
  return (*a < *b) ? -1 :  (*a > *b);
}
```

FIGURE 13.9. Sorting **long**s using the built-in routine **qsort**.

TABLE 13.3. Sorting time for longs using the built-in routine qsort.

Number of Values	Time (secs)
100	0.15
200	0.25
400	0.52
800	0.95
1000	1.32
5000	6.98

to compare the key fields in the records. For efficiency, the comparison function takes pointers to the values to be compared.

The values in Table 13.3 show that the computing time is proportional to about $n\log_2 n$, where n is the number of values to be sorted. Note particularly the time to sort 1000 values—1.32 seconds, compared with the previously noted linked-list insertion sort, using our own free storage manager, of 5.4 seconds. Sorting using the built-in qsort is a factor of four faster.

The same routine can be used to sort strings. Suppose lines is an array of strings. Each string is a fixed size array of MAXSTRING chars, so lines is a two-dimensional array.

```
#define  MAX          1000        /* max nbr. of lines to sort */
#define  MAXSTRING     80          /* nbr. of chars in a string */

char    lines[MAX][MAXSTRING];     /* fixed-length strings */
```

Then we can sort lines with a call to qsort (where n is the actual number of strings in the array, which must be less than or equal to MAX):

```
qsort((char *)lines, n, MAXSTRING, strcmp);
```

Several additional library routines for manipulating complex data structures are provided in the standard libraries that come with some C compilers. These include bsearch, hsearch, tsearch, and lsearch for managing search tables, curses for screen manipulation, getopt for obtaining the next optional argument in an argument list (as we did in Chapter 12), plot functions for generating device-independent graphical output, and others.

PROGRAMMING PRACTICE

13-9. Insertion sort is said to be an n^2 algorithm because computing time goes up as the square of the number of inputs. Run insertion sort with data sets that are *nearly sorted*. Nearly sorted arrays are ones in which no value is more than K places from its final resting place, for some small K. What is the time complexity of insertion sort for nearly sorted arrays?

13-10. Repeat the previous exercise for qsort.

WRAPPING UP

We will finish by discussing several common myths about C. The first is that C programs are difficult to read. In truth, some programs are unreadable. This is not a flaw of the language, however, but of its programmers. While it may be fun to make a program as compact as possible—we admit that we have had a chuckle or two nesting ?:s four levels deep and then secretly watching someone try to understand our code—doing so is not conducive to being a productive programmer. Just because C allows us to write incredibly concise programs does not mean we have to do so. While writing code, remember that someone else may have to read it, and your C programs will be as easy to read as programs written in any other language.

The second myth is that it is difficult to write portable programs in C. Just as it is possible to write unreadable C programs, it is also possible to write nonportable C programs. But again, this is not a fault of the language. (After all, it is easy to write programs in any language that simply do not work. Is this the language's fault?) Think about portability as you code, follow the guidelines in this chapter, and it will not be difficult to write programs that port to a wide range of machines, operating systems, and run-time environments.

Although C is not without its drawbacks (as anyone who has ever tried to declare an array of pointers to functions returning pointers to doubles has quickly discovered), and there are many areas where the language could be improved (a more consistent syntax, better type checking, and so on), it is a surprisingly pleasant language to program in. Why? Because it is compact, yet powerful. Because it is relatively simple in its capabilities, yet comes wrapped in a set of useful tools. Because it allows access to low-level machine details when necessary, yet allows us to ignore them the rest of the time. And finally, because it is applicable to a wide range of programming tasks, yet is not difficult to master. We hope we have prepared you not only to write and understand C programs, but to have *fun* writing them as well.

APPENDIX 1

OCTAL AND HEXADECIMAL NUMBERING SYSTEMS

There is a class of representations known as the *base systems*. Some commonly used bases are binary (base 2), octal (base 8), decimal (base 10), and hexadecimal (base 16). Each of these systems is centered on an integer, other than zero or one, called the *base* or *radix*.

Each base uses a finite number of symbols. In binary the allowable symbols are 0 and 1. In octal the symbols used are 0, 1, 2, 3, 4, 5, 6, and 7. In hexadecimal we need a way to represent the values 10, 11, 12, 13, 14, and 15. The letters A, B, C, D, E, and F, respectively, have been chosen to symbolize them.

In a base system, a value is represented by a string of symbols. Each place occupied by a symbol corresponds to a power of the base. The rightmost place corresponds to the base raised to the zero power (which is 1 for any choice of base). Each move to the left multiplies the current place value by the base. In octal, the rightmost place corresponds to 1s; the next place to the left corresponds to 8s; the place one more to the left corresponds to 64s, and so on. In hexadecimal, the rightmost place also corresponds to 1s, the next place to the left corresponds to 16s; the third place to the 16×16s, or 256s, and on up.

The following table illustrates the correspondence between position and value in binary, octal, and hexadecimal. It is convenient to start numbering the positions at zero from the right so that the position value will be equal to the power of the base.

Position:	n	4	3	2	1	0
Binary	2^n	16	8	4	2	1
Octal	8^n	4,096	512	64	8	1
Hexadecimal	16^n	65,536	4,096	256	16	1

To compute the base 10 value of a number $a_n a_{n-1} \cdots a_1 a_0$ in base B, compute

$$\sum_{i=0}^{n} a_i \times B^i.$$

To convert the number 742_8 to base 10, evaluate $(7 \times 8^2) + (4 \times 8^1) + (2 \times 8^0)$ to obtain the value 482_{10}. To convert the number $A2C_{16}$ to base 10, you evaluate $(10 \times 16^2) + (2 \times 16^1) + (12 \times 16^0)$ to get 2604_{10}.

There is a simple and direct relationship between binary, octal, and hexadecimal numbers. To convert from binary to octal, group the number from the right in three-bit units and convert each to an octal number. To convert to hexadecimal, group in four-bit units, and convert each group in turn. For hexadecimal, values from 0 to 9 convert to the same digit; 10 converts to A, 11 to B, 12 to C, 13 to D, 14 to E, and 15 to F.

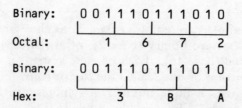

To convert a number, X, from base 10 to base B, recursively divide X by B. The remainder becomes the leftmost digit of the converted number and the quotient becomes the next X. When the new quotient becomes zero, the process is complete.

APPENDIX 2

THE ASCII
CHARACTER SET

0	1	2	3	4	5	6	7	8	9	10	11	12	13	14	15
^@	^A	^B	^C	^D	^E	^F	^G	^H	^I	^J	^K	^L	^M	^N	^O

16	17	18	19	20	21	22	23	24	25	26	27	28	29	30	31
^P	^Q	^R	^S	^T	^U	^V	^W	^X	^Y	^Z	esc				

32	33	34	35	36	37	38	39	40	41	42	43	44	45	46	47
sp	!	"	#	$	%	&	'	(	)	*	+	,	-	.	/

48	49	50	51	52	53	54	55	56	57	58	59	60	61	62	63
0	1	2	3	4	5	6	7	8	9	:	;	<	=	>	?

64	65	66	67	68	69	70	71	72	73	74	75	76	77	78	79
@	A	B	C	D	E	F	G	H	I	J	K	L	M	N	O

80	81	82	83	84	85	86	87	88	89	90	91	92	93	94	95
P	Q	R	S	T	U	V	W	X	Y	Z	[	\	]	^	_

96	97	98	99	100	101	102	103	104	105	106	107	108	109	110	111
'	a	b	c	d	e	f	g	h	i	j	k	l	m	n	o

112	113	114	115	116	117	118	119	120	121	122	123	124	125	126	127
p	q	r	s	t	u	v	w	x	y	z	{	|	}	~	del

THE EBCDIC CHARACTER SET

0	1	2	3	4	5	6	7	8	9	10	11	12	13	14	15
NUL	SOH	STX	ETX	PF	HT	LC	DEL			SMM	VT	FF	CR	SO	SI

16	17	18	19	20	21	22	23	24	25	26	27	28	29	30	31
DLE	DC1	DC2	TM	RES	NL	BS	IL	CAN	EM	CC	CU1	IFS	IGS	IRS	IUS

32	33	34	35	36	37	38	39	40	41	42	43	44	45	46	47
DS	SOS	FS		BYP	LF	ETB	ESC			SM	CU2		ENQ	ACK	BEL

48	49	50	51	52	53	54	55	56	57	58	59	60	61	62	63
		SYN		PN	RS	UC	EOT				CU3	DC4	NAK		SUB

64	65	66	67	68	69	70	71	72	73	74	75	76	77	78	79
SP										¢	.	<	(	+	|

80	81	82	83	84	85	86	87	88	89	90	91	92	93	94	95
&										!	$	*	)	;	]

96	97	98	99	100	101	102	103	104	105	106	107	108	109	110	111
/											,	%	-	>	?

112	113	114	115	116	117	118	119	120	121	122	123	124	125	126	127
										:	#	@	'	=	"

128	129	130	131	132	133	134	135	136	137	138	139	140	141	142	143
	a	b	c	d	e	f	g	h	i						

144	145	146	147	148	149	150	151	152	153	154	155	156	157	158	159
	j	k	l	m	n	o	p	q	r						

160	161	162	163	164	165	166	167	168	169	170	171	172	173	174	175
		s	t	u	v	w	x	y	z						

176	177	178	179	180	181	182	183	184	185	186	187	188	189	190	191

192	193	194	195	196	197	198	199	200	201	202	203	204	205	206	207
	A	B	C	D	E	F	G	H	I						

208	209	210	211	212	213	214	215	216	217	218	219	220	221	222	223
	J	K	L	M	N	O	P	Q	R						

224	225	226	227	228	229	230	231	232	233	234	235	236	237	238	239
		S	T	U	V	W	X	Y	Z						

240	241	242	243	244	245	246	247	248	249	250	251	252	253	254	255
0	1	2	3	4	5	6	7	8	9						

THE MATH LIBRARY

Here is a list of the C mathematical functions found on our UNIX system. Not all of these functions may be available on your system. We have, for example, noticed that many personal computers provide only the most basic math functions. On the other hand, we have also noticed systems that have a more comprehensive math library than ours. You should consult your reference manual to find out which math functions are provided by your environment.

To use these functions, include *math.h*. Some of the functions expect a `double` as an argument, but because of C's automatic type conversions, a `float` can be passed instead. Most of them return a `double`, so be careful of the type of the variable being assigned to.

```
int abs(x)
int x;
```

Absolute value of x. Cannot be used to take the absolute value of a `long`.

```
double acos(x)
double x;
```

Arc cosine of x in radians. Returns zero if x not in range −1 to +1.

```
double asin(x)
double x;
```

Arc sine of x in radians. Returns zero if x not in range −1 to +1.

```
double atan(x)
double x;
```

Arc tangent of x in radians. Sometimes called arctan.

```
double atan2(y, x)
double y, x;
```

Arc tangent of x/y in radians. Result machine dependent if x and y are both zero.

```
double ceil(x)
double x;
```

x rounded up to the nearest integer.

```
double cos(x)
double x;
```

Cosine of x (x in radians).

```
double cosh(x)
double x;
```

Hyperbolic cosine of x. Returns largest possible double on overflow.

```
double exp(x)
double x;
```

e to the x power. Returns largest possible double on overflow.

```
double fabs(x)
double x;
```

Absolute value of x.

```
double floor(x)
double x;
```

x rounded down to the nearest integer.

```
double fmod(x,y)
double x, y;
```

Remainder when x is divided by y.

```
double frexp(x, nptr)
double x;
int    *nptr;
```

Finds f and n such that f is between 0.5 and 1.0, and $f \times r^n = x$, where r is the radix used by the internal representation; returns f, and puts n in the place pointed to by nptr.

```
long labs(x)
long x;
```

Absolute value of x.

```
double ldexp(x)
double x;
```

$x \times r^y$, where r is the radix used by the internal representation.

```
double log(x)
double x;
```

Natural log of x. Returns largest negative double if x is less than zero.

```
double log10(x)
double x;
```

Base 10 log of x. Returns largest negative double if x is less than zero.

```
double modf(x, nptr)
double x;
int    *nptr;
```

Splits x into a fraction and an integer; the fraction is returned, and the integer is put in the place pointed to by nptr.

```
double pow(x, y)
double x, y;
```

x to the y power. Returns largest possible double on overflow; returns largest negative double if x is negative and y is not an integer, or if x is zero and y is not positive.

```
int rand()
```

Random number between zero and the largest positive double (inclusive). May be initialized with srand(x).

```
double sin(x)
double x;
```

Sine of x (x in radians).

```
double sinh(x)
double x;
```

Hyperbolic sine of x. Returns largest positive double on overflow; unpredictable results on underflow.

```
double sqrt(x)
double x;
```

Square root of x. Returns zero if x is negative.

```
srand(seed)
unsigned seed;
```

No value returned; initializes rand. Same seed produces same numbers.

```
double tan(x)
double x;
```

Tangent of x (x in radians).

```
double tanh(x)
double x;
```

Hyperbolic tangent of x.

THE CTYPE LIBRARY

Here are the C character testing functions. As with the math library, not all of these functions may be available on your system. We have simply listed all of those that we are aware of. Consult your local reference manual for details. To use these functions, include *ctype.h*. In the declarations below, assume that c has been declared as a `char`.

isalnum(c)

Nonzero if c is alphabetic or numeric; zero otherwise.

isalpha(c)

Nonzero if c is alphabetic; zero otherwise.

isascii(c)

Nonzero if c is an ASCII character; zero otherwise. isascii also works on any `int`; if c has no ASCII value, zero is returned.

iscntrl(c)

Nonzero if c is a control char; zero otherwise.

iscsym(c)

Nonzero if c can be a valid character within an identifier; zero otherwise.

`iscsymf(c)`

Nonzero if c can be the first letter of an identifier; zero otherwise.

`isdigit(c)`

Nonzero if c is a digit; zero otherwise.

`isgraph(c)`

Nonzero if c is any printing character other than space; zero otherwise.

`islower(c)`

Nonzero if c is a lowercase letter of the alphabet; zero otherwise.

`isodigit(c)`

Nonzero if c is an octal digit; zero otherwise.

`isprint(c)`

Nonzero if c is printable; zero otherwise.

`ispunct(c)`

Nonzero if c is a punctuation character; zero otherwise.

`isspace(c)`

Nonzero if c is any white space character; zero otherwise.

`isupper(c)`

Nonzero if c is an uppercase letter of the alphabet; zero otherwise.

`isxdigit(c)`

Nonzero if c is a hex digit; zero otherwise.

`toascii(c)`

ASCII value of c; if c is not in the range of ASCII characters, truncates to lowest seven bits.

```
toint(c)
```

Decimal value of a hex digit; minus one if c is not a hex digit.

```
tolower(c)
```

c in lowercase

```
toupper(c)
```

c in uppercase

```
_tolower(c)
```

c in lowercase; defined only for uppercase c.

```
_toupper(c)
```

c in uppercase; defined only for uppercase c.

THE STANDARD I/O LIBRARY

Here is a table of the standard I/O library functions. Most implementations provide all of these functions, but once again, to be on the safe side, you should consult your reference manual.

You should include *stdio.h* when using any of the standard I/O functions. Unless otherwise stated, these functions assume that all of the files passed to them have already been opened for input or output.

    EOF

Returned by functions when end of file is reached.

```
int fclose(file)
FILE *file;
```

Closes a file that was open for input or output.

```
int feof(file)
FILE *file;
```

If end of file is detected on an input file, a nonzero value is returned; otherwise zero is returned.

```
int fgetc(file)
FILE *file;
```

Returns integer value of next character of input file. The macro version is **getc**.

```
        char *fgets(s, n, file)
        char *s;
        int n;
        FILE *file;
```

Reads n characters from file into s; stops reading on newline or end of file.

```
        FILE *fopen(path, type)
        char *path, *type;
```

Opens a file for input and output. type is one of "r", "w", or "a". "r" means open the file for reading from the beginning. If the file does not exist, NULL is returned. "w" means open the file for writing. If the file exists, it is truncated to zero length. If it does not exist, it is created. "a" means open the file for updating. If the file exists, writes will occur at the end. If it doesn't exist it is created. Both "w" and "a" return NULL if there is an error.

```
        int fprintf(file, format, arg1, arg2,...)
        FILE *file;
        char *format;
```

Writes arguments to a specified file using a given format (see printf).

```
        int fputc(c, file)
        char c;
        FILE *file;
```

Writes the character c to the file and returns the value of c as an int.

```
        int fputs(s, file)
        char *s;
        FILE *file;
```

Writes the string s to the file.

```
        int fread(ptr, ptr_size, n, file)
        char *ptr;
        unsigned ptr_size;
        int n;
        FILE *file;
```

Reads a block of binary data into a buffer from a file and returns the number of items read.

```
int fscanf(file, format, ptr1, ptr2, ...)
FILE *file;
char *format;
```

Reads formatted input from a specified file (see scanf).

```
int fseek(file, offset, type)
FILE *file;
long offset;
int type;
```

Allows positioning within a file for input or output.

```
long ftell(file)
FILE *file;
```

Returns current position within an open file.

```
int fwrite(ptr, ptr_size, n, file)
char *ptr;
unsigned ptr_size;
int n;
FILE *file;
```

Writes a block of binary data from a buffer to a file; returns number of items written.

```
int getc(file)
FILE *file;
```

Macro version of fgetc; true function equivalent to fgetc in operation.

```
int getchar()
```

Returns integer value of next character from standard input, or EOF on end of file.

```
char *gets(s)
char *s;
```

Reads a string from the standard input until newline or end of file.

```
int printf(format, arg1, arg2,...)
char *format;
```

Formats output and writes to stdout; choices for format include:

    %d   signed decimal
    %hd signed short decimal

```
%ld  signed long decimal
%u   unsigned decimal
%hu  unsigned short decimal
%lu  unsigned long decimal
%ou  unsigned octal
%ho  unsigned short octal
%lo  unsigned long octal
%x   unsigned hex
%hx  unsigned short hex
%lx  unsigned long hex
%c   character(s)
%s   right-adjusted string
%-s  left-adjusted string
%f, %e, %g
     signed decimal float or double
%%   percent sign
```

```
int putc(c, file)
char c;
FILE *file;
```

Puts character c into specified file; returns character as a value of type int.

```
int putchar(c)
char c;
```

Same as putc but writes character to standard output.

```
int puts(s)
char *s;
```

Writes string s to standard output.

```
int scanf(format, ptr1, ptr2,...)
char *format;
```

Reads characters from standard input according to a specified format; choices for format include:

```
%d   signed decimal
%hd  signed short decimal
%ld  signed long decimal
%u   unsigned decimal
%hu  unsigned short decimal
%lu  unsigned long decimal
%ou  unsigned octal
%ho  unsigned short octal
%lo  unsigned long octal
%x   unsigned hex
%hx  unsigned short hex
```

```
%lx  unsigned long hex
%c   character(s)
%s   right-adjusted string
%-s  left-adjusted string
%f, %e, %g
     signed decimal float
%lf, %le, %lg
     signed decimal double
%%   percent sign
```

```
int sscanf(s, format, ptr1, ptr2, . . .)
char *s, *format;
```

Reads characters from string s according to specified format (see scanf).

```
extern FILE *stderr;
```

Stream to which error messages may be written.

```
extern FILE *stdin;
```

Stream from which normal input is read, usually the terminal.

```
extern FILE *stdout
```

Stream to which normal output is written, usually the terminal.

```
int ungetc(c, file)
char c;
FILE *file;
```

Next character c is put back on the specified file; getc from same file will return this character.

```
system(command)
```

An operating system command is run, and its exit status is returned. Though originally defined for the UNIX operating system, system is now found on most others.

A P P E N D I X 7

THE STRING LIBRARY

Here is a table of C string functions. The available string functions vary quite a bit between systems, and your system may not support the complete set of functions listed here or may have different names for some of the functions.

All strings should end with the null character ('\0'); if a string without a null character is passed to one of these functions, the results are unpredictable at best. You should include *string.h* before using any of these functions. Some systems call this file *strings.h* and others do not have it all. If the file isn't present, you must explicitly declare the return type of these functions before using them.

```
char *strcat(s1, s2)
char *s1, *s2;
```

s2 appended to s1. Returns a pointer to s1. Unpredictable results if s1 and s2 share any memory.

```
char *strchr(s, c)
char *s, c;
```

A pointer to the first occurrence of c in s; a null pointer if c does not occur in s. Sometimes called index.

```
int strcmp(s1, s2)
char *s1, *s2;
```

An int, less than zero if s1 is less than s2, zero if s1 equals s2, and greater than zero if s1 is greater than s2.

```
char *strcpy(s1, s2)
char *s1, *s2;
```

The contents of s2 are copied into s1. Returns a pointer to s1. Unpredictable results if s1 and s2 share any memory.

```
int strcspn(s, set)
char *s, *set;
```

Number of characters in s before encountering a character in set. Returns length of s if no characters in set are also in s; sometimes called instr.

```
int strlen(s)
char *s;
```

Number of characters in s before the terminating null. Sometimes called lenstr.

```
char *strncat(s1, s2, n)
char *s1, *s2;
int n;
```

First n characters of s2 are appended to s1; returns pointer to s1. Unpredictable results if s1 and s2 share any memory.

```
int strncmp(s1, s2, n)
char *s1, *s2;
int n;
```

Compares first n characters of s1 and s2. Returns an integer less than zero, zero, or greater than zero depending on comparison of the first n characters, as with strcmp.

```
char *strncpy(s1, s2, n)
char *s1, *s2;
int n;
```

Copies n characters to s1 from s2; if s2 is less than n, s1 is padded with null characters to length n; returns a pointer to s1. If s2 greater than or equal to n, s1 is not null terminated.

```
char *strpbrk(s, set)
char *s, *set;
```

A pointer to the first character in s that is also in set; NULL if s and set have no intersection.

```
    int strpos(s, c)
    char *s, c;
```

The position of the first occurrence of c in s; minus one if c is not in s. Some versions have a variant called scnstr.

```
    char *strrchr(s, c)
    char *s, c;
```

A pointer to the last occurrence of c in s; NULL if c is not in s.

```
    char *strrpbrk(s, set)
    char *s, *set;
```

A pointer to the last occurrence in s of a character in set; NULL if s and set have no intersection.

```
    int strrpos(s, c)
    char *s, c;
```

The position of the last occurrence of c in s; minus one if c is not in s.

```
    int strspn(s, set)
    char *s, *set;
```

Number of characters in s before encountering a character not in set. Returns length of s if all characters in set are also in s; sometimes called notstr.

A P P E N D I X 8

STORAGE ALLOCATION FUNCTIONS

Here are the functions provided for allocating and freeing storage. The storage allocation functions all return a pointer to a contiguous block of storage of at least the requested size. The functions return type char *, and should be cast to the appropriate type. The storage is guaranteed to be properly aligned to the requirements of the underlying hardware. These functions return NULL (defined in *stdio.h*) if there is not enough free space available.

The storage freeing routines require a pointer to a contiguous block of storage previously allocated by one of the storage allocation functions. They return the pointed-to block to the free storage pool. The type of the argument is char *, and should be cast as appropriate.

We hate to tell you this and we know you hate to hear it, but once again, some systems do not provide all of the functions listed here. In fact, most systems do not provide the functions allowing a long to specify the number of bytes to allocate, although they are in the proposed C standard. One final time, you get to check your local reference manual for the details.

```
char *calloc(n, size)
unsigned n, size;
```

Allocates n blocks of storage, each of size bytes. All bits in the allocated space are set to zero.

```
cfree(ptr)
char *ptr;
```

Returns space previously allocated by calloc to the free storage pool.

```
char *clalloc(n, size)
unsigned long n, size;
```

Similar to calloc, except the arguments are longs allowing for larger blocks of storage to be allocated.

```
free(ptr)
char *ptr;
```

Returns space previously allocated by malloc to the free storage pool.

```
char *malloc(size)
unsigned size;
```

Allocates a contiguous block of storage of at least size bytes, and returns a pointer to the first byte in the block, or NULL if there is not enough space.

```
char *mlalloc(size)
unsigned long  size;
```

Similar to malloc, except that the argument is of type long, so that more space may be requested.

```
char  *realloc(ptr, size)
char      *ptr;
unsigned size;
```

Takes a pointer to a block of storage and "grows" it to the requested size. A pointer to the new block is returned. Returns NULL if the amount of space requested is not available. In some environments, if realloc fails, the original space may be lost.

Index